An American Journey

THE SHORT LIFE OF WILLY WOLFE

By Jean Kinney

SIMON AND SCHUSTER
New York

Published by Simon and Schuster
A Division of Gulf & Western Corporation
Simon & Schuster Building
Rockefeller Center
1230 Avenue of the Americas
New York, New York 10020

Photo editor: Vincent Virga

Manufactured in the United States of America

1 2 3 4 5 6 7 8 9 10

Library of Congress Cataloging in Publication Data

Kinney, Jean Brown.
  An American Journey: The short life of Willy Wolfe

  1. Wolfe, Willy, 1951–1974. 2. Symbionese
Liberation Army—Biography. 3. California—Biography.
I. Title.
F866.4.W64K56   322.4'2'0924 [B]   79-16577

ISBN 0-671- 22857-9

Acknowledgments

When Patty Hearst told the world that "neither Cujo nor I had ever loved another individual the way we loved each other," I called the mother of Willy Wolfe (Cujo) and asked if she objected to my writing this book. When she said no, I began my search for reasons why an attractive boy from an apparently responsible and well-to-do family should have joined up with a group of West Coast "crazies" who terrified (and fascinated) the world as they murdered, kidnapped, robbed. Little did I know that my quest would take me to all parts of the United States where I would meet hundreds of persons who knew Willy (or could help me understand him) to whom I owe thanks.

I could not have written the book without the help of the Wolfes— Virginia, Willy's mother, who lives in Litchfield, Connecticut, not far from me; John, Willy's musician brother in Philadelphia; Ben Cheney, Willy's older half brother, who lives with his wife, Mary Ann, and their four children in New Hampshire; and most of all, Roxie, Willy's tall, handsome sister, who looks enough like Willy to be his twin and has the insight of a psychiatrist. And then there are Sharon, Willy's stepmother, who received the last letter ever written by Willy; and Dr. Wolfe, Willy's father, who couldn't believe until Patty's love message that his son was a terrorist; and black Mike Carreras, who is not a blood member of the family but has spent time with the Wolfes off and on for thirty years since he went to them as a *Herald Tribune* Fresh Air Fund kid from New York.

Friends of Willy talked to me in the East—Kirk Johnson and Eric Whyte, classmates at Mount Hermon who will be doctors with Harvard's help; Nick Monjo, his roommate, now a publisher; and a half a dozen others in his class of '69; Willy's first girl; teachers who remember Willy from public school, prep school and Berkeley.

Members and friends of members of the Symbionese Liberation Army gave me letters, memories, confidences. Bill Harris and Russ Little at San Quentin; the mother of Bill Harris in Indiana and the sister of Russ in California; Elena DeAngelis, the sister of Angela Atwood; Gary Ling, brother of Nancy Ling Perry; Fred Soltysik, brother of Patricia (Mizmoon) Soltysik; friends of Camilla Hall; sorority sisters of Emily Harris; Colston Westbrook, who took Willy to Vacaville to meet prisoners; Willie Hearst, who was the first in the family to know that Patty had been kidnapped; Sara Jane Moore, who worked as a volunteer accountant for the Hearsts during the food giveaway; Jack Scott, who protected Patty after the fire; Steven Weed, who lived with Patty.

With all of this help, I still could not have written the book without the aid of professionals who were deep into the story before I tuned in. Reporters Joyce Hoffman at Allentown's *Call-Chronicle*, first to interview Dr. Wolfe; Bob Simmons, who televised the fire in Los Angeles; Bill Hazlett at the Los Angeles *Times*, who went out of his way to get me police and FBI reports, legal documents, his own on-the-scene accounts. Then there were James L. Browning, Jr., who as U.S. Attorney prosecuted Miss Hearst for bank robbery; Public Defender Jim Jenner in Oakland, who helped me to understand the trials of Little and Remiro, now in San Quentin and Folsom; and California's Deputy Attorney General Howard Schwab, who provided me with a copy of his appellate brief in the case of *People vs. William and Emily Harris*; FBI Case Agents Richard Fritz in Allentown and Joseph Alston in Los Angeles.

I gained insight from psychiatrists Dr. Frederick Hacker, who has negotiated with terrorists around the world and told the Hearsts early on not to be surprised "if Patty develops an affinity for her captors" and told me I was bound to find "all in SLA had an upset family background"; from Yale's Dr. Robert Lifton, who believes Patty was brainwashed and suggests the same could have happened to her father at her age "who would have felt equally terrified and disoriented and could have been made to feel guilty for his wealth and dubious family background"; from Dr. Frank Bolton of Phoenix, who urged me to remember "the SLA flourished in California—which is as far west as you can go in this country without jumping off the Golden Gate Bridge, which many do"; and from Nelson Shields III, who resigned from a comfortable job at E. I. Du Pont after his son was killed senselessly by San Francisco's Zebra Gang and who now is in Washington to head the National Council to Control Handguns.

Finally many of my friends helped me in practical ways. In San Francisco, I stayed with Kay Linz as I did my research and was driven by Doug Rederer to the houses where Willy lived in the Bay Area with and without Patty, to the California Medical Facility at Vacaville where Information Officer Thomas Charleston re-created for me the climate of the prison when Cinque and Willy and others in the Black Cultural Association were making plans for the Symbionese Liberation Army, and to the prison at San Quentin where Information Officer Bill Merkle got me in to see Bill Harris and Russell Little and told me what he remembered of George Jackson. In Los Angeles, I stayed with Marcia Binns, whose sleuthing, along with that of Lisa McNeal, took me to George Martin, who lived next door to Willy in Berkeley; and to many in Watts, including Christine Johnson, who was with Willy the night he burned to death.

Through the entire project I had the help of Julian Bach, my agent; Alice Mayhew and John Cox and Vincent Virga at Simon and Schuster; and my husband, who has been living with Willy Wolfe as I have for a long time now and may deserve the most thanks of all.

Contents

Prologue

March 1976

Tania loved Cujo
. . . but during her trial
for armed bank robbery,
she called him a rapist.

Patty couldn't stand Willy Wolfe
. . . but when she was captured,
she carried on a silver chain
the little stone face
he had given her in the underground.

On Thursday, March 18, 1976, U.S. Attorney James Browning, Jr., stood in front of seven women and five men in the jury box at the trial of Patricia Campbell Hearst for armed robbery. Now or never, he would convince the jury that the defendant had gone with a gun to rob a bank of her own free will and not because she was afraid of reprisal from rapists and murderers in the Symbionese Liberation Army. In his hand he held a small stone face (found with Patricia's things at the time of her arrest) that had been given to the defendant by Willy Wolfe, who had raped her, she said, a year and a half before she was captured.

Browning, as prosecutor, had lacked the dazzle of Boston's fast-thinking, high-paid F. Lee Bailey, who represented the defendant, but he had worked hard and had recognized luck when it came his way in the form of a small Mexican art object. With good timing in his closing argument, he let the small black curio drop from his hand as he held on to the silver chain that Patricia had threaded through the strange little face.

"She couldn't stand him," Browning reminded the jury, harking back to Patty's testimony about Willy under his cross-examination, "and yet there is this little stone face that can't say anything, but can tell us a lot." He showed a blowup then of a picture of Patty which was found at the scene of the fire in which Willy died "where you will see around her neck an object that is identical with the little black stone face that Cujo gave her." With this, he asked the jury to reject the defendant's entire testimony as not credible.

"She asks us to believe that she didn't mean what she said on the tapes. She didn't mean what she wrote in the documents." The attorney raised his fist in a power salute. "She didn't mean it when she gave this clenched fist salute after her arrest. That was out of fear of the Harrises, she tells us. She didn't mean it when she told the Deputy Sheriff she was an urban guerrilla, that was her occupation." As he talked, he let the little face dangle from his hand. "She says the Mel's Sporting Goods store shooting incident was simply a reflex; the untruths in the affidavits simply some attorney's idea. She was in such fear that she couldn't escape in nineteen months while crisscrossing the country or even get word to her parents or someone else." Now Browning swung the silver chain so that the little face moved slowly back and forth like a pendulum. "She couldn't stand Willy Wolfe, yet she carried this stone face with her until the day she was arrested. It's too big a pill to swallow, ladies and gentlemen, it just doesn't wash."

Would this line of reasoning bring a conviction? If so, Browning had two women to whom he owed thanks. The first was Carole Westrick, his bright young associate who concentrated in this case on the "woman's angle"; the other was Emily Harris, who unwittingly provided the clue that led him to the most important exhibit he would present at the trial. The break that every prosecutor waits for but knows he can't count on had come to him a couple of weeks back. He remembers that he was listening in the courtroom to an attack by Bailey and his associate, Albert Johnson, on the professional qualifications and ethics of a psychiatrist who had testified in court for the prosecution. During his examination of Patricia, the doctor had told the court, "She said Willy Wolfe had been nice to her, been kind, shown an interest in her along with Angela Atwood and Nancy Ling Perry, and she indicated having had intercourse with him twice." This did not necessarily suggest a love affair, but it appeared to conflict with Patricia's testimony of February 17, in which during examination by Bailey she had for the first time seemed to be saying that she had been, in effect, raped by both Willy and Cinque:

12

BAILEY: Did there come a time when one of the women came to you and talked to you about getting it on with someone?

PATRICIA: Yes.

BAILEY: All right. Can you remember where you were at the time?

PATRICIA: I was in the closet.

BAILEY: Were you blindfolded?

PATRICIA: Yes.

BAILEY: Do you remember who the speaker was?

PATRICIA: Yes.

BAILEY: Who?

PATRICIA: Angela Atwood.

BAILEY: Can you tell us what she said as best you can remember?

PATRICIA: She said that I was going to sleep with William Wolfe.

BAILEY: Uh-huh.

PATRICIA: And so I did.

BAILEY: Did she explain to you any of the customs of the SLA, what their sexual pattern was that you were to be aware of?

PATRICIA: Yes, she said that she and everybody else wanted me to know more about what it was like being in the cell with them.

BAILEY: Uh-huh.

PATRICIA: And that everyone had to take care of the needs of other people and that sexual freedom was a part of the functioning of the cell and that since I'd been there, even though I was in the closet, that I should know more about them.

BAILEY: Uh-huh. How long after she had this conversation with you did Willy Wolfe come in?

PATRICIA: Not long after that. I don't know exactly. It was the same night.

BAILEY: Was your blindfold removed?

PATRICIA: Yes.

BAILEY: What clothing had you been using since your captivity?

PATRICIA: They gave me clothes.

BAILEY: Do you remember what kind? Can you describe them in any way?

PATRICIA: No.

BAILEY: When Mr. Wolfe came in the closet, what did he say
    and do?

PATRICIA: I don't really remember what, if anything, he said.

BAILEY: Did he take you out of the closet?

PATRICIA: No.

BAILEY: What did he do?

PATRICIA: He came in the closet and he closed the door and—

BAILEY: Did he make you lie on the floor?

PATRICIA: Yes.

BAILEY: And then what did he do?

PATRICIA: Had sexual intercourse.

BAILEY: At some time after that, did someone else come to the
    closet for the same purpose?

PATRICIA: Yes.

BAILEY: How long after?

PATRICIA: Maybe a week.

BAILEY: Who was it?

PATRICIA: It was Cinque.

After that, Browning needed more than an "it isn't so" answer, and as he sat with Carole at the prosecutor's table, he saw a way to present tangible proof that Patty had not taken part in the robbery because she was afraid of Willy and the others.

"How was the mail this morning?" he remembers asking Carole.

"Three letters wanting to know how you screw in a closet."

"Same as in the back seat of a car."

Carole laughed. "Somebody in the office said, 'Easier than in the front seat.'" Then she handed Browning the March 5 edition of *New Times* magazine, which had a picture of Emily and Bill Harris on the cover. "This gives the Harrises' version of Patty's love affair with Willy Wolfe. There might be something here." And, now, as Bailey went on with his cross-examination of the psychiatrist, Browning scanned the Harris interview where this statement by Emily jumped out.

"Once Willy gave her a stone relic in the shape of a monkey-face that he had bought when he was in Mexico—he called it an Olmec or something. He had fashioned a macramé chain for it out of some waxed brown string that was lying around the house, sort of a thick thread used for sewing on leather. Anyway, Patty wore it all the time around her neck. After the shootout, she stopped wearing it and carried it in her purse instead, but she always had it with her. Willy also made her a ring out of the same string."

Browning went back and reread the sentence that had made him catch his breath. *"After the shootout, she stopped wearing it and carried it in her purse instead, but she always had it with her."*

Could the face have been in Patricia's purse when she was arrested? Could he get hold of it now? Browning would find this out from Thomas J. Padden, special agent for the FBI, who had been involved with the SLA case since the night of the kidnapping and was at 625 Morse Street in San Francisco on the day Patricia was picked up.

"Yes," Padden told Browning, "the stone face was in the purse." And, "Yes, I can bring it as an exhibit." Then, in another week, Padden and Raymond Callahan, sergeant of police for the Los Angeles Police Department, and Clement Meighan, professor of anthropology at UCLA, turned up in court to be witnesses for the prosecution. While the backgrounds of the three men were not the same, the pieces of knowledge they possessed about one or more artifacts from Mexico would help Browning to sell the point that Patricia Hearst had felt affection for Willy.

On the day the three were to testify, Browning introduced the blowup of the photograph of Patricia which was found after the Los Angeles fire that killed six members of the SLA, including Willy. Next, he presented to the jury the stone object (stipulated now by Bailey as "once having belonged to Willy Wolfe, now deceased") that had hung around the neck of the defendant. And then he examined his first witness as follows:

BROWNING: With respect to Exhibit No. 176 [Olmec figurine] which once belonged to William Wolfe, can you tell me where you found the object?

PADDEN: I got it out of the purse of Patricia Hearst.

BROWNING: And at what time did you get it out of her purse?

PADDEN: That would have been on the 19th of September, 1975.

BROWNING: How do you know that was her purse, incidentally?

PADDEN: On the 18th of September, she told me it was her purse.

That was all; then Browning called Sergeant Callahan, who took the stand for about thirty seconds.

BROWNING: On May 17 of 1974, following a shootout on West 54th Street in Los Angeles, did you have occasion to be present after the fire died down?
SGT. CALLAHAN: Yes.

At this point, Browning gave his witness Exhibit 178 (a small stone object) and asked him if he could identify the object.

SGT. CALLAHAN: Yes, this is an object that was found at the scene.
BROWNING: And where, precisely, at the scene did you find that object, or where did you first see it?
SGT. CALLAHAN: This was beneath the body of one of the deceased, William Wolfe.
BROWNING: Do you know which body that was?
SGT. CALLAHAN: William Wolfe.
BROWNING: And you say beneath the body?
SGT. CALLAHAN: Yes, it was.
BROWNING: Did you actually see it beneath the body?
SGT. CALLAHAN: When the body was turned over, I saw it beneath the body at the time, yes.
BROWNING: And is that the same object that you see on the stand today as Exhibit 178, the small figurine?

When the sergeant said yes, he was excused by Browning, who offered the two artifacts (one from Patricia Hearst's purse and the other from under Willy Wolfe's body) as plaintiff's exhibits, after which he called Clement Meighan, the anthropologist from Los Angeles.

BROWNING: Do you have a field of specialization in anthropology at UCLA?
PROF. MEIGHAN: It's archaeology. I deal with prehistoric human remains of the New World.
BROWNING: And what are your duties at UCLA?

16

PROF. MEIGHAN: I teach classes in archaeology and deal in matters of archaeology, do field work in archaeology.

BROWNING: Have you also published archaeological materials, Professor Meighan?

PROF. MEIGHAN: Yes, sir.

BROWNING: Can you describe briefly for the jury, Professor, how archaeology relates to art?

PROF. MEIGHAN: Well, art objects are, of course, part of archaeology. It deals with the physical things that people manufactured in past times and that includes art objects.

BROWNING: Have you, heretofore, while teaching at UCLA, been called up to identify ancient Mexican artifacts?

PROF. MEIGHAN: Yes sir, frequently.

BROWNING: And during your career have you had occasion to become familiar with the sale of Mexican artifacts in Mexico?

PROF. MEIGHAN: Yes, sir.

BROWNING: And are you generally familiar with the sale of Mexican art objects, both authentic and simulated, to tourists in Mexico?

PROF. MEIGHAN: Yes, sir.

BROWNING: Are you familiar with the language and terms used in referring to Mexican art objects?

PROF. MEIGHAN: Yes, sir.

BROWNING: Are figurines from ancient civilizations recovered quite frequently in Mexico?

PROF. MEIGHAN: Yes, they are.

BROWNING: Are they easy to find?

PROF. MEIGHAN: Yes, they are easy to find.

BROWNING: How are such items described in Mexico, Professor?

PROF. MEIGHAN: The local term used in Mexian-Spanish for these is to refer to them as *monos*, which means monkeys in English, although in Mexico that term includes figurines and also includes anything that is found at an archaeological site.

BROWNING: I see. Let me show you Exhibits 178 and 176, and ask whether either of those items might be described as monkeys in Mexico?

PROF. MEIGHAN: Yes. On the market from an uneducated person in Mexico they would both be referred to as *monos* by the people who sell them.

BROWNING: All right, Professor. At this time I want you to listen to just a sentence or two on a tape and ask if you can define one of the words on the tape?

Here Browning played a portion of the tape that was made by Patricia Hearst after Willy had died in the fire. *"The pigs probably have the little Olmec monkey that Cujo wore around his neck. He gave me the little stone face one night."*

BROWNING: Will you define the word, Olmec, on the tape?

PROF. MEIGHAN: Olmec is a style named for very early culture in Mexico for a particular class of archaeological artifacts.

BROWNING: And would either of those items that you have before you there be commonly described by a non-expert, let us say, as Olmec?

PROF. MEIGHAN: Yes, they could be.

BROWNING: In your experience, would it be uncommon to have a piece such as you see there, either of those two pieces, sold in Mexico as Olmec monkeys?

PROF. MEIGHAN: No, sir. I have seen such things sold under those terms.

BROWNING: In your opinion, are either of those, in fact, Olmec monkeys?

PROF. MEIGHAN: I doubt it, in my opinion they are not.

BROWNING: Would it be possible for a person to have obtained both of those items in the same area in Mexico, the same geographical area?

PROF. MEIGHAN: Yes.

BROWNING: I have no further questions.

The questioning ended at 4:37 P.M. on Monday, March 15, 1976, and now on Thursday, three days later, Prosecutor Browning was urging the jurors to remember. "She couldn't stand Willy Wolfe, yet she carried that stone face with her until the day she was arrested. . . . I ask whether you would accept this incredible story from anyone but Patricia Hearst, and if you wouldn't, don't accept it from her either."

He said that Patricia Hearst had voluntarily joined the SLA and committed that bank robbery, "and we ask you to convict her of the bank robbery." He finished with, "The doctrine of our criminal justice system is that guilt shall not escape or innocence suffer." Now, had he made his point? Had he convinced members of the jury that Patricia was not telling the truth about her relationship with Willy Wolfe? And, if so, could he count on their not accepting the theory that the defendant had robbed the bank because she feared for her life?

On Friday, Judge Oliver J. Carter, who had heard the case, advised members of the jury to consider first the offense charged in Count One of the indictment against Patricia Hearst, to wit, *armed bank robbery*. "If you find the defendant guilty of that count beyond a reasonable doubt, you may then proceed to consider the offense charged in Count Two of the indictment, to wit, *use of a firearm to commit a felony*." He said that if jurors found the defendant not guilty of the offense in Count One, "you must find the defendant not guilty of all the charges in the indictment, including the offense charged in Count Two."

That evening and the next morning, newspapers and networks speculated about the trial's outcome and many mentioned the little stone face. "Isn't this proof from the dead that Patty is lying?" asked one. But others did not buy. "Patty kept the curio because she is an art history major and appreciated the *object*, not the donor." Or "In Mexico, *monos* bring good luck, and who more than Patty needed that!"

On Saturday, as the jury deliberated, a reporter called Willy's mother in Litchfield, Connecticut, for her feeling about the trial and Patty. "I wish Patty Hearst no harm, but my gentle Willy could never have committed rape. Maybe he was in love, but he would never force himself on someone—I know that. It wasn't in his nature." On the street, others weren't so sure. "After all he was in it with all those crazies, and he could have been full of dope . . . "

Patty crocheted in her holding cell as she waited for the verdict that was announced in Judge Carter's big chilly courtroom at 4:10 on Saturday afternoon. "Guilty," said the crier, and then again, "Guilty." The little stone face had made its point. Patricia had not stayed with the SLA because she had been threatened with death and had been raped.

Listening to the verdict in prison were Russell Little and Joe

Remiro, two former SLA members who are serving time for the murder of Oakland's black superintendent of schools, which they and the Harrises and Patty Hearst say they did not do. Both remembered that Willy wore a little stone object around his neck. "But neither of us knew that Willy had two of those things," Russell Little told a visitor, "but we're awfully glad he did."

Bill Harris, another former comrade-in-arms, laughed when he was asked if Patty was raped. "If anyone raped anyone, she raped Willy."

"Cujo was the gentlest, most beautiful man I've ever known," Patty had said on tape. "He taught me the truth as he learned it from the beautiful brothers in California's concentration camps. We loved each other so much, and his love for the people was so deep that he was willing to give his life for them. The name Cujo means 'unconquerable.' It was the perfect name for him, Cujo conquered life as well as death."

Confronted with this declaration during her trial, Patty said yes, she made the tape, but no, she had nothing to do with the authorship of what she said on that tape. Her examination by her defender went like this:

BAILEY: Who was the architect of the taping process?
PATRICIA: William and Emily Harris, mostly William Harris.
BAILEY: How did they go about it? What preparations did they make prior to the actual recording of the tape?
PATRICIA: They wrote like speeches.
BAILEY: Speeches for whom?
PATRICIA: Each one wrote one for themselves and then both of them wrote one for me.

Later Bailey asked, "Was any of what you said Patricia Hearst speaking or was it all something that was written? In other words, were you reading throughout the recording of this tape?" Patricia said, "Yes," there was nothing on the tape that was in her own words. "I might have changed a phrase to make it easier to read, but—none of it was my own words."

Accept that, and Patty becomes the ingenue who scored a hit on the evening news in a part written for her by revolutionaries. And the lover she introduced as a figment of another's imagination. There was no Cujo.

Still we know better. Cujo was Willy Wolfe, the doctor's son from the East who had died a few days earlier at twenty-three. His prep school classmates say he was "strictly apolitical" and his mother remembers him as "the gentlest of my six children." One school adviser says, "He was the sweetest kid you can imagine," yet Willy died in a blaze of gunfire as a most-wanted terrorist. What happened?

In 1974, when the Symbionese Liberation Army was challenging Watergate as a top news story, Willy was the army's mystery member whose name was never mentioned in a communiqué from the underground. Then, when he was mourned on tape by Patty, he became known to millions as the lover of a kidnapped heiress, which to most who knew him is ironic. "He was such an innocent kid," says a young instructor at Andover who went to school with Willy. "I don't think he even kissed a girl until his senior year—not that he didn't want to, but he was timid." And Willy's younger brother shakes his head. "*Willy, the lover*—that was a new one to me."

Until the Cujo announcement, Willy's father had refused to believe his son was mixed up with the kidnappers. "He would never get himself into a thing like that." Then came the tape from Patty and hard evidence from investigators that Willy was not just a member of the SLA, but one of its originators. Still Dr. Wolfe, going back over what happened, wonders if Willy, like Patty, could have been a hostage. "I just can't think he joined up."

Willy's mother is more realistic. Yes, Willy was in the SLA, but why? What did he think he could do that way for himself or anyone else? She thinks about Willy's last week, when he must have sensed that he was cornered, and feels sad. Did Willy wonder then how he ever got into such a deal, which is something Patty Hearst, in jail, did a lot of thinking about in regard to herself.

According to one psychiatrist who talked with Patty shortly after her arrest, "She seemed to get upset and deeply moved when I asked [after hearing her speak tenderly about Willy Wolfe on tape], 'Is that the way you felt about him?'—I felt she was sobbing inside." The doctor said that at the time "I described her—thought of her—made a note she was crying but no tears ran down her face.

"She seemed so upset and she said, 'I don't know how I feel about him.' And I said, 'I am not asking you how you feel about him.' This is now a year and a half later. 'All I am asking is how you felt about him at that time.' She again became very much upset, began to shake and quiver, obviously suffering. And she answered, 'I don't know why I got into this goddamn thing, shit'—and then got up and left the room, terribly upset."

PART ONE

Home to Say Goodbye

Chapter One

On January 2, 1974, eight weeks after the Symbionese Liberation Army sent its Communiqué #1 to Berkeley's underground radio station KPFA claiming responsibility for the murder of Dr. Marcus Foster, Oakland's black superintendent of schools, Willy Wolfe awakened in the guest room of his mother's apartment in Litchfield, Connecticut. In the next five months the SLA, of which Willy was the youngest member, would become as familiar to TV watchers as the FBI, but now no more than two dozen people, if that many, could have told you anything about the group. Certainly no one in his family had any idea that twenty-two-year-old Willy, along with a hodgepodge of California terrorists, would soon be competing with the Watergate clique for top billing on the evening news; the boy-man in the bedroom was just a kid like other kids home for the holidays.

This Wednesday morning when Willy opened his eyes a little after 8:30 he said happy birthday to his tall, handsome sister. Roxie was tying a long green kimono-type robe over her nightgown in front of a full-length mirror beyond the other bed. For most of this vacation their younger brother, John, had spent his nights with Willy. Now John had taken off for Philadelphia, where he was studying music, and, a houseguest having come and gone over New Year's Eve, Roxie had slept in the room with her brother, who showed no surprise. In Willy's life, such body switching was not rare.

For as long as Willy could remember, the people around him had not stayed put. When he was a little kid in New Milford, where his father had his office in the big house on the river, his brothers and sister and half brothers from his mother's first marriage to Dr. Cheney and his dad's ambulatory patients and a summer *Herald Tribune* Fresh Air kid or two made for perennial flux. Then, later, in the Wolfes' showplace home outside of Utica, when all the kids in the house were in different schools, somebody from Andover or Taft or Abbot or Yale was always coming or going. After that came prep school in Massachusetts, not exactly an isolation unit, and then, for the past few years, there was California.

Out on the Coast, Willy and his good friend Russ Little and Russ's girl from Florida had roomed for a long time near Berkeley at Dave Gunnell's place on Chabot Road in Oakland, which was really a kind of commune, and then just recently he and Joe Remiro had lived in a bungalow on Bond Street which Cinque and Mizmoon and all the others had used as their drop. And now, in the Bay Area, there had been another shift. Last he heard, his stuff was stored in Angela Atwood's room at the Harrises', but by now it probably had been taken to the Concord house thirty miles to the east where Nancy Ling Perry was keeping his car. So why should he care at this place who slept where?

For Willy, just as inconsequential as the apartment's shifting personnel was the per diem mileage he clocked up as a matter of course on whatever car happened to be available wherever he might be. Since his arrival on December 20 at his dad's house in Pennsylvania (after hitchhiking in from the West) he had driven his stepmother's car to New York to have a talk with his black Puerto Rican friend and mentor Mike Carrerras, an executive of the telephone company who had come years before as a poor city kid to spend his summers in Connecticut. Then he had headed north to see his mother and after that had moved on to New Hampshire for Christmas with the family of his brother, who was his half brother, really, old, straight Ben. And, finally, he had returned to Litchfield, from which he would be taking off today for another stopover with his dad's young family near Allentown. But for now he would relax, which was easy to do in his old four-poster in this room with its antique chests and polished brass lamps and the Oriental rug from his grandmother's house in Torrington.

Yawning, he let the muscles of his neck and shoulders relax and turned his head toward his sister. Sensing that she was considering what twenty-five years had wrought, he told her, "Not bad." Then, smiling at her in the mirror, he said, "Name one person as good-looking as you." And when Roxie smiled back, he gave her a sleepy salute. In the past two weeks, everywhere these two had been together, someone had told them they looked enough alike to be twins.

At the time of their parents' divorce in 1966, when their father gave up his job as staff anesthesiologist at St. Lukes Memorial Hospital in Utica and moved to another state, these lanky middle kids in the foursome of Wolfes looked more like LeRoy S. Wolfe, M.D., than like their smaller-boned mother, and the resemblance grew. Their dad (christened Peter and known to friends as Pete in spite of his having adopted his father's name of LeRoy before going to Pennsylvania's Hill Boarding School) is six feet five, and Roxie and Willie stood tall. By ninth grade, Roxie had reached her present height of five feet nine, and by prep school Willy pushed six feet.

More than the others, these two, born two years and one month apart, were the inheritors of their father's dark good looks (strong features, even white teeth, purplish eyes and curly black hair), which—along with the name, Wolfe—made many wonder if they were Jewish, which they were not. On the Wolfe side, they were descended from Pennsylvania Germans with names like Shupe who were lured to the Commonwealth by William Penn and whose grandsons and great-grandsons married the granddaughters and great-granddaughters of Scottish transplants from northern Ireland. On their mother's side, their forebears, the Lawtons, were a sturdy line of Connecticut Yankees who worked hard, made a shrew deal whenever they got the chance, took out patents, acquired land and big houses, and sent their children to eastern schools. For the boys, this last meant Yale, where at weekend house parties, they met girls of their own kind. And for the girls, this meant boarding school instead of public high school, followed by college sometimes if marriage did not come early, as it did for Virginia Lawton, known from babyhood as Honey.*

In her young girlhood, the mother of the Wolfe children lived in

---

*When Honey's father, who sired this child late in life, looked at his new baby, he said, "This one's a honey." And the name stuck.

Torrington, where brass strip casting was big business and everyone understood the Lawton Mold (invented by her father). She was known also in Waterbury, where her father commuted daily to work for the Anaconda Copper Company. Honey enjoyed the respect that is usually accorded the banker's daughter in small towns.

Charles Lawton, whom everyone looked up to, was twice the age of the fathers of Honey's friends, and her mother, too, was old enough to be her grandmother. So Honey, the adored child of her parents, looked to her sister, Kate, who was eighteen years her senior, for guidance. She was happy and to outsiders for a long time she seemed to be taking one light-footed step after another into a just about perfect future.

When it came time to go away to school, Honey chose Abbot Academy (now integrated with Phillips Academy at Andover, Massachusetts), the oldest incorporated school for girls in the United States. There she was a good student, laughed a lot and was an excellent dancer during the Big Band era. She did not lack for dates then or later. But the prom-trotting role was not for her for long. At twenty-one, she married serious-minded Charles B. Cheney, a graduate of the Taft School and a pre-med student at Yale, whose mother was a Farrel (one of the wealthiest families in Connecticut) and whose father was Dr. Benjamin A. Cheney, chief of staff at New Haven's Grace Hospital and later director of the prestigious Yale-New Haven Medical Center.

In the next six years, during which time Charles graduated from Yale Medical School, the Cheneys had two boys, Ben, born in 1937, and Charlie, born in 1941. Then came the attack on Pearl Harbor and, with it, the end of predictability to Honey's life. During the war, she and her husband, who served in the Army Medical Corps, were sometimes apart and sometimes together, and found along the way that both could be as comfortable without as with each other. The marriage ended in 1945, the year when collapsing war marriages sent the American divorce rate up to a historic high, not to be duplicated again until the 1970's.

Like many couples who had lived separately during the war years, the Cheneys could find logical reasons for not getting back together without one person's embarrassing the other, and they managed this. And soon both were looking ahead to new marriages that each believed could be better. With concern for each other, which Charles and Honey still express more than thirty years later, they arranged a support plan for the boys, who would stay most of the time with Honey. Then Charles married a second girl from the East, a Smith graduate and Yale nurse, and Honey married a second Yale man who was studying to be a doctor. Unlike her first husband, this one was unconventional and six years her junior.

"Everything Pete and I did in those early years was so much fun," Honey remembers. Her second husband agrees. "No two people were ever so much in love."

The Wolfes' first child, Peter, was born in 1947 in Cuba, where Pete was a lieutenant (jg) at Guantanamo Naval Base. The next five children (two were stillborn twins) came along after the young doctor had become a practicing GP in the country town of New Milford, Connecticut, where farmers, factory workers, and a few exurbanite artists and writers worked hard and stayed to themselves. There, Roxie came along in 1949, Willy followed in 1951, and John arrived in 1953.

Like many fathers twenty-five years ago, Pete Wolfe did not share child-care duties with his wife and by today's standards, according to Roxie, was "a real male chauvinist pig." Occasionally he sailed on Candlewood Lake with Honey's oldest son, Ben Cheney, or played ball in the schoolyard with her second boy, Charlie, and he served as resident doctor for the brood, which in the summertime included Brooklyn-born Mike, a *Herald Tribune* Fresh Air kid whom Pete invited up with his sister on impulse one year "to compensate," as he told friends, "for Honey's loss of the twins." But he depended on Honey as a matter of course to take care of the house and his office, do the laundry, ironing, cooking, and bookkeeping, and bathe and feed the children. Although close with money and not as wealthy as Honey's first husband, who sent a chauffeur for the two older boys when they were due to go to New Haven, Pete was a responsible provider and early in his professional career commuted to Hartford to take a special course in anesthesiology from internationally known Dr. Ralph Tovell that could lead to a higher income. The boost came when Pete left New Milford to become a staff member of a hospital in upstate New York, where he moved with his wife and a scramble of kids along with a horse, two dogs, a couple of cats and a parrot to a big house in a small town near Utica.

Sometimes, Dr. Wolfe shocked orthodox doctors with his garb (he

29

wore sandals and an open shirt in the office) and startled some of his women patients with remarks remembered as "a little too sexy," but he was a vital husband and colorful father, and for the first few years the Wolfes went happily along until fate dealt Honey a painful blow. Without warning, she was stricken with a type of polyneuritis (now Legionnaire's disease) that paralyzed her respiratory system.

Diagnosed correctly by Dr. Wolfe as Landry-Guillain-Barré, which was to become a household conversation piece in 1976 when it occurred in a number of recipients of swine flu vaccine during the nationwide inoculation program, his wife's peculiar ascending paralysis called for mechanical ventilation in a hospital. During Honey's three-month stay in an iron lung and the long ambulatory recuperation period thereafter, Dr. Wolfe's mother, who was her daughter-in-law's good friend and companion, came from Buffalo and took over as the children's caretaker-counselor.

Crediting her husband for saving her life, Honey fought with all her spirit to get back to her family, but when she returned, the old wife-and-mother role wasn't as easy to perform as it had been. Her body after her illness was emaciated and one leg was thin and permanently crippled, so household chores, which had always been simple, now became difficult. But her husband was doing well at his work at the hospital and in private practice and she could afford a housekeeper, so she could cope, but some of her zest was gone. For one thing, she couldn't dance anymore, and sitting on the sidelines of life in any department was difficult for someone who had rollicked along like Honey.

Even in this period, according to Roxie, "no children ever had a happier life," but eventually Honey's depleted vitality along with a work load that was larger than life and a new worry about another woman who was of interest to her husband left her defensive and nervous. Then the frustration she felt brought forth explosions, with talk of separation, which started as a threat but soon became a thrust. The result was divorce and the end of carefree living for the Wolfe kids.

When the family split up, Roxie, who was away at Abbot, was regretful but not shocked because she had been alerted by Peter, her older brother, that their father was "fooling around." But Willy, who was fourteen and in ninth grade, had refused to see signs of the coming break and was staggered. "Willy had a bad time," says his father, who was married soon after the divorce to a slim blond nurse twenty-one years his junior. And says Willy's mother, "His grades began to show it."

Willy's honor-roll record in junior high reveals grades in accelerated math and earth science and biology of 94 and above. But afterward, when he moved with his mother and John to Litchfield, his marks dropped to the 80's—good enough B grades but not up to Willy's usual A standard, which may account for his not being accepted at Exeter or Andover, where he applied for his eleventh and twelfth years. He got into Mount Hermon Preparatory School, however, owing to his IQ of 133, his high verbal and nonverbal Lorge Thorndike scores, and his recommendations from well-known persons in Utica and Litchfield, who assured the school "this one is quality."

As a good-natured boarder at the school in Northfield, Massachusetts, which is now coeducational but in Willy's day was a home nine months of the year for 650 boys, he was a disappointing underachiever in the classroom. Still the faculty, which gave him special encouragement and even suggested during his senior year that he come back for another year before going on to college, knew he was immature but believed he was one of those late bloomers they had known before who could go on to a good small college and eventually find himself. "A one-word description of Willy when he was here would be 'winsome,'" says William Morrow, longtime director of the alumni office. "So you can see why the entire faculty was dumbfounded a few years later to find that the Willy Wolfe we heard about in the Symbionese Liberation Army was *our* Willy, as sweet a boy as any of us can remember."

"He *was* sweet," Roxie says, as she thinks about that last morning in Litchfield when she told Willy as she was leaving the bedroom that she was glad he seemed to have recovered from whatever had hit him on New Year's Eve and asked if he wanted coffee.

"I hear the percolater; want me to bring you a cup?"

"Mmmmmmh," her brother said. "And when you come back, I've got a present for you."

In the kitchen, Roxie could hear Willy moving around in the bedroom and when she returned he was back in bed and leaning on one elbow with a long, flat newspaper-wrapped package beside him. "You can leave this with Mom or take it to Pennsylvania today, whichever you like."

Roxie sat down on the bed where she had slept and kept saying as she unwrapped her gift, "What in the world?" And then, finally, "Not your gun!" The old .41 caliber rifle had been Willy's prize possession since the day a dozen years before when the Swiss bridegroom of twenty-two-year-old Karen Gabrielson, Willy's special friend in Utica, sensed at the wedding the boy's feeling of loss of the "older woman" in his life with whom he thought he was in love and gave him the antique Vetterli. "Why do you want me to have it?" Roxie asked her brother now.

"Not to shoot, that's for sure; you'd blow yourself to pieces."   ·

"But you liked this gun so much."

"So did you."

"I know, but . . ." Roxie had gotten up and was walking slowly across the room with the gun hanging down by her side in her right hand and the fingers of her left hand spread across her mouth as she tried to figure this out. "If you ever want this . . ."

"I won't want it," Willy said as he put his head down and pulled up the covers to sleep some more, but Roxie in the doorway went on talking. "Dad said when he came back from California a couple of months ago that you might marry a girl out there from Sweden; why wouldn't you give this to her?"

"Oh, come on, Roxie," Willy said, yawning deeply now, "didn't anyone ever give you something for your birthday before?"

"Not anything like this," Roxie said, as she looked down at the weapon, and now she was talking as much to herself as to Willy, who had closed his eyes. "Never thought I'd own a gun, but I can think of one day I would have been glad to have had it." At other times, recalling her abduction in Philadelphia in 1971, Roxie had cried.

Chapter Two

In 1971, when she was a student nurse in Philadelphia, Roxie was dragged into a van by a quiet-talking man of twenty-six or twenty-seven who stopped to ask directions. For the most part, she has blocked out the memory of being driven for miles with a switchblade pressed against her ribs to the back entrance of a motel across the river in Pennsauken. But sometimes, when she is overtired or finds herself in a life situation that seems too big for her to handle, she screams out in the night at the wet, grim nightmare face of a light-skinned black man who slashes through her leather coat with a sharp knife, tears at her skirt and stockings and encircles her throat in a viselike grip as he forces her back and down. . . .

For a long time, Roxie, whose given name, Roxanna Whitney, came down to her from a great grandmother on her mother's side, did not tell Honey that the man who had left her choking and half-unconscious in the motel was black "because I couldn't bear to stir up a prejudice that she didn't know was there." But she needn't have worried. "White men do cruel things, too," Honey said.

Many years before, Honey had shocked a mother in New Milford who had children Roxie's age when she said that she wouldn't make a fuss "if my daughter grows up and marries a colored man if he's a nice

man and they love each other." And this was more than no-risk
dramatic talk that a bright young woman might send out as a shocker
to the wife of a stuffy, standpat Republican in a town with no more
than one or two black families.

With Mike around during the summer, Honey had become color-
blind. "He's just like the others who come to play," she told a niece,
"only quieter and better mannered." And says Roxie today, "My
mother really loved Mike, and I think she hoped that some day I
would marry him. Certainly she would have had no racial objection."

After her divorce from Pete in the sixties, Honey did not march
with civil rights protesters and was all for law and order, but she knew
that integration in schools and neighborhoods and voting rights for
blacks were long overdue and was glad that the government was doing
something about both. And while she had been upset when Willy
dropped out of Berkeley, she had been rather proud at first of the work
he was doing at Vacaville prison, where, as she gathered, he was
helping black prisoners to prepare for life outside. And then, after
Roxie had told her about the abductor, she had been glad that she had
not taught the children to hate a man for the color of his skin. (She
realized that a deep-felt prejudicial fear along with real physical terror
would have been too much for her daughter to bear.) She talked about
this to Willy, she remembered later, who had been deeply affected by
what had happened to his sister. ("A guy would have to be crazy to do
a thing like that," he told Mike.) And she was glad that her daughter
had felt free to talk to her about the assault.

Today, on the last morning of Roxie's holiday, Honey was sitting at
her desk in the little room where she did her letter writing, checkbook
balancing and bookwork for the selling · job she did for a local
advertising sheet. When Roxie appeared at the door, she was just
hanging up the telephone. "Nobody thinks you can make it to
Allentown," she said. "Kate says to turn on the TV." And in seconds
Roxie was looking at cars lined up in the snow to buy gas at a filling
station in Pennsylvania where there was none. Still, gas shortage or no
shortage, Roxie said, she had to report at the Allentown Hospital the
next morning "or shoot myself," whereupon she held up Willy's gun,
and Honey did a double take. "Is that Willy's?"

"He gave it to me, which makes me think my hunch is wrong and
he *is* getting married."

"Sometimes I think yes, but the rest of the time no, because why wouldn't he be calling the girl?"

"Way over in Sweden?"

"I'm not sure that Eva's gone back to Sweden or even that Willy's in love with her."

"He was with her all the time in California when Dad was there."

Honey turned back to the desk and slowly shook her head. She said that a few nights before, when everyone was out, a collect call had come from California "that I thought was going to be from Eva." She hadn't accepted the charges because Willy wasn't home. "But the call wasn't from Eva, anyway, but from one of Willy's roommates." She said she thought sometimes that Willy wasn't going to Sweden at all "but is planning something that he can't talk about."

"I wish you wouldn't worry."

This, Honey said, she couldn't help. On New Year's Eve, when she was alone, she had reread all of Willy's letters from California and the talk of revolution in the last ones had frightened her. "The whole story is in these letters that have come in the last few months," she said, holding up a small packet that she placed now in the little right-hand drawer of her desk. "Ever since he's been in California, he's been getting more and more radical," she told Roxie. "First he moved from the dormitory to Peking Man House, and then he dropped out of school because 'it isn't relevant,' and then he started quoting Mao and talking about revolution, and I though that was just a phase. But now I'm really scared, because in these last letters he's been saying that the prisoners he's working with should be organized to overthrow the government." She turned her face toward Roxie, who had switched off the television and was drinking coffee in the doorway. "I'd like to think of a way to keep him here but I don't know how." Roxie did not interrupt as her mother continued to think out loud. "And why is he so involved in all this now, that's what I'd like to know. The war's over, and he isn't going to be drafted and Nixon's about finished, everybody says. So what does Willy want?"

"A perfect world where everybody practices self-denial and has a big breakfast," Roxie said with a laugh as they listened to Willy's heavy footsteps in the kitchen and smelled bacon frying out there. "And if Willy marries a Swedish waitress, so much the better, because somebody's got to keep those old short orders coming." Then she walked over and bent down and kissed her mother as they waited for Willy. "He'll find himself; think how long it took me."

Seven years before, after Roxie had graduated from Abbot, she had gone on for her freshman year at Briarcliff, where she felt ungainly, unattractive and unlike the other girls who were proper, snobbish and, she thought, dull. She had switched to nursing school in Philadelphia, but found her classes a bore. So in her third year, she had dropped out of college to work with juvenile delinquents in a drug-rehabilitation program, but now she was in Allentown where she could work in the hospital where her father was on the staff and take courses at the same time at Cedar Crest College, where, finally, if all went right, she would get her B.A. in June.

"A sweet girl graduate at twenty-five," she said to her brother, who had come to the door with his plate heaped high. "And what are you going to do?"

"He's going to clean up the mess he left in the kitchen," said Honey.

"Don't dream," said Roxie.

"First, I'm going to eat," said Willy, "and then say goodbye to Lydia."

"I thought he did that the night before last," Roxie said when her brother had gone back to his room.

"And the night before that and the night before that."

"So, maybe Lydia right here in town is the one Willy loves."

"I used to hope so . . ." Honey began but Roxie was shaking her head.

"Lydia's had a lot of terrible things happen to her in the last few years, and she has a lot of problems."

"So does Willy," said her mother.

"And together they'd have bigger ones."

Honey agreed, but she said she couldn't help remembering long ago, before she had moved to Litchfield, when Lydia had come here with her parents from Boston to spend the holidays in their second home, and Willy had come with her to visit Aunt Kate, and both children had their portraits painted. "And everyone who saw the paintings thought they were the most beautiful little girl and boy anyone ever saw."

"And you dreamed they would grow up and marry and live happily ever after."

"So, I'm a romantic," said Honey, "but don't laugh. If things had been just a little bit different for both of them, that is what could have happened. And I've been thinking a lot about that this week as I've watched Willy and Lydia together and—funny thing—I know Willy's been thinking about that too."

Chapter Three

On the last day of Willy's visit, eighteen-year-old Lydia Brickley awakened in the antique French bed next to the window in the back bedroom, which had been her mother's room in the last years before the accident, and listened to the ringing of the telephone. When she heard her brother tell Willy that she wasn't available, she did not move her head or call out. Lying still, she looked down into the blue-white valley to the west where children were skating on the black ice of Cranberry Pond, knowing that her brother and his new wife would be going soon to her grandmother's house; then she would call Willy to come over.

Ever since she had run away to California from boarding school two years before, Dick, who was here this weekend, and her younger brother, Jim, had despised the boy she had been writing to out there. That Willy had nothing to do with her taking off from Westover they did not believe and she no longer tried to sell. Instead, she ducked the issue, as she was doing now, arranging to meet Willy in his mother's apartment or here when the others were out.

As she pulled on her blue jeans, she thought of other holidays when she had come to Connecticut with her family and had dressed in a hurry on mornings like this to go with one of the boys to Crutch &

MacDonalds Drug Store for *The New York Times*, which they took to their grandfather in his big white house with its tall classical columns on Prospect Street. But that was long ago, and Grandfather Hickox, who had been sick even then, had been gone a long time now, and her mother was dead too. Up in Boston her father had remarried, and up there or here her older brother, who was a stockbroker, and the other, who would be going into her dad's law firm, were not fun anymore. It was vacation time and Willy was home, but he was talking more and more about going to live in Lapland, and nothing, she sensed, would ever be the way it had been. Nothing, that is, but the village. Litchfield, high on its rocky ridge above the rest of Connecticut, looks now as it did when its great houses were built two hundred years ago.

"But where did people way back in the hills get the money to build houses like this?" someone always asks as hundreds go from mansion to mansion when the town has its annual July Open House. And the guide, busy with a thousand details, says "Merchants here imported from China" or "We had a great law school" or "Washington and Hamilton came here a lot," fast answers that leave the puzzled more puzzled. But who can blame the volunteers when people from New York are parking every which way and wanting to go to the toilet and trampling all over the flower beds? On such a day, no one has time to quote from an editorial written by Lydia's great-great-grandfather in the Litchfield *Enquirer*, which he owned and edited for twenty-five years following the Civil War. "Things have a way of coming out right if they start right." Unlike other towns in western Connecticut, this one, with its huge trees and broad streets, was not settled helter-skelter; rather, it was laid out around a green in sixty fifteen-acre lots by a group of able men, approved by Hartford's General Assembly, who set aside three lots for a school, a meeting house and a homestead for the minister from the state-supported Congregational Church. Then they sold the other parcels and the farmland behind each to fifty-seven "proprietors."

Nothing trashy mars the look of Litchfield (pop. 7,500). The few old houses that had turrets and domes, added in the late 1800's by disciples of Stanford White, have had the clutter removed. Other houses, like the one belonging to Lydia's father, which was built in 1876, have been done over as his was renovated in 1948 to harmonize with authentic Colonials. So on street after street one gleaming white house with dark shutters after another stands as a monument to worldly success.

Some of the old mansions are owned by the town or by descendants of early settlers, but most have been purchased and restored by weekenders from New York or Boston, who have also done over the old stables, which are finished in black walnut. Once, when Willy and Lydia first knew each other, they went to a party in a converted barn, and as they stood looking up at the huge beams, Willy said that he would like to come back here as an archaeologist and live in a stable and write a book on the mica schist rock under the town. But that was long ago, and, if reminded, Willy would not have remembered the dream as he walked between the round pillars into Lydia's house which was watched by police driving slowly down North Street.

Once inside, Willy stood in his heavy jacket and red knit cap in the center hall with his back against the heavy front door. He watched as the fragile-looking girl with long pale hair who was buttoning her flannel shirt came lightly down the stairs. "What's with the pigs?" And now as Lydia moved past him to look out through the handmade lace curtain in the left front window, he told her, "They're watching the house."

The girl shook her head. "Why?"

Willy stiffened but relaxed when he saw that the cops were studying Lydia's brother's Massachusetts license. Remembering talk around town that kids here were getting deliveries from South Boston, he may have wanted to warn Lydia, "Now, they'll say you're dealing." Instead, he laughed, then stopped. "And you *like* this town. Come on. You better go with me to Lapland."

"I'm beginning to think you mean it." Willy had told her before about having met an old man in upper Sweden when he was exploring there in 1970, a person who was kind and wise "and can do absolutely anything." Now he said that he and Lydia could stay with his Laplander friend "in his clean little house that has nothing around it but white snow for as far as the eye can see."

When she looked back later, Lydia believed that Willy had been fantasizing, but at the time she accepted what he said as truth. "What's there that we don't have here?" she asked.

Willy took off his jacket and dropped it on the hall love seat and followed Lydia into the living room where they sat together on the sofa. "This country's corrupt, and it's going to get worse. In Lapland there's freedom."

The headmistress of Lydia's Windsor Mountain School, a boarding school in Lenox, Massachusetts, had studied under Freud, and the girl said now that freedom was something you had to find inside yourself. "The last time I went looking for it someplace else, I didn't have much luck." She was referring to the spring of '72 when she had run away to California in search of Willy.

"You didn't have things planned right," Willy said with his arm around her shoulders.

When Lydia smiles, her lips part to reveal small, straight, evenly spaced teeth and her large blue eyes become beautiful. "That's for sure," she said, beginning to laugh now with Willy at the child she had been on the February morning when a classmate at Westover had come to her room and begged her between sobs to escape from the school "which I loathe so much I'm going to commit suicide if you don't run away with me." So Lydia had agreed to help. "The place is a prison," she had told her mother more than once. "They've got guards at the gate." And her mother had said, "It will get better." But it had not, and now Lydia could remember the elation that she had felt when she and her friend (bundled up in all the shirts and sweaters they could button themselves into) had gotten past the unsuspecting guards and slipped around the corner and were free of the place.

"Isn't this fabulous?" she kept saying all the first day as she and the girl from Detroit rode along to New York State in the cab of a truck with a driver who had been delivering something not far from the school and had agreed to give them a lift. "We're *free!*" But her pal with the suicide bent had wept then about something new. "I'm killing my folks," she had wailed, "how are they going to feel?"

"They way you felt when they left you in that prison," Lydia told her, "so stop crying; you're the one who wanted to come." But in the night, as her friend lay sniffling beside her under a blanket in the back of a second westbound truck, Lydia assured her that she didn't have to go all the way to California. "After our next ride or the next, we'll be near Michigan, and you can call home." And that's the way it worked out.

At Youngstown, Ohio, after promising Lydia that she wouldn't tell where her old schoolmate was headed, the girl called her parents, who wired money for her to get home. Lydia understood but didn't relent.

Waving goodbye, she continued west with a pair of other runaways about her age who called themselves Tim and Terry.

A long time later Lydia told Willy that those weeks on the road with the boy and girl hitchhikers from the Middle West were the happiest she had known. "We'd meet a truck driver at a weighing station and he would give us a ride and a couple of dollars, and then we'd stop in a little town and talk to kids on the street and maybe get invited to a diner for a hamburger or to a cabin for a meal and it was wonderful." In New Mexico, Arizona and Southern California the trio found other young people in communes who gave them food and directions to more groups up ahead, and every day along the highway brought adventure. But when they hit Los Angeles, their luck ran out.

Even before they got to the city, Tim had lost his zest, and by the time they were in the outskirts, his skin had turned yellow and he could hardly drag himself along the road. Finally, he told Terry that his stool was whitish-looking and sometimes tinged with blood and that he was afraid he was going to die. The frightened girl appealed to Lydia, who asked the next driver who picked them up to let them off at a hospital if he knew of one, which he did, and there the doctor said that Tim had hepatitis. As welfare workers got busy trying to locate Tim's parents, Lydia bid Terry goodbye and went to a pay phone and tried to call Willy in Berkeley, where the operator at the university kept cutting her off. Then, when she tried to reach him where she had been writing, she found that the telephone was not listed under Wolfe, and not knowing the name of the owner of the rooming house, she had to give up.

Thereafter the sky caved in. Heading north alone, she accepted a ride from a salesman, who threatened to abduct her, and returning terrified to her friends in Los Angeles, she begged two other runaways to take her to Willy. But by then she was ill herself, and while she waited for treatment at a Los Angeles clinic, one of her companions for the trip north was killed on the highway while changing a tire. With this news, Lydia was drained of any desire for more adventure. Sobbing, she told a nurse at the clinic the names of her parents and their telephone numbers and within hours was on a plane to New York. Her mother didn't come down on her when she arrived in Litchfield. "After I took a bath and got into bed, she brought me tea and toast and sat without talking until I went to sleep." In another ten days, when Lydia continued to feel ill, her mother took her to the doctor, who lived next door "who found that I had hepatitis and put me in the hospital, which is something I go over and over when I think of all that happened because of that."

On April 21, Lydia had dramatic proof of what Sartre meant by "it is our presence in the world that multiplies relations," which a graduate student from Santa Barbara had pondered with others beside a bonfire in an Arizona commune where she had stayed one night with Tim and Terry. At three o'clock that Friday afternoon two persons were killed and two others critically injured in a collision on the road between Torrington, where Lydia was in the hospital, and her home in Litchfield. Because of who she was and whom she knew, traffic was tied up for several hours between the two towns as ambulances carted away the stunned, unconscious or lifeless bodies of five persons.

Shortly after lunch that day, Litchfield's young Dick Reventlow, whose father, Court Haugwitz Reventlow, had been married to Barbara Hutton, and whose half brother, Lance, was as well known to most Americans in his babyhood as the kidnapped Lindbergh baby, had gone with his friend Tommy Bowers, grandson of a wealthy member of the New York Stock Exchange, to visit Lydia in her hospital room. At the time, Dick, who would be identified in newspaper accounts after this afternoon as "Miss Brickley's boy friend," was twenty-four and Tommy was twenty-six. For a year or more, both had been drop-in friends of Lydia's mother, an obese, discontented woman who once had been as slimly beautiful as her daughter.

Lydia Hickox Brickley, the mother, who was a bridge table pal of Honey Wolfe's, was the only daughter of doting parents who owned handsome houses in New York and Litchfield. She was the inheritor of an adventurous intellect as well as good looks and wealth from both sides of her family. Instead of going with her friends to a conventional finishing school, talented Lydia Hickox went to Bennington College, where she studied art and modern dance and met Richard Brickley, a handsome, athletic Irish Catholic law student from Boston who was an intimate friend at Harvard of Joe Kennedy's boys. With the blessings of her parents, she married, had three children, ran homes in Boston and Litchfield, and at the end of twenty-five years found herself filled with a vague unrest which she quelled with the help of tranquilizers and alcohol.

"She's spoiled," said the jealous ones who envied her money and her physically fit successful husband. Or "The marriage isn't working out," said the catty ones at cocktail parties who noted Richard Brickley's increasing interest in the widow of Marshall Field III who had bought a big house next to Lydia's grandmother's place. "Who can blame him, letting herself get so fat," said the vicious ones.

In the spring of '72, when Dick Reventlow and his friends discovered that Mrs. Brickley was fun to talk to, they sat often on her big glass porch on North Street, which brought more gossip. "Who do the boys like over there, anyway, the mother or the daughter?" In truth, the bright young men liked both Lydias, and when the younger Lydia went to the hospital, they stopped as often to see her as they did to see her mother. In fact, on the day of the accident, Dick and Tommy were saying goodbye to young Lydia in the hospital about the time the older Lydia was leaving Litchfield to go to the same place.

When young Lydia's callers left her, they got into Dick's Mercedes-Benz, drove to Toll Gate Road and started up one of the two long southbound lanes that climb the steep hill between Torrington and Litchfield. At the same time, unseen by them but coming up the single northbound lane in a van on the Litchfield side of the hill was local florist Ralph Wadhams, fifty-eight, with his wife, Evelyn, fifty-seven, who were delivering roses to Miss Brickley at the hospital. And two cars back of the van, traveling in the same "no passing" northbound lane at a reasonable speed, was Mrs. Brickley, in her Mercedes-Benz on her way to visit her daughter.

Later the coroner's report would say that at a few minutes before three o'clock, Mrs. Brickley approached the crest of the hill and moved into the lane for southbound cars to pass a small passenger car in between the florist's van and her car. Then, apparently seeing Dick's Mercedes coming toward her, she veered to the right, struck the left rear fender of the florist's van and lurched into the path of the oncoming car, colliding with it head-on. All three vehicles went out of control, and the rest was a bloodbath.

The florist's van turned over and righted itself on the shoulder of the road, throwing Mrs. Wadhams through the windshield to the pavement as it bounced her husband to his death. In the same pileup, Dick Reventlow's car was demolished, and his passenger and he were taken by ambulance back to the hospital, where Tommy was released after treatment but Dick was laid up for months. And the blood-soaked car belonging to Mrs. Brickley had to be pried open so that its crushed occupant could be transported to the hospital's emergency room, near which Lydia was having tea and cookies with her grandmother, who had driven past the carnage on Toll Gate Road, not knowing that her daughter was its cause.

Late that afternoon when Mrs. Brickley was pronounced dead, Lydia's doctor came to comfort his patient. "She had a tumor that would have killed her soon," he told Lydia, whose guilt, he knew, might very well plague her for years.

Within a year, Tommy Bowers, who miraculously escaped serious injury in the accident, was struck by lightning inside his house in New Hampshire and was killed. Lance Reventlow, half brother of Dick, who had walked unhurt from the world's fastest speedways, died in a plane crash out west. Lydia found the tragedies in her life almost too much to bear. "It seems that something terrible happens to everyone connected with me," she had told Willy on the afternoon of New Year's Eve.

People who saw Willy that evening at a party where he spent much time with Lydia, who had come with another date, have prismatic versions of his mood on the last night of 1973. According to Honey, Willy told Roxie that he would go along with her and some visiting cousins to a nearby pub that night. "But I could tell from what he'd been saying to Lydia he would be giving them the slip later on to go to a party at the Mosleys', who own one of the big houses here."

"And that's what happened," says Roxie. She and her mother and Willy had supper at the apartment with their cousin, Mary Brooks, a young member of Honey's clan from a prominent Torrington banking family, and then all but Honey went to Mitchell's Pub to meet Pete Zimmerman, the son of Aunt Kate's daughter, Addie, a publisher's wife in England. "Pete and his two brothers had come from London to visit often when they were growing up, but it wasn't until that Christmas vacation that Pete and I became good friends," says Roxie. "My mother had taken him up to Ben's for Christmas, and he and I had driven back together a few nights before and stopped and talked for hours over Harvey Wallbangers at the Publick House in Sturbridge."

This Pete, who was then living in Los Angeles, remembers having a drink on New Year's Eve in the pub with Ron Anderson, a bachelor artist (who occupies a studio duplex next to his grandmother's house) whose portraits of Willy and Lydia and many others from the town's old families were known to Pete. "We'd hardly got settled when a fellow at the bar who had on a white turtleneck with a big silver medallion around his neck got to talking with us and sat down. About that time, Roxie and Brooksie blew in with Willy, who began acting fruity. I remember he started lisping and making eyes at the new fellow to get at Ron. And that made Roxie mad."

Roxie remembers too. "I ordered a mix of vodka and Galliano but I didn't sit down. Instead, I stood behind Ron and motioned for Willy to lay off."

"Maybe Willy's in the closet and doesn't know it," Pete whispered to her, but Roxie shook her head.

"Grade-school stuff, and all I can say is the great liberal's got some growing up to do." As a distraction, she put one knee on a dish cart parked at the end of the bar and began coasting along. "Whee!"

"Everybody's nuts in this town," Pete said to Ron, who paid for the drinks. "Why do you stay?"

"Good living," Ron said. He told Pete that he was going to a party that night at which supper at midnight would rival any dinner Pete had ever eaten at Simpsons. "Litchfield people know how to live." In another few minutes he excused himself and left Willy sitting face to face with the young homosexual he'd taunted.

Now, alone with the man, Willy muttered a quick "so long" and followed Ron to the door where he mumbled an apology. "I thought the guy was visiting you."

"So you were safe." Then Ron smiled and wished Willy a happy new year and left. Willy, too embarrassed to return to the table, hurried out into the cold and soon appeared at the house where he had agreed to meet Lydia.

"He got very sick that night," Lydia remembers, "and afterward, Roxie thought somebody had put turpentine or something in his drinks, but I think he just had more to drink than he was used to." With this, Russ Little, who knew Willy well and heard the story years later in San Quentin penitentiary, agrees. "That was probably just a night when Willy felt like getting drunk." Whatever the cause, by midnight, when the whistles blew and everyone was kissing everyone else, Willy was smashed.

"Shall we burn your parents' house down?" he asked his host, Michael Moseley, who did not take him seriously. "I though that kind of talk was a façade to hide insecurity," Michael said later when it was rumored that Willy was a member of the SLA. "I heard him say that he was thinking about getting some dynamite to blow the place up, and I laughed. I couldn't believe he was somebody the FBI would ever be looking for. He wasn't big time."

Anne Moseley, Michael's sister, home for the holidays from the University of Wisconsin, was more impressed. Afterward, remembering Willy's good looks and his stand against corruption, she wrote him to say that "of all in the room, you're the only one who had things together, and when I come to California, I'm going to look you up." This she did not do because by the time the letter arrived at Willy's old boardinghouse in Berkeley, Willy was underground. Still unbelieving about what happened to Willy after that night, Lydia says, "None of us could have imagined that he would be involved with the kidnappers of Patty Hearst anymore than I could believe he wanted to go to Lapland."

At five in the morning, when Willy, supported by Lydia and her date, stumbled into his mother's apartment, he still was mumbling to Lydia about going to where "there's miles of snow and no tracks."

"He's had too much to drink," Lydia said to Roxie and Honey, who came into the hall, but neither Willy's sister nor his mother believed it.

"Somebody's put something in his drinks," Roxie said.

And Honey, coping as usual with what had to be done, said in a puzzled voice, "This isn't like Willy."

Telling Lydia's date, who didn't want to make the long cold drive home to Greenwich, to get into Willy's bed near one where Roxie would sleep, she made a makeshift bed on the floor for Willy. Lydia put a little pan beside his head "in case he gets sick."

And about then the telephone rang.

"He can't talk," Lydia and Roxie heard Honey say. Seconds later she was back and looking down with Roxie and Lydia at Willy. "He'll have to talk tomorrow to Joe Remiro."

Within two weeks Honey would read that Joe Remiro had been arrested for murder, but by then it would be too late to ask Willy about this friend in California who had been his roommate, because by then the tall, innocent-looking kid with the crinkly black hair who had lain sprawled in the hall would be nowhere to be found.

47

Chapter Four

"What about the Movement?" Lydia asked Willy on their last day together when he had asked her one last time if she would go away with him. "Don't you believe in that anymore?"

"Sure," he said, forgetting about Lapland. "But every step we take has to be right."

"One mistake and you could get yourself killed, right?"

Willy said that didn't worry him. "One life doesn't matter anymore than if a pebble over there rolled off the side of the mountain." But he believed that anyone working for a classless society had to avoid turning away sympathizers. "We've got to make sense to people on the street."

"To the ones like my brother?" Lydia was looking out a window at carefully groomed Dick and his wife, who were approaching the front walk.

"Oh, Christ," Willy said. "I don't need a confrontation with that arrogant bastard again."

Lydia told him to go out the side door. Touching his face, she said not to be too hard on Dick "because if it weren't for him, we wouldn't know each other."

Four years earlier, Lydia had tagged along with Dick when he went to see Roxie at Honey's place. There she struck up a conversation with Horace, the parrot, in order to draw out Willy, who was up from New York, where he was working that year. Later that spring and summer she and Willy had followed the activities of campus protestors and she had listened wide-eyed as Willy talked of protestors who thought school was kid stuff and were dropping out to be revolutionaries who would do more than toss bricks at ROTC buildings.

Now she watched him leave without for a moment imagining that she would never see him again.

"So what's with the Brickleys?" Roxie asked Willy when he got home. Then, observing the weather through the open doorway, she didn't wait to hear. "A bitch of a day to drive," she said, looking out at the ice, "especially when we don't know where we'll find gas."

"A mess," Willy said, entering and closing the door.

"So too bad John isn't here; he could chant a mantra." She said that on the day her mother and Pete Zimmerman had gone to New Hampshire, John had chanted "and the sky cleared right up . . . "

"And the ice melted off the roads; that's a lot of shit." He went toward his bedroom.

In the living room, Honey took a handsome tweed skirt from the front closet. "I can't match Willy's birthday present," she told Roxie, "but I hope you like this." Roxie went to change for the last family gathering, and Willy reappeared from his room with the old duffel bag that his father had used in the Navy. "For a man who's supposed to be going on a wedding trip," said his mother, "you don't look very dressed up." She tucked an envelope into his outside pocket. "Here's four hundred dollars. Use it for new luggage or anything else you have to have if you're really getting married . . . or . . . "—she moved closer to Willy—"or use it in California or in Sweden to go on with archaeology."

"I won't ever be an archaeologist," Willy told his mother, "but some day you'll be proud."

Roxie put on a jacket and a crocheted cap and went out front to put her bag and antique gun in her father's wife's red VW. She was joined minutes later by her mother and brother, who drove them for a goodbye drink in the restored parsonage (c. 1830) owned by Aunt Kate and Uncle Pete, a succesful antiques dealer. There, as they stomped off snow in the vestibule, Honey cautioned Willy, who was wearing combat boots but not challenging his mother's world with his Mao headgear. "No leftist talk!" she said. "Nobody needs an argument on your last day here."

The message got through. For the next forty-five minutes Willy, sitting in a tapestry wing chair away from the others, who included the painter Ron Anderson, said little as he nursed a Coke. And when it was about time to leave and Roxie was telling Ron that they would be going south to 84 and then west across the Hudson before turning south again at Port Jervis, Willy talked about their itinerary as if he were as interested in this trip as any in his life. Then he got up like any well brought-up young man and kissed his Aunt Kate, shook hands with Uncle Pete and said a polite goodbye to courtly old-world Ron, who did not refer to Willy's gleeful performance in he bar on New Year's Eve. After that, Pete Zimmerman, who was going with them, went out with his bag and got in the back seat of the car, and Roxie followed and got in front behind the wheel. Willy stood for a minute on the porch with Honey, who had come out in the cold to say goodbye.

"You know I want you to be careful," she said, and, as Willy put his arms around her, she asked him to call before he left Pennsylvania.

Willy kissed the top of her head, nodded with his chin against her hair and seconds later released her gently and said, "I've got to go now, Mom." Then, carefully picking his way down the steps and not looking back, he skidded along the drive to the car. Roxie bent down to smile goodbye as Willy climbed in beside her, and as the VW moved off, Willy waved through the front right window to the mother he would not see again.

"Over and over," Pete said as they drove south on 25, "we all come back to this womb."

"Who can knock Litchfield?" said Roxie.

"Me for one," said Willy. "Nobody in the whole crappy town knows about anything that matters."

"Not even Lydia?" Roxie asked him.

"She's not part of the town," Willy said, "and I wish Mom wasn't, because then maybe she'd change."

"She'll change sometime the way my grandfather's changing," Pete said. "She'll get old and her plumbing will wear out . . . "

"Good night," Roxie said, "how did we ever—"

But Willy interrupted. "Watch behind," he said quickly to Pete, who looked back and saw a police car.

"They're not after us."

"Step on it," said Willy in an agitated voice as Roxie, who had made a left signal, turned off Route 25 as the car behind moved up to pass on the right. "The gun; they'll find the gun."

"What the hell was that all about?" Pete asked when the police car had gone on and they were traveling on 209. "What gun?"

Before Willy could answer, Roxie told Pete about the antique gun "that hasn't been fired in seventy years," that was on the floor in the back. "So get ready, any minute now we all might be sent to the hole."

"You're really wacky, do you know that?" Pete said to Willy. "Talk about Berkeley paranoia, you've got it." Willy turned his eyes toward his cousin, who was leaning forward. "Hey, take it easy, man," Pete said as he drew away. But the fuse had been lit.

"You fuckin' idiots don't know where it's at." Willy said they ought to be followed by a couple of pigs sometime "the way a salesman who picked me up in Ohio a couple of weeks ago and I were followed clear into Pennsylvania; then you'd know who's paranoid."

"But you didn't even have the gun with you then," said Roxie. And "What kind of a salesman?" asked Pete.

"Who the hell cares?" Willy said. "The cops were following *me*."

"But, Willy," Roxie insisted, "ask yourself why."

"I know why," Willy told her. "They were tailing me because I believe—and a lot of my friends believe—this government's got to come down."

"You're heading for trouble," Pete said.

"He doesn't believe that at all," Roxie replied. "He just talks that way to stir people up."

Willy leaned toward her as if he were going to hit her. "I don't say things I don't believe, and you know it," he said. "Goddamn it, you'll see." He pushed his right fist into his thigh. "I've got friends who believe in what they're doing so much they're going to be dead in a couple of months."

After that Roxie and Pete sat silently as they rode on to the Hudson and across into Newburgh, where they left the highway to find a gas station. As Roxie asked if they could possibly have more than three gallons, the kid at the pump did a double take. "Hey," he said, taking in Roxie's dark good looks and her thick hair tucked under the loosely-woven cap pulled down on her forehead, "you look like Ali McGraw."

"Ten gallons instead of three means never having to say you're sorry," said Pete from the back seat.

The boy laughed but shook his head. "Not allowed."

"That kid wouldn't have given us an extra gallon if he knew we would be freezing to death without it." Willy said to Pete when they were back on the highway again. Roxie and Pete had switched places.

"His old man probably owns the station and told him what to do," Pete guessed.

"Sure," Willy agreed, "and the old man's been conditioned not to question the gas shortage so that before you know it the government can build nuclear plants that will exterminate half the people."

"What!" the other two said at the same time.

"Okay, but that's what a lot of people in California think." He paused and then challenged the others. "So, what do you think? That the oil companies couldn't see that we'd be running out of gas, do you actually buy that?" When no one answered, he went on. "Or are they driving up the price so a few people can get rich and the rest can stay poor?" He shook his head. "It's hard to believe everybody will stand still for all this, but here we are, going along as if nothing's happening."

"What's happening is that we'll be running out of gas unless we find a place to buy three more gallons in the next sixty miles."

"That's all anyone wants—something for themselves in the next sixty miles," sighed Willy. "And that's why the oil guys have got us."

But Roxie wasn't listening. "If we can't get to Dad's house," she said from the back seat, "we'll stay at his country place. What do you say, Willy, shall we show it to our cousin here?"

They found gas for sale south of Stroudsberg where Roxie, who moved up to drive again, told Pete, "Now, I'll take you to where we could have stayed." And soon they were sitting on a byroad, peering through leafless black trees toward the Delaware River beside which a snow-covered cottage, a separate outdoor solarium and a privy could be seen. "Dad rents out the cottage in the summer and stays weekends in the topless wonder where we all go outdoors to the privy that Willy built, isn't that right, Willy?"

But Willy was looking at the cottage. "That little house would be perfect if you were hiding out," he was saying more to himself than to the others. "Nobody would find you for years."

"And when they did, you'd be frozen to death," said Pete. "I hope your dad's home in town has heat."

"It's warm enough, but strictly Dick Van Dyke," Roxie said, drawing a square in the air. "But, anyway, Willy is the only one who'll stay there; you'll stay with me."

When they reached Roxie's apartment in Allentown, she gasped. "My key to the apartment! It's in Litchfield in the pocket of my other skirt."

Willy was halfway out of the car. "Give me a credit card," he said. "I'll get us in."

"Apartment C," Roxie said as she handed over her American Express card, which Willy took with him to the apartment house, which his father owned. Calling back to Pete to bring the luggage, he headed confidently toward the flat, and, sure enough, when Roxie and Pete arrived at the door, it was open and a triumphant Willy was standing inside with the lights on. "All I had to work with was this little piece of plastic," he said as Roxie wondered aloud if she could have forgotten to lock the door in the first place.

"Willie Sutton," said Pete, who noticed that Willy's long fingers, which had been raking the space behind the books on a shelf, had come to a stop. "Find something?"

"A stash," said Willy. "That's where they always keep it."

"And that's where it stays," said Roxie. "It must belong to my roommate."

"What's she like?"

"A good gal who's for Pete. Come on, we're due at Dad's for dinner."

Willy held back. "Looks like there's going to be a lot going on here tonight."

"You're going to be baby-sitting, remember?" Her father and stepmother, Sharon, and Sharon's parents from upstate New York were leaving in the morning for a holiday week, Roxie explained to Pete, leaving Willy in charge of Anne and Diane, his preschool half-sisters. "And I'll move in too when the rest have cleared out," she said, adding that they were now late for dinner.

"Your old man scared the shit out of me when I was seven," Pete said as they continued toward Emmaus, the Allentown suburb where Dr. Wolfe lived. "What's he like now?"

"All right unless you let him get to you," Roxie said.

"He was out to prove we were spoiled English brats who didn't know what was up."

"Did he win?"

"Like shootin' fish in a pond. I was the oldest, so I really got hit. Once he handed me a can of frozen orange juice, which I'd never seen before, and told me to fix everybody a drink. So I went to the kitchen and hacked away . . . "

"And he let you!"

"And laughed . . . "

"And you cried, so he proved his point, which is the way he plays."

"His trouble is he's a capitalist," said Willy, "who keeps pushing for more money . . . like what does he need all those apartments for?"

"To support his family if his job goes down," said Roxie, "which it might do if the board at the hospital takes a notion. And to pay the alimony he's supposed to pay Mom and for your dentist and for John's music—"

"Keep it up," said Pete, "and I'll feel sorry for the guy."

They turned into a middle-class residential development, then down a curved street flanked by long, low houses, each with a Christmas tree in its wide living-room window, and a crescent of snow underneath. A minute later they were inside one of them, kissing two jumping little girls and saying hello to Dr. Wolfe's wife, Sharon, who looked about Roxie's age, and shaking hands with Sharon's parents from Canastota, who were contemporaries of Honey. And, finally, they confronted Pete Wolfe, whom Willy called Ace.

"You remember Pete Zimmerman," Willy said.

"Of course," said the towering doctor, whose penetrating eyes seemed never to blink, "how could I forget old O.J." Then he told his wife's mother that young Pete was so rich that until he came to America he had never seen orange juice outside of an iced glass in a silver bowl. "So when I told him to mix frozen juice and water together, he was lost."

"You know how it is when your nanny does everything." Pete Zimmerman said to Sharon's mother, who saw the game and smiled.

But big Pete Wolfe didn't let go. "Well, tonight I've got a

contraption out in the kitchen I think you can handle," he said to young Pete. "It's a winemaker, and all you have to . . . "

But his guest shook his head and moved to the cheese board. "Want some Brie?" he asked Roxie, who said, "Good boy; Willy's never learned to do that."

Dinner was served at an extended table set up for the occasion in the front room between the Christmas tree and a fire-lit fireplace. Conversation was dominated by Dr. Wolfe, who praised Sharon's crab-meat casserole and other good things, poured homemade wine into crystal goblets and talked of exotic dishes prepared elsewhere for him—by Honey in Utica, by an admiral's chef on a yacht, and by the residents of Peking Man House in Berkeley "where Willy's Commie friends know how to fix vegetables in a wok but not much about saving the world."

"Lay off Willy or he won't baby-sit," Roxie said, to which the host replied, "Oh, yes, he will, or he won't get any pie and cake," and the little girls laughed and called out, "Willy can't have pie and cake." Sharon moved quietly to the counter that separated the living room from the kitchen, returned with a pumpkin pie and a chocolate cake, and set them in front of Willy. Then, while she and Roxie cleared the table and Sharon's mother leaned toward Willy and cut the desserts, attention moved to the children, who were then playing with a helium-filled red balloon trailing a string.

The girls passed the balloon from one to the other until Diane, an elf of two, receiving from Anne, aged four, fumbled. The balloon rose out of her reach, and when Anne recovered it, Diane began to cry. "That's not fair," she protested. "Anne's too tall."

And as everyone around her laughed, Willy went to her and picked her up and asked, "Do you want to be tall?" He told her that in a minute she could be as tall as Anne.

Now the older child became interested too and let go of the balloon, which rose to the ceiling again, forgotten as Willy picked up some crayons from under the tree and began drawing a face on a long paper sack that he withdrew from the kitchen counter.

"Blue eyes," he said, "and a red mouth, and brown hair and two slits at the bottom for your real eyes to see through." Then he placed the sack on top of Diane's head and tied a kitchen apron around its base like a cape which hung down to hide Diane's face. Then, arranging the slits cut in the paper for Diane to see through, he took her and Anne to the mirror in the hall and said, "Now, everything's equal; Diane is as tall as Anne."

Shouting victoriously, Diane raced back to the living room to recover the balloon only to find that her arm was no longer than before, whereupon she burst into sobs again.

"So now she's back where she was," said Dr. Wolfe, "which ought to show you, Willy, you can't make things equal—not with cosmetics, anyway," He turned to the girls. "So, I say, toughen 'em up. C'mon, little people, who wants the beanbag?"

The girls rushed to their father, who picked them up and hurled them one at a time toward a big beanbag chair that they had gotten for Christmas.

As each girl flew into the bag, Pete Zimmerman turned and said to Roxie, "He can fracture their skulls."

"They'll be all right," Roxie told him.

"How do you know?"

"I've been there, and the scars hardly show."

As the hurling and screaming went on, young Pete told Willy he'd be glad when the baby-sitter took over, and Roxie, who overheard, told Sharon, "We childless ones are a little squeamish," and asked it if wasn't about time for bed.

When Sharon called, the flushed children went to Willy, who picked one up in each arm and carried both to the bedroom, where their mother laid out their night things. Then, when they were in bed, Willy calmed them with a story about when he was a little boy and lived with his sister and brothers by a great river where they skipped flat stones on the shining water the way Anne and Diane did on the Delaware. And Sharon, listening, knew that her children would be in good hands, which she told her mother when she returned to the living room. "He's wonderful with children."

"He'll be a good father," Sharon's mother agreed, adding that someone ought to tell that to the girl Willy was going to marry.

"If he's going to marry," Roxie thought to herself as she watched her father and brother begin a familiar scene with three twenty-dollar bills.

"Here's something in case you and Roxie and Pete want to go out," Dr. Wolfe said, handing over the cash, "with enough in the kitty to pay for our regular sitter."

Taking it, Willy said he might opt to stay home with the sitter. "What's she like, ho ho."

And his father exclaimed that some guys were never satisfied. "You ought to see Willy's blonde at the other end of the line."

A half hour later, when Roxie and Cousin Pete were en route to Allentown, Pete said he thought Roxie's father had laid out the bills to impress Sharon's parents, "if you'll pardon the observation." And Roxie said, sure, and at the same time Willy was being macho to please his dad. "And the whole song and dance was as phony as Willy's wedding plans."

"You don't buy Sweden?"

"No, but why's he saying that?"

Roxie pondered the question again as they unlocked her apartment with a key borrowed from her father. Then, calling Honey, she asked her to send the other key and some letters she had left in her skirt pocket, which Honey promised to do.

Then Honey said that a few things that day had her puzzled. First, at three, when she got home from Kate's the telephone was ringing with another collect call from Joe Remiro for Willy, who she said could be reached later at his father's house. As she was reading off the number, she said, Joe told the operator he couldn't call later, and asked that Willy get back to him as soon as possible. Then, when she opened her desk drawer to get a pad and pen to write down the message, she found a big square of paper in the drawer with a name and address written on it in Willy's handwriting.

Eva Olsson
Svesgagen 15
19144 Sonetunsa, Sweden

"And then I noticed that all the letters from Willy that I read on New Year's Eve were gone," she told Roxie. "Those last ones that scared me, they're missing. So what do you think?"

"Well, the address in the drawer is to make you think Willy's going to Sweden," said Roxie soothingly, "and the letters contain information that somebody wants destroyed."

"Sounds like Hitchcock, but I guess I agree."

57

"But the caller from California, he's just a guy who wants to borrow Willy's car or something. What's his name again?"

"Joe Remiro."

"I say he's not part of the plot."

Until then, Roxie's deductions had been on target. But this one was wrong.

Chapter Five

At nine the next morning, California time, Russ Little called Willy collect in Emmaus, where Willy, at noon, was dishing up spaghetti for four in the kitchen. "I'll take it on another phone," he told the operator as he accepted the charges and said "Put my spaghetti in the pot" to Pete, who had dropped Roxie off at the hospital that morning and moved in with Willy and the kids, whose parents and grandparents had taken off. Then he handed the phone to Anne and told her to hang up when she heard him say hello. So a few seconds later, when Russ said, "What gives, Cujo?" it was Anne's small voice that answered, "Now, Willy?"

"Saaay," Russ said from three thousand miles away, "I'll bet your father's name is Ace."

"My father's name is Dr. Wolfe," Anne said.

"Dr. *Ace* Wolfe."

"Just Dr. Wolfe," the little girl explained, "although some people call him Pete."

"Wouldn't you know," Willy broke in from his father's bedroom, "the old lady killer's at it again!"

"*Now*, Willy?" Anne asked again.

"That's right, Anne, you can hang up now," Willy said and, when the click came, "How are you, man?"

"Okay," Russ said, "But what the hell are you doing?"

"What I came for."

"Both deals?"

"One's taken care of; the other's taking longer."

"You've said your goodbyes," Russ guessed.

"Pretty much—with Sweden thrown out as a camouflage."

"But you haven't got the money?"

"Not enough, but I'm working on it."

"Like how?"

"You'll have to trust me."

"Goddamn it, Willy," Russ said, "we've been working things out up in Concord over the weekend, and we're ready to move."

"So'm I, but Ace is away."

"Till when?"

"Next week."

"Then, boy, you gotta get your ass out here."

"It'll be ten days at the latest."

"Okay," Russ agreed. "And you can leave word at the drop about what time." Then he was all business again. "Now you haven't forgotten the pickup place."

"Oakland station," Willy replied. "I'll be yawning and chewing gum."

"So what else is new?" Russ was laughing, and when he spoke his voice was fond. "Everybody misses you, Cujo, especially me."

"Same here, Osi." Willy used the diminutive for Osceola, his friend's adopted name, which back in the 1800's was the name of a Seminole chief in Florida who stood up to the U.S. Army. "I'll be seeing you." He hung up the phone, mistakenly confident that they would soon be reunited in the underground, and returned to the kitchen, where Anne asked, "Who was that?"

"Osceola."

"That's a funny name."

"Once upon a time an Indian had that name." He told the girls he would tell them about the first Osceola when they went in for their nap.

Just then, Pete, who was scraping more spaghetti out of the pot, made a suggestion. "When you're getting the girls settled, why don't I call your brother in Philadelphia and ask him if he wants us for dinner tonight?" As he dipped out more sauce, he said Roxie would be working until nine or ten o'clock. "So why don't we see if John's available and bring over the baby-sitter your dad told us about?"

"Fine with me," Willy said. "If you work out the logistics, I'll get the kids in the sack." He gave Diane's shoulders a gentle squeeze. "Finish up your milk, and I'll tell you about the Indian down south who wouldn't let the Army push his people off their land."

In their room, the girls took off their shoes and lay in their playclothes on top of their beds. Both kept their eyes on Willy, who tucked a small blanket around each one and sat down on the bed beside Diane. Then, with his hand on the smaller girl's arm and looking over at Anne, he began his story.

"This brave Indian named Osceola lived a long time ago in a grassy place beside a river."

"Like where we go in the summer," said Anne.

"That's right," Willy said, "and Osceola was the strongest and wisest Indian around so he was the chief. And under him, the people in the tribe were happy. All the children played and swam and paddled their canoes in the water, and the big Indians caught fish and found berries and other things to eat in the forest. And nobody bothered anybody until the government wanted the Indians to give up their land and a lot of American soldiers came *tramp, tramp, tramp* through the trees."

"Is everybody going to get killed?" Anne asked, putting her hands over her ears.

"No, but they could have been if it hadn't been for Osceola."

"What did he do?"

"He sharpened up his arrows and told the other Indians to do the same, and they shot at the soldiers and chased them away."

Diane sighed. "I hope they didn't come back."

"But they did," Willy said. "And this time the soldiers brought more soldiers, and they told the Indians to go find a new place to live out west or they would kill them all. So most of the Indians packed up their things and left, but Osceola and a few others hid in the woods and shot arrows at the soldiers who were camping on their land. This scared the soldiers and they sent a scout to invite Osceola to come to their campfire to find a way for him to bring the others home."

"Did he go?" Anne asked.

"Yes, but when the young chief got to the soldiers, they dragged him off to prison, and there he stayed for the rest of life."

Diane was letting herself go to sleep now that Willy seemed to be ending his story, but Anne had more questions.

"Is that where he called from?"

"Who?"

"Osceola on the telephone, did he call from prison?"

"Oh," said Willy, smiling now. "That was a *different* Osceola. The one you talked to just took the first Osceola's name because he wants to be brave like him."

"Will this one go to prison?"

"I hope not," Willy said, "not for a long time, anyway. But it wouldn't matter, would it, if he was fighting for what is right?" He stood up and went over and looked down at the little girl. "And, now, you close your eyes and pretend you're lying in the sunny grass by a river." At the door he asked if she could hear the water rippling by.

"Kind of," said Anne with her eyes closed. And then, as Willy was going out the door, "Are you brave like Osceola?"

"I try to be."

Back in the kitchen, Willy said he hoped plans for the night hadn't gone too far because "my fucking ulcer is giving me hell." His face was damp and he bent forward over his right arm, which he held across his stomach. "The goddamn thing is a bloody mess and me the son of a doctor."

"Have you talked to your old man about it?"

"For about five years."

"What does he say?"

"Not much—sends me Maalox once in a while."

"You ought to lay out what's the matter; this could be serious."

"Yeah," said Willy, "could be." Then he asked Pete, "What did you do about tonight?"

"I got things set, but I can switch; how about tomorrow, think you can make it then?"

"If I work at it—no booze, lots of milk—"

"—and a couple of swigs of Maalox."

"That's right," said Willy, "and I'll be my old macho self again." Then he went into the bedroom and wrapped himself in his father's bathrobe and came back and watched an old Fred Astaire movie. "That guy can really dance," he said later as he drank milk at the table where they had shoved aside the dirty lunch dishes, and the children spread jelly on bread and Pete opened a can of soup. Then, after telling the girls "can't do" when they asked for another story before bed, he slumped again in front of the TV where he watched a western film until Roxie came in at 9:30 and threw up her hands at the mess.

"My God, you've been in the house one day, and look at the place."

"Willy's incapacitated," Pete said, "and I'm incapable, remember?"

"What's the matter with Willy?"

"Ulcer."

"So? Can't he walk to the dishwasher?" She stood in the middle of the kitchen and stared at the cluttered stove and table. "C'mon, you guys, start cleaning; I'll look in at the girls." As her cousin reluctantly left the living room, she went to the bedroom and came back shaking her head. "They're asleep in their clothes, not even undressed."

"I never had any sisters," Pete said, "and Willy's feeling bad."

"Willy's a slob," said Roxie, "so, come on, you rinse, I'll load." As they did so, Roxie told Pete that her roommate had come back from vacation. "So too bad you aren't still at the apartment."

"Then I could tell Willy how I'd been into your roommate, and he could tell me how he'd been into the baby-sitter, and neither of us would have been into anything."

"Chauvinists!"

"Country boys." Pete told Roxie they needed a trip to a big city. "So we're thinking of going to see John tomorrow. Want to go along?"

"Maybe," said Roxie.

But on Friday, she worked at the hospital and the boys took off for Philadelphia alone, arriving at about six o'clock at John's apartment building near Rittenhouse Square. In the hallway above the doorbell, they found a scribbled message: "Bell broken, call from across street."

"So we start a goddamn treasure hunt," said Pete.

As they headed for the telephone booth across Walnut, Willy, who followed, was laughing. "This is neat—when somebody goes over to call, John can look out the window and see who's there."

"The Wolfe arrogance is showing tonight," Pete said after their host had announced "I'll be waiting on three" and they were again in the building and climbing the stairs. At the third landing they were greeted by John, at twenty-one some two years younger than Willy, equally handsome and more poised.

"Good you can be here," John told the pair. "Come see how I live."

His room was simply furnished, cleanly swept and had a Gohonzan scroll on the big wall by the front window as its only decoration. "Don't know if you know much about Nichiren Shoshu," John said as Pete studied the scroll, "but that's the focus."

"Where you chant," Pete said.

John nodded. "But really we can chant anywhere. Right, Frank?" The younger Wolfe introduced a quiet black man coming out of the kitchen, a companion he explained whom he had met through NSA.* Frank said hello and told Pete and Willy that he and John had thought of going to dinner at a Thai restaurant in the neighborhood. "But, if you'd rather, we can eat in, but, then, we've got to go to the deli." He asked for a show.

"In," voted Willy, "and I'll fix the kind of meal I put together sometimes in Berkeley." So they went for food and along the way John bought a bottle of Soave Bolla, and in another hour they sat down to a dinner of ground beef mixed up with tomatoes, served with wine for all but Willy, who drank milk, and topped off with some stewed fruits for dessert. Then they smoked a little grass and talked about the differences in the childhoods of Frank, who grew up in the South, and Pete, who lived outside of London, and the Wolfes, who had done a lot of bouncing around. Then Frank, who was an accountant, left to get some rest, "so I can head into my boss's tax problems tomorrow," and John and Pete drifted into talk about NSA.

"I wanted three things three years ago when I got into Nichiren Shoshu," John said, "and I got them all—money, women, drugs." He went on to explain how his chanting and his faith ("that some day I might gain a little of Buddha's wisdom") had changed his life. "Little things like avoiding accidents don't sound like much but can straighten out your days. And the other things"—he paused—"like losing a need for drugs can make for something big." He said best of all he now had hope.

"Hope?" Pete wondered. "Don't most people have hope?"

"Not me," John said. "I used to spend about half my time thinking about suicide." He said he used to go down in the subway and try to analyze what was the best way to make a sure-fire death dive.

"My God," Pete said.

* Nichiren Shoshu Academy.

"I don't think about suicide anymore," John assured him, "and not much about drugs—or which sex I like."

"Which sex?" Willy was surprised. "You weren't thinking about which was for you up in Litchfield when Maggie was around."

John leaned back with a rapt smile on his face as he thought of his high-school love. "Mmmmmmh, wasn't she a moist plum?"

"What happened to her?"

"She graduated from Shipley out here in Bryn Mawr and went on to school up in Boston, and I see her sometimes. She's still buxom and sophisticated, and God did I love her!" John licked his lips. "But I had other interests."

There was a pause until Pete asked his cousin about his work at the John Neubauer School of Music, where John was enrolled year around.

"That's for me for life," John said, "*music*. Especially the composing end." He got up and got his guitar and played a composition he had worked out for his first concert, scheduled for May.

When he finished, Willy, who had said little, suddenly burst out. "You think only about yourself. What are you doing for anybody else?"

"Developing a talent that I can give to people."

"That's a bunch of high-sounding shit," Willy said. "And, anyway, the way things are going there aren't going to be any people to give your talents to; did y'ever think about that?" He tried for a hit. "You know who you're like? Nero, that's who, strumming away while your country falls apart."

Pete tried to mediate. "Why don't we say music is one kind of shit—"

"And revolutionaries who run around with bombs are another," John interrupted, "and which shit's better?"

"We better push off," Pete told Willy, but John had felt the goad.

"I'm registered as a conscientious objector," he reminded the other two, "and I don't believe in blowing things up." He turned to his brother. "I suppose you like the way we bombed Cambodia."

Willy stood up. "Now you've got things twisted and you're happy," he said. For years he had actively opposed the war in Vietnam, and his brother knew it. But what was the use of arguing against John, who liked to manipulate? "What the hell," he said, "you're a hefty dude with a guitar, and maybe that's all that matters." By then the brothers were at the door, saying their last goodbye, although neither knew it. "I guess that chanting's paying off the way you want it to," Willy said. "You got your life working, so it's right for you, anyway." He frowned, then, remembering something, and asked, "That money you talked about, where you getting it?"

"Driving a laundry truck."

"Isn't that pretty slow?"

"Fast enough for what I'm trying to do." He looked slyly at his brother. "Course, I'm not trying to save the world." At the stairs, he gave Willy's arm a farewell jab. "Don't get yourself killed in a movement nobody knows we need."

"John's a little flaky but he's got a point," Pete said the next midday when Willy was driving him to a roadside restaurant to catch a bus to New York. "Why let a bunch of heavies talk you into trouble?"

Willy didn't answer until they were walking to the Greyhound. "Nobody's talking me into anything."

"That's good," Pete told Willy as he started up the steps. Then, just before the bus door closed, he called down an invitation he would remember and worry about later. "Come to see me in L.A.; Roxie's got my address."

"It's in my little black book," Roxie told Willy that night as they had dinner with their half sisters. "But if you're going to be in Sweden, how can you call Pete in Los Angeles?"

Willy talked no more about the future, and shortly after the children had gone to bed, he told Roxie, "I don't feel so good," and went down to the lower level, where his bed was made up.

On Sunday, Willy didn't appear until afternoon. Then, wrapped in his father's old bathrobe, he entered the living room where Roxie was reading the paper and complained, "God, you wouldn't come in to see what was the matter if I were dying."

"If a man wants to sleep, I'm not one to . . ." Roxie began and then she looked at her brother's flushed skin and bright eyes and cut herself short. "You look awful."

"Got some kind of a bug," Willy told her as he dragged himself out to the refrigerator.

"Lots of liquids, good boy," Roxie said when Willy came back through the living room with a glass of orange juice. "Got any aspirin?"

Willy nodded. "When's Dad coming home?"

"Tomorrow night. Think you can take care of the girls when I'm in school tomorrow?"

Willy, breathing through his mouth, nodded. "But Sharon won't think I'm much of a baby-sitter."

"I'll tell her."

And Roxie did so the next night when her father's wife thanked her for taking care of things. "Willy was the chief cook and bottle washer."

"More cook than washer," her father said as he looked around the kitchen. "Not much of a swab."

"But an awfully good storyteller; ask the girls."

"If he feels better tomorrow, he's going to tell us more about Osceola," Anne told her mother.

But the next day and the next, Willy lay in bed with Hong Kong flu, and it wasn't until breakfast on Thursday, the tenth, that he joined his family at the table.

"I'm going to be pulling out in a day or two," he told his father, adding, "and sometime before I do, I'd like to get together with you."

"It's usually the bride, not the groom, who needs advice," Pete said, winking at his wife, but then he was serious. "How about meeting me for dinner in Allentown tomorrow night?"

Willy smiled. "I'll be there."

But he wasn't there because later that day, at a little after noon, he received a collect call from California that changed his life. It was Bill Harris, calling from Redwood City to report that Osi and Bo had been busted in Concord early that morning.

That Willy had been pressured earlier in the week to get himself back to California is confirmed by Russ Little, who says he told Willy he had been gone long enough and "what are you waiting for, for Chrissake?" and by Bill Harris, who told Willy to "get your butt back out here," and by Dr. Wolfe's telephone bill, which records two collect calls from California on Sunday, January 6, which is the day Willy became ill, and a last one four days later.

On the tenth, no call other than the one from Redwood City was recorded, so presumably Bill Harris gave Willy a number where he could reach Mizmoon Soltysik, Nancy Ling Perry, or Donald DeFreeze, the black escaped convict whom Willy had met at California's Medical Facility at Vacaville and who shortly would become world-famous as the SLA's General Field Marshal Cinque.

By the morning of the eleventh, Willy must have known from calls to the Coast that the boardinghouse he had lived in in Oakland had been raided, that the bungalow in which he had lived with Joe (Bo) Remiro had been searched, that Mizmoon and Nancy Ling Perry had set fire to the SLA safe house in Concord, that his Oldsmobile had been used as the getaway car and then abandoned, and that therefore he was in this thing up to his neck. But he showed no agitation when he told Sharon that he wouldn't be meeting his father for dinner. "A friend of mine's sick in New York," he told her, "and I've got to get in there."

"Somebody else has the flu?"

"More serious," Willy explained, "so I can't meet Dad."

A few minutes later, when Pete called to remind Sharon that he and Willy wouldn't be home that night, Willy came on the line and said, "I'm sorry. I'll be in touch," And, calling Roxie, he asked her to go with him to the bus.

"Why in the name of God do you always have to bitch things up?" his sister asked. "Now I'll have to switch things around to get off work to do what you want."

"It won't happen again," Willy told her. "It's the last time."

"That'll be the day," Roxie said, but she agreed to go to the bus stop with Willy if he would pick her up in Sharon's car.

"This is easy," Willy said when he and his sister were on their way. "You can take the car back anytime."

"Anytime, so long as it's tonight," Roxie said with sarcasm. "Because tomorrow Sharon's got to work in the operatoring room in Quakertown. But what do you care about that?"

"I care about things, Roxie," Willy said. "Lots more than you know."

Roxie said no more as she rode in the car beside Willy, who said nothing more himself until they reached the bus stop and saw the bus approaching a mile down the highway. Then, reaching in back of the seat, he pulled out his father's old duffel bag. "Here," he said, "I want you to have it."

"Your duffel bag?" Roxie was as startled as she had been when Willy gave her the gun. "But this is your other favorite thing."

"But that's all it is, a thing," Willy said, "and you're my sister." He leaned over and kissed Roxie's cheek as he lugged a knapsack from in back of the seat. Then he opened the door.

"But, Willy," Roxie objected. She got out with the duffel bag and followed him to the bus. "I'm not mad at you, or anything. You don't have to give me this."

"I want you to have it," Willy said. He climbed the steps. Then, at the last minute, he turned and said, "Take care."

"After Russ and Joe were arrested and my dad heard portions of the communiqués that were sent out by the Symbionese Liberation Army," Roxie remembers, "he believed that the SLA was a big operation like the Mafia and that anyone who knew too much about the group could be killed." She says that when the first reports came in, her father thought that Willy was hiding from terrorists, not from the police. "He didn't think for a minute that Willy was a terrorist, but he thought he might have met some terrorists in his prison work who would want to shut him up." She says that when her father told her this "his theory made sense to me too." She remembers that when he heard about Russ and Joe, "He called and I went over and tried to figure with him and Sharon where Willy might be. It never occurred to us that he would be heading for California. We thought he was in New York, where he probably would be calling Mike."

Apparently, the FBI had the same notion. "Because not long after Willy took off, two agents came to see my sister and me," says the black man who became part of the Wolfe family before Willy was born. "I hadn't heard from Willy and I didn't expect to when his dad told me about his friends out there who had been picked up because Willy would know the FBI would look for him with me." He says he did not go along with Dr. Wolfe's theory about his young friend's escaping from terrorists.

"I knew Willy had friends in California who meant as much to him as his family, and if they were in trouble he would go to them." He said he told his older sister, whom Willy liked, and her daughter to call him if they heard anything from Willy, "but I didn't think he'd call." He says he had a feeling Willy was on his way west "and, if so, he was in terrible danger." In fact, the more Mike thought about Willy and the Symbionese Liberation Army, the more he was afraid he would never see his longtime friend again.

PART TWO

Willy's Merry Way

Chapter Six

In the summer of 1949, Mike Carrerras, ten, born in Brooklyn of Puerto-Rican parents (his mother was descended from an African Negro and a native Borinqueños Indian and his father was Spanish), arrived in Connecticut with his sister Mary, twelve, to stay with the Wolfe family.

Honey at the time was a slim, pretty, quick-moving woman in her mid-thirties who had borne six children, four of whom were living. A year and a half earlier she had lost twins, born prematurely, but in the house now were Ben and Charlie Cheney (by her first marriage), aged twelve and eight, and Peter Wolfe, who would soon be three, and Roxie, who was "not long out of the oven," as her father liked to say. Still to come were Willy, who would arrive in '51, and John, who would follow in '53. And in the years to come, all of Honey's children would become as close to Mike as were his brothers and sisters and cousins back home.

In that long ago July, when he walked into the low, red New Milford station that smelled of wood and chocolate and coal dust, the wiry, big-eyed boy (who was wearing a tag bearing his name and destination) squeezed his fingers into his hands as he anticipated what would come next. Only a few hours earlier, he had said goodbye to his mother in Grand Central and climbed into a railroad coach with his sister and a dozen or more strange kids of assorted shapes and colors to go to the country for a couple of weeks of "fresh air." Never before on a train, he had sat with his face next to the window as his car on its elevated track passed Harlem tenements where his eyes met those of black women in short sleeves who leaned out of high windows to get away from the inside heat. And he had stayed close to the glass as he was rushed on to a world of leafy trees and stretches of green where stops were made at neat stations surrounded by shining cars and laughing people who called out hellos to passengers getting off. Along the way, some from Mike's group had gotten off and he had watched as they were greeted by white men and women who patted the arms and heads of the kids like a new teacher.

Sensing after the train had left Danbury and he was passing fields with cows and horses that his journey was about to end, he became nervous and had asked Mary over and over who was going to meet them. And finally, after they had moved through an aisle of green where little trees and big poles came close to his window and had come at last to their destination, he hung back. Mary had to pull him by the hand to get him to jump down the steps.

Then, he was in the station and everything was happening fast. Suddenly he was boosted high in the air and swung out the door by a giant of a man who wore shorts and had a crew cut. After that he was tumbled into a big car with its top down, where he found himself taking the measure of a quiet white boy who was as tall as Mary, even as that boy and two smaller kids were taking the measure of him. Finding them to his liking, he jabbed at conversation the way he did with new kids on the playground of his school in Brooklyn, which was integrated. That he had no fear of the others and they had none of him was established by the time the convertible had reached the big white house (c. 1775) by the rushing river where he and his sister were greeted by Honey and would spend their vacation.

At first Mike was homesick for the sounds and smells of their flat, even as he was awestruck by the great white father "who is so rich," he told his mother later, "he can go out and buy a motor for a boat the way we buy a head of cabbage." But unlike his sister, who felt lonesome when night fell and was afraid of the huge doctor who sat at the head of the table (like the leader of a cult, Mike remembers) and tapped the boys on their heads with the bowl of a big spoon when their manners needed correcting, he soon got used to the Wolfes and had the time of his life in New Milford, which is only a few miles down in the valley from Litchfield but is a far different town.

Intersected by the Housatonic River, the once predominantly agricultural community is crisscrossed by branches of the Aspetuck, Rocky and Still Rivers, as well as by smaller brooks and creeks that empty into its main stream. In 1949, when northwestern Connecticut was still country, Mike and the Cheney kids could climb a rise and look out for miles over rolling hills and the exposure of Candlewood Lake. And there were no people visible for as far as the eye could see—just meadows and water and fields of grain and other plants, which Mike learned to identify as alfalfa, corn and tobacco.

But the simplicity of the place had begun to change long ago. About a mile from where the Wolfes bought their home, a deep slash of a valley separates the Candlewood and Guardian mountains. This ancient gorge, known as Rocky River Valley, was selected in the late 1920's as the site for a reservoir to be created by an immense core dam and five smaller dikes. The result is Connecticut's largest lake, which covers six thousand acres and has a sixty-mile shoreline in and around New Milford.

Applauded as a come-on for new industries, the Rocky River project pumps water from the Housatonic up and over Candlewood Mountain and dumps it into the lake when the river is high and brings it back down to generate current during peak-load periods. The resulting cheap electricity proved to be attractive to the Nestlé Company and Kimberly-Clark, which put up plants by the river. But it was the lake itself that from the first proved to be the boon.

Begun in 1927, it was completed long enough before the Depression for real-estate brokers and developers in five towns to have the time of their lives. They sold choice lake sites for large homes on promontories above the water, and they put up small vacation houses in beach-front communities that sold out in a week with an ad in *The New York Times*.

In the thirties, the boom slowed down, but vacationers from the city still came up with their swimsuits and water skis to rent whatever cabin or house was available. And at the same time, others from Manhattan were discovering New Milford's hills and streams and were scouting the countryside for inexpensive property which many found.

Then came World War II, and when it ended, the farm town of New Milford, which still had more than six hundred working farms, had close to six thousand full-time residents and a new personality.

As before, the community had its old-family mainstays, who lived on the green or on Aspetuck Hill, went to the Congregational or Episcopal church, and ran the town. But with renewed interest in Candlewood Lake, New Milford also had summer people who dashed in and out of each other's glass-fronted houses for cocktail parties and barbecues. And it had an ever-increasing number of part-time exurbanites restoring its rural Revolutionary houses. In this last group were Hollywood's Fredric March and Florence Eldridge, who came to the country between pictures, the Malcolm Cowleys, Van Wyck Brooks and Peter Bloom, who lived nearby, Rex and Paula Stout and many Jewish intellectuals like Dr. Burrill Crohn (the discoverer of ileitis) and a host of New York's independently rich like the Jack Leons.

Occasionally members of one set mixed with those of another, but as a rule the townspeople, who ran the Rotary and Lions clubs, Town Hall, Planning Commission and hospital, as well as the Republican Town Committee, saw little of the lake people, and the intellectuals and creative people saw few from either of the other groups at their Community Center, a renovated Grange hall in the Merryall farm district where 250 members met (and still meet) on Saturday nights to hear the Berkshire String Quartet from nearby Music Mountain or listen to a talk by Margaret Mead, Harrison Salisbury, William Styron, Arthur Miller, Tish Baldrige, Isaac Stern, Bill Blass, Dore Schary or some other houseguest or neighbor.

For the last thirty years nobody in New Milford has had to make much of an effort to find others with his interests. The new dentist who likes to play golf buys insurance from the local mainstay who takes him to the Waramaug Country Club. The vacationing bachelor looking for a date finds out-of-town girls at the Racquet Club. And the writer back in the hills who wants to hear Merle Miller's talk at the Community Center bumps into a retired professor at the Country Store who takes him along. Within weeks a newcomer instinctively finds his place.

So it was with Pete Wolfe, who became "thick as thieves," as one dowager reports, with the town's brightest and most ambitious young businessmen. Fresh from the U.S. Naval Base at Guantanamo Bay,

Cuba, Pete bought the house, where he would have his office, for $26,000. Like Pete, the man who sold it to him had graduated from an eastern school (M.I.T.) and had served as an officer in the Navy with the same rank as Pete (Lt. jg). And through this friend and patients in his office who came from prominent local families, Pete soon knew other well-educated fellows who were moving in or coming back to New Milford after a stint in the military and, like him, ready to get cracking.

Hanging in Pete Wolfe's study in Hellertown, Pennsylvania, near a picture of his late son, Willy, is a yellowed certificate of membership in Five Friendly Farts, a poker club the doctor belonged to back in New Milford when his life was young and upbeat. One of the group, who designed the certificate and sat down once a week for a game of penny ante, was artist Bob Kuhn, a discharged merchant marine who became one of the country's leading animal illustrators. Another, a discharged Army major, ran the Housatonic Tractor Corporation. The others, both former Navy officers like Pete, were the real estate friend and a lawyer.

None of the four who played with Pete in one or another's home, where the host each week laid out beer and sandwiches, can remember talking much in those days about politics. Still, all knew instinctively that the artist in the group was an Independent, the corporation man a conservative Republican, the realtor and lawyer the same but not so far right, and that Pete might vote for God knows who. The doctor, who delighted in making waves, might say in a crowd of leftover Roosevelt haters that he had been all for FDR, but most of his friends, who, along with his poker pals, included two automobile dealers, a free-lance New York media man and the town's leading young dentist, believed that inside the voting booth the doc probably voted the same as his neighbors, who up to that time had never voted for a Democratic President.* Rather than furrowing their brows over issues of the day, the Farts talked less about the Marshall Plan and McCarthyism than about fly-fishing and sailing, which were Pete's favorite sports and which he shared with his kids.

On his first visit with the Wolfes, Mike stood on the bank of the river in back of the house and caught perch, catfish and, on one occasion, with the help of Dr. Wolfe, a large-mouth bass, which

---

* In 1964 the town finally went Democratic in the Lyndon Johnson landslide.

Honey fried for supper. This back-to-basics approach to food was a delight to the boy, as was going to a farm to pick corn, which Honey wrapped and roasted later at a picnic by Candlewood Lake. Such experiences made Mike want to come back, but it was sailing on the lake toward the end of his stay that clinched his inner commitment. He vowed to return again and again, if the Wolfes would have him, whether his sister came back or not.

As it worked out, he did, they would, and his sister did not. And so it was that Mike Carrerras came to know firsthand the short, tragic life of the next child to be born to his friends.

Chapter Seven

On February 17, 1951, Virginia Wolfe went into her husband's office and told his assistant that she was in labor and would meet Pete later at the hospital. Then she went out and got a fellow who was shoveling the walk to pilot her in her Austin down snowy Route 7 to New Milford's new hospital and checked herself in. There, a half hour later, she was delivered of a six-and-a-half-pound boy by Dr. John Street, who was thirty-six years old, compulsively hardworking and not an admirer of young Dr. Wolfe.

"The man was smart enough," he recalls, "but he was a put-down guy."

Completely dedicated to his profession and with Deerfield Academy, Yale and the Medical School of Duke University in his background, Dr. Street resented the younger doctor's flippancy and arrogance. "And so did all the other doctors," he says thirty years later. "I can't remember any doctor who was more unpopular." He explains why: "The man was a terrible bullshitter, and when you get one of those on a hospital staff, you're in trouble because the fellow's values are bound to be off." He said that outside the hospital none of the staff was much bothered by Wolfe "because he didn't associate with other doctors."

But Mary Miller, the widow of a successful surgeon who left a large

New Jersey practice in the early fifties to lead a less harried life in northwestern Connecticut, has a different recollection. "When we came to New Milford, the doctors were not too cordial, but Pete and Virginia Wolfe were most cordial." She said the younger couple invited her husband and her to "a lovely dinner that Virginia prepared" and later "gave a beer party in our behalf." This last was pure Pete. To send out come-and-get-it invitations to a party for a prestigious surgeon whom the other doctors stood back from was his way of one-upping the others. And an even deeper dig was to call the occasion a beer party when there was no need.

"I was offered sherry," says Marian Piper, a retired teacher whose favorite all-time pupil was Virginia's son Charlie. She remembers the party because on that afternoon she had three invitations—to the Wolfes', to a reception at the Congregational Church for the new pastor, and to lunch at the home of a "colored child," which she couldn't quite work in. "At the party, I think I drank ginger ale," says Marian, "but no matter. The gesture was gracious."

In the next few years Pete often assisted Dr. Miller in surgery, the anesthetic for which at that time was given by nurses. (This was not any more unusual then than to have a dental assistant help an extractionist put a patient to sleep with nitrous oxide in a dental office.) Eventually, as he worked with his mentor, Pete learned to give ether, gas and local anesthetics. Knowing that surgery there and everywhere would become more sophisticated with the passage of each year, he sensed that there soon would be a need in New Milford for a trained anesthesiologist. So, about the time Willy was born, Pete started thinking seriously about becoming an anesthesiologist, which he says now "is the easiest specialty in medicine."

"It is if you're good at it," says Dr. Street, conceding Pete Wolfe's ability. "He had a natural talent." He shakes his head. "Too bad he wasn't liked by other doctors; we needed what he could do."

According to another doctor-surgeon who was assisted by Pete in the operating room at that time, "Someone applying for a staff job in a hospital like ours has to be recommended to the Board of Managers by doctors on the staff before he or she can be considered for the job of anesthesiologist. And I have the feeling that after Dr. Wolfe had taken his advanced training from Dr. Ralph Tovell up at Hartford and got around to applying for a job with us some of the doctors on the staff would not have given him a recommendation." This may or may not be true, but certainly Pete Wolfe was no politician. Although he had been accepted as a friend almost immediately by up-and-coming young fellows in town who considered him a "character," he had an arrogance and a way of life that mocked the ingrained attitudes of Main Street's white Protestants who collected the mortgages, elected the town selectmen, and decided who would serve on the library, school and hospital boards. Early on, all got the idea "this new doctor has an awful good opinion of himself."

"He was an overbearing fellow," remembers Ben Stone, longtime president of the Litchfield County National Bank, "who had a way of looking down on everybody, physically and every way." And "He was kind of a show-off," says Building Inspector Charlie Treat. "When he came to a party or a meeting, you couldn't miss he was there." And Mike remembers that when he took all the kids to the movies, he would hold one of the youngest on his shoulders which meant that nobody could see in the seats behind.

Social leader Helen Mygatt, who lives now in the same mansion at the north end of the green where she lived when the Wolfes were in town, says that when the tragedy came, people from way back who had known the family weren't all that surprised. "A lot of young parents were more permissive in that day than in the generation before," she says, "but permissive wasn't the word for the way the Wolfe children were raised." *

A Wolfe loyalist is Virginia McKee, who worked for Dr. Wolfe as his assistant and says she never knew a woman who was as proficient as Virginia Wolfe at everything she did. "I marveled at the way she kept her house in order, did the laundry, was a good cook and hostess, and at a party could talk about everything that was going on in the world. And besides that, she did all of the extra things that a lot of mothers don't do—like having a special christening party for every new baby."

Pete and Honey's newest baby was named William Lawton Wolfe. The William came from Pete's side; the Lawton came from Honey's—and William was shortened immediately to Willy. This was not an intentional diminutive. Bequeathed to the little boy by his Uncle Willy, the name was associated in the minds of the family with

---

* "Not so," says Roxie, "our father ruled with an iron hand."

Pete's enormous older brother, who, like his father before him, had gone to Yale.

As Mike remembers, Yale was as important to the Wolfes as the Catholic Church was to his family in Brooklyn. And Mrs. McKee says, "I don't know about Willy's room, but when I was at the house, Ben and Charlie had navy-blue bedspreads with big Y's on them and were expected to take care of their digs like college men." According to Mike, it just kind of went without saying in that house that any boy in the family would go to college in New Haven. And he said that by the summer after Willy came, Ben was ready for Andover, where he would begin preparing in the fall to go in a few more years to Yale.

"All of us knew we were expected to go to college and had to do well in school," says Roxie, "but I can't remember any 'do this and study that' kind of stuff. We just kind of learned as we lived—like the Bobbsey Twins."

"The place was a real 'you can't take it with you,'" says an electronics expert who went to the house after John, who followed Willy by two years, had been born. "My job was to repair a hi-fi set the doc had rigged up in a bathtub to broadcast classical music through an interroom communications system." He said the doctor told him that the children could do whatever they wanted about music later on "but at least they'll know what good music is." The repairman went away with admiration for the young father, but said he had to step over bodies to get his work done. "The place was wall-to-wall with kids with animals to match."

"There was a parrot named Peppy in the reception room that was supposed to have been trained by some old salt to say dirty words," says Will Webster, a social worker with Torrington's Catholic Charities, who was taken to Dr. Wolfe when he was a small child with asthma. "I used to jiggle the cage to get the bird to talk." He said he got to know Willy, who was a couple of years younger, and "I don't know why, but, years later, when I heard the name Willy Wolfe in connection with the SLA, I knew right away that was the boy I got to know when I was going to his father for scratch tests."

Unlike doctors who stick to the tried and true, Dr. Wolfe as a GP liked being first with a new treatment or technique and became known in town as a faddist. "Maybe so," says Will Webster, "but when he was into scratch tests, he found I was allergic to grasses, timothy and alfalfa and gave me shots twice a week that helped me to breathe." He said he loved to go to the office and the only time he had a bad time there was when the doctor had to stitch up one of his hands that he had stuck through a window without giving him an anesthetic because of the asthma. "That was rough, but Dr. Wolfe made me laugh by pretending he could see through my ears," Will says, "and Willy stood behind me and patted my good arm to show he was sorry."

"Willy was a sweet little boy, but his nose was always snuffly," remembers Henry Allsop, a neighbor who was called in as caretaker--baby-sitter when Willy's parents were busy or away. When asked why he didn't put Kleenex in the little boy's pocket, Henry paused for effect. "He never had a pocket," he explained; "he was naked. And so were all the other Wolfe kids."

Henry, in his fifties now, says he wasn't surprised to learn that Willy was a member of the bizarre SLA gang. "No, I can't say I was surprised at all." He says this has nothing to do with Willy's running around "naked as a jay" as a child (although Henry's own little girl, Susie, thought it was terrible that Willy didn't wear any clothes). "Willy was brought up to think for himself and not to be like everybody else, so, of course, he was going to do something different."

Even though the Wolfe kids "ran around like gypsies," they were obedient ("they never went to the river unless they were with an older person because they knew they could be hurt"), Henry remembers, and they were polite to older people and generous. "When Susie had the chicken pox, Willy sent her a Siamese kitten from a litter born to their cat, which had run out on the highway and committed suicide. And do you know that crazy cat of Susie's, which she called Peppy after the Wolfes' parrot, had every kind of accident, even broke its jaw and had to have its mouth wired shut, but lived to be nineteen years old and didn't die until the very month that Willy burned up in Los Angeles." He says, "You just kind of expected something strange to happen with anything connected with the Wolfes."

Henry is not anti-Wolfe, however. "When you did anything for that family, they really appreciated you." Henry says Dr. Wolfe loved roses and told him he'd like to have roses in the yard as late in the year as possible. "So," says Henry, "I grafted a rosebush onto a rose tree, and we had flowers until September, and Dr. Wolfe never got over talking about it." He said half the town owed the man money because he didn't push to collect. "And it was those very people, out of guilt or whatever, who did the most talking about his not going to church and having a colored boy in his house and letting his kids run around naked."

"Ben and I were too old not to wear clothes," says Mike, "and Charlie didn't buy the idea." He says that Charlie and his stepfather clashed anyway, and Virginia McKee sensed there was "a personality conflict." She says that once when Charlie wanted to go with friends to the Congregational church, Dr. Wolfe said, "Only if you go for the church itself, not to socialize." She says that he told her he would take the kids to the Congregational, Baptist, Christian Science, Quaker, or Catholic church or even a Jewish synagogue if they really wanted to go to church, but he wouldn't take them across the street if they weren't sincere.

Both Mrs. McKee and Mary Miller say Pete had a tendency to be "short" with anyone who didn't agree with him and this included his patients. "Some of them couldn't take it when he didn't beat about the bush," says Mrs. McKee, who tells about a woman who came to the office with a heart problem she didn't know she had. "When Dr. Wolfe prescribed digitalis and said 'You'll have to take it the rest of your life,' she stomped out of the office and never came back. But you know what happened? She took digitalis for the rest of her life."

"The doctor was just as short with people who called him for a problem he thought insignificant. I called in a panic when one of our boys got hit in the head with a swing and I thought he had a concussion," remembers Grace Hotchkiss. "And Pete took one look at the bump on his head and yelled, 'You mean you called me here for *that*.' I ended up apologizing."

"So did I," says Mrs. McKee, "when my husband had some kind of muscle spasm one weekend and I got him to a chiropractor." When she told the doctor on Monday that the other man had fixed up her husband, whose diaphragm was in spasm, he shouted, "In spasm! Well, then, he's dead; so, tell me, is he dead?" "I never mentioned the word 'chiropractor' again."

"He was so big, you didn't talk back," says Warren Kohler, the dentist. "The day that he became president of our Exchange Club, he stuck his finger in my chest and said, 'Build a ski tow for the kids here in town.' I didn't know how, but I did it."

"He was always on stage," says his old poker friend Bob Kuhn. "And he tried to keep everybody off balance. If a hostess asked us all to come in evening clothes to a fancy dinner, he would get his wife to appear with him as pirates."

"But we had a lot of fun," remembers poker pal and real estate friend George DeVoe, who sailed in the summer of '51 from Rye, New York, to Block Island and back with Pete and Pete's stepson Ben and lawyer Hank Anderson, another member of the card-playing quintet. "We went in a rented forty-three-foot ketch," says Hank, "with George as our captain for obvious reasons." (Hank was essentially a powerboat man, and Pete, although a good sailor, was impulsive.) "We took turns being cooks, part-time sailors and swabs."

"I arrived for my third trip to the Wolfes about the time the sailors got back," says Mike, who remembers that first summer of Willy's life as the beginning of the family's happiest time. "The doc had a lot of patients and was feeling good about the hospital. Ben had been accepted at Andover, and Willy, who looked like Roxie, was healthy and didn't cry much." Still, older now and familiar with his surroundings, Mike noticed little contradictions he hadn't seen before. "The house had as many magazines as a newsstand, but nobody had time to read. And when Dr. Wolfe hit the kids on the head for not having good manners—he said we had to use one hand, not two, to pick up an ear of sweet corn—he made Charlie mad and pretty soon he'd be yelling, 'You're not my father,' and be crying to go to his real dad in New Haven." He says he got the feeling that summer that Honey was afraid of getting old. "I don't like to go into the new A&P store," she told me, "because everyone who shops there looks so *old*." Still, he had enough sense to know that living with this family ("which was probably better than most") was teaching him a lot.

Mike thinks it was that summer that he made up his mind that he would get an education. "What the Wolfes had that my parents didn't have, I began to see, were space to move around in and money, and I decided that the key to both was an education. And for that awareness I can thank the Wolfes."

"That's a lot," says Tony award-winning Tom Meehan, author of the book for the Broadway hit *Annie*, who lived and wrote on the outskirts of New Milford and knows from his own experience that the Wolfes had to stand up to prejudice when they brought black children into their home. "Twenty years later," says Tom, "neighbors thought the price of the houses near us would go down when we brought two black kids up from New York, and cars would drive slowly by our house when we were playing ball out front with them. I give Dr. Wolfe credit for courage."

"That he had," says an old-time nurse at the hospital. "That's not all," says another, who thought he looked "devilish," like Clark Gable. "He was certainly good-looking," says Helen LaTaif, whose late husband was chief of staff at the hospital when Pete came to town. She says she'll never forget the night the new doctor came to the house in his Navy uniform to make a courtesy call. "I thought he was the biggest, darkest, best-looking man I had ever seen." And Honey says after all these years, "In that uniform, he was really somethin'."

"But he wasn't God's gift to all women," insists Bob Kuhn, who once took his wife's amply endowed cousin, who was suffering from a head cold, to the doctor's office. "Apparently Pete couldn't help but exclaim over the girl's pulchritude, and she came out furious."

"His attitude wasn't always professional," believes George DeVoe's mother, who says a young woman might go to him to find out if she were pregnant and hear that she had beautiful legs.

"But that was just his way," says ever-loyal Mrs. McKee. "He'd say 'You have beautiful legs; come into my Casbah' the way another man might tell a hostess he liked the rug on her floor." She says that women on the make got their jollies by pretending he made passes at them when he did not. "So he had to have someone like me in the office in case some 'cry-rape woman' tried to get something on him."

"He was magnetic, that's for sure," says a woman from Gowanda, New York, who went to Dr. Wolfe two days after she had become engaged to be married. Twenty-three years old, fresh from Utica College and "a virgin, I'm ashamed to say," Hildegarde "Bubby" Lahvis was her college's sweetheart of Sigma Chi and the winner of a half-dozen beauty contests. She was also a doctor's daughter and had a history of kidney stones and on the day in question had a pain in her back and side. "So I went to the office expecting to have something to dilate the kidney and a urinalysis but instead I had a vaginal examination and psychoanalysis."

In the next two weeks the doctor went four times to talk with Bubby about sex, snakes and dreams at the home of her future mother-in-law, "whose eyebrows had arched up to her widow's peak." Believing that fear of sex was Bubby's problem, Dr. Wolfe told her that he and his wife went naked around the house and that she had to get rid of her repression as his wife had gotten rid of hers if her marriage was to be successful, which she reported to her husband-to-be, who thought the whole approach was baloney. "So the sessions ended and I got a bill, when I asked for it, for one hundred and fifty dollars, which my mother-in-law paid." Years later, when her marriage was over and Bubby had moved back to New York State, she wondered if the doctor could have known what he was talking about. "But anyway I never forgot him or my analysis."

"We were all getting into Freud," says a woman who liked to dance with Dr. Wolfe at the Fireman's Ball, the town's big social event, "and Pete could talk more convincingly than anyone else about frustrations and all that, so some of us found him fascinating. But at the same time, this made him a pain in the neck to old-guard doctors, and at the end of his time here, he was about as controversial a figure as his friend Parker Dooley* up in Kent."

"Dr. Wolfe didn't have anything to do with that Dooley business," says an older woman who baby-sat for the Wolfes. "But when the whole story came out in William Buckley's magazine,** the doctor was tarred because he was different from the other doctors, the way he wore shorts and all. And she added, "Then there was the business of the horse."

When the children wanted a pony, Dr. Wolfe sent for a Montana range horse, which supposedly could fend for itself throughout the year. He put it out to graze on land that happened to be next to Mary Miller's, "who worried about that horse," says a friend, "all one winter long. Night after night, she would go out with a lantern and try to coax it into the barn where there was hay." Mary herself says, "The horse wouldn't eat the hay, though, and it did survive, so I guess what Pete believed was right." Another neighbor disagrees. "The man was a madman and was going to make that horse live the way the ad said it could if it killed it, which I understand it eventually did."

"So the doctor was different," admits one baby-sitter, "but he must have done something right, because the children were wonderful."

---

* A celebrated doctor who had been arrested and charged with indecent assault in connection with his treatment of young boys.

** The *National Review*, edited by William F. Buckley, Jr., who has a country place at Sharon, Connecticut, not far from New Milford, carried the story of Dr. Dooley in its December 7, 1955, issue.

She says the first time she stayed for a weekend when the parents went away, she was astonished. "Everything was casual, and I couldn't find enough sheets or pajamas, but the kids didn't care, and with help from Roxie, who was just a little girl then, we made do." She said some kittens were born to the Siamese cat while the parents were away and Henry Allsop had to dispose of them because they were mutant freaks. "And the children didn't cry because they knew those cats weren't normal." She says Willy was wonderful with animals and would have made a great veterinarian.

Years later, she found it hard to believe that Willy had become a terrorist because he and all the others played like kids in a storybook when they were with her. "They had a lot of freedom, but they didn't abuse it. And nothing bothered them, and they didn't argue and fight with each other or me, or with their mother when she was home. And their father was strict, but they loved him."

"They thought he was God," says Mike. "And then, a few years later when God fell with a thud, Willy had a hard time. But that wasn't what led him into the SLA and all the rest. He was so mesmerized by his father, he was just kind of set adrift when his Dad wasn't there anymore." He says he gets the feeling that out in California "Willy was swept along with the SLA the way cows we saw once in the river in New Milford were swept along in the flood. And once he got caught in the current, he couldn't turn back." Mike believes it wasn't just one thing but many things that led Willy to a life in California that few could understand.

Chapter Eight

"Willy's most vivid memory from his time in New Milford," believes Mike, "was the Connie-Diane flood that hit the town in 1955 when he was four, which we talked about when he got older."

In August, just before the closing that ended the Wolfes' ownership of the house in New Milford, two hurricanes in three days deluged much of New England and sent the Housatonic River over its banks all along its course. At the time Mike, who was heading for his senior year at Brooklyn Technical High School, was getting away from the city, courtesy of the Wolfes, just as he had done for the last six years. "And we had a flood for a finale, which was about all the doc needed after what had happened at the hospital."

As Roxie heard it, once her father finished his training in Hartford and returned to the New Milford Hospital, he heard from the board, "Sorry, we've already hired an anesthesiologist." According to Virginia McKee, "He got caught in small-town politics." And from Mike: "He lived as he wanted and didn't care what anyone thought, and for a long time people in the town let him alone, but when that didn't bother him, they got him another way."

Mike remembers a day when a woman on the street rushed up to Dr. Wolfe and told him he ought to take his children to church, and when he kept on walking, she stumbled and said he pushed her into the gutter. And when author Hila Colman's son collided on his bike with Dr. Wolfe's car, many accused the big man of running the little kid down. "And," Mike adds, "I suppose *I* was a nail in his coffin."

Sometime in the week before the hurricanes when Ben Cheney was getting ready to go to Yale and Charlie was about to enter the Taft School, where his father in New Haven had prepped before him, the boys told the town barber that they would be coming in with Willy the next day for three haircuts. And when Mike said, "Make it four," the barber suggested he come out to the Wolfes' house to do the haircuts, which he did. Mike said that because he had felt no prejudice at the Wolfes' he hadn't felt conspicuous in town, but thereafter he knew the Wolfes must have taken some flak. "This made me protective, and you can bet that when the river started up, I was praying as hard as the doc that it wouldn't pour into his house."

The first night of the storm, when Hurricane Connie hit, Willy cried when the lights went out and the big house shook in the pounding rain and wind. And he was more upset the next morning when he saw dead squirrels, rabbits and other animals all over the lawn, which was strewn with blown-down branches. Then when Mike took him to the riverbank where a few days before he and his sister and brothers had searched for wolframites in the rocks below, he couldn't believe his eyes. The swollen stream, carrying dead dogs and cats and uprooted trees and sheds, turned to kindling wood, went crashing along only a few feet below the rim of the bank, which usually stuck up as high as a house over the water. "But, anyway, the storm's over," Mike told Willy; "now the water will go down." Three days later Hurricane Diane came barreling in, to demolish downtown Torrington and other Litchfield country towns and send the Housatonic behind the Wolfes' house up to within inches of the rim. And now when Mike and Willy went outside, the yard was filled with snakes and turtles; and the river, roaring along like a fast train, was loaded with trailers, broken bridges, barns, dead rats and even cows. "And the cows, flailing their legs as they tumbled along, were what got Willy, and me too, because once caught in the current, no cow could get out alive. And, of course, farmers whose cows had been swept into the water knew this, so they were running up and down the bank with rifles to put the cows out of their misery. And when a shot would come and a cow would stop kicking as the water around it turned red, Willy would cry and hang on tight to my hand. Still, he was fascinated and so was I as we watched one cow after another die that day in the river."

All that afternoon they kept hearing that dams on smaller rivers upstream were going out and that any minute the water in New Milford might go over the bank, so they piled sandbags around the house. But before night the water crested and the house was safe. "Hallelujah," cried the doc, "the Wolfes are heading into a lucky streak." And for a year or so thereafter, that seemed to be true.

In September the family moved into a large house in Frankfort, a workingman's community outside of Utica, where the doctor was to take a year's residency and eventually go on staff as an anesthesiologist at St. Lukes Memorial Hospital. Now, with his professional work in a town of one hundred thousand separate from his home in the suburb, Pete Wolfe had a certain amount of anonymity. And Honey, with Willy in kindergarten and his older brother and sister in grade school and two-year-old John in nursery school, had an easier time than ever before in this marriage. But the lull was short; in no time the Wolfes were back in their Mary Hartman way of life.

First came Honey's peculiar paralysis, which followed a viral infection and started in her legs. Then the paralysis ascended to involve the nerves controlling the muscles in the upper part of her body and her breathing muscles became involved, and her husband was sure the symptoms meant Guillin-Barré, which occurs in approximately five thousand persons each year. A test of Mrs. Wolfe's cerebral spinal fluid substantiated the doctors diagnosis and sent Honey into the hospital where mechanical respiration saved her life and underscored the children's belief that their father was a genius.

In a new school in a new town and with his mother away, Willy, whose bedwetting was a bother, had his usual night problem, but in the daytime he had none of the physical, emotional and learning problems of the other boys. (Peter, who was an average student in the fifth or sixth grade by this time, wept in rage when his father put him down and ended arguments with "we should have thrown this one back." And John, the littlest Wolfe, frightened the family with a breath-holding act when he was frustrated. And Charlie Cheney, whose conflict with his stepfather had been severe, had asthma attacks when he was in the house that caused him to moan with pain and panic and required drastic hot-water-and-steam treatments from Dr. Wolfe, which he battled.) Not Willy. This one, who looked like his dad, got credit from him for being the smartest of the brood and lived up to his reputation. Beginning in kindergarten, he walked into a classroom with an assumption of success, and sailed along as one of the brightest without half trying. But shortly after his mother came home from the hospital, he suffered an accident that was traumatic. Again, Mike, who by then was putting himself through New York's free City College as he supported himself with odd jobs, had driven up to see the Wolfes and was on the scene.

"The doc had a new rotary mower with so much power it snapped the pipe of the sprinkler as easy as a weed when he accidentally ran over it in the yard. And he was on this day out in front racing along after the mower, and Willy and I were reading something under a tree. And then Willy ran over to tell something to his dad, who before I knew what happened began yelling 'Mike, Mike, help!'

"I looked over and saw the mower slashing its way over Willy's foot, not once but three times as the doc pushed and pulled and pushed again to get the mangled foot untangled, so I ran and helped get the motor turned off, but by this time Willy's foot was just hanging there by some muscles."

The doctor held his son's foot to the stump and, with Mike's help, got Willy to the hospital, where surgeons saved the foot and dealt with the child's shock. But the doctors couldn't prevent physical impairment (Willy limped slightly after that) and, possibly, psychological damage as well.

Willy's father, who competed with the others, did not pick on Willy, whom his brothers came to resent. "So they would go after Willy," says Honey, "and he would manipulate around until he got everybody fighting with each other." She remembers that when she and her husband went away for any reason, the other kids said "take Willy" because he always stirred things up. "He was just plain smart, that's all."

Willy's grades were excellent during his first couple of years in Frankfort, and he got along with the kids in his classroom, but his lagging foot and his inclination to be by himself kept him from excelling in schoolyard athletics until the family took off for a year in Puerto Rico. By this time, his freak accident and Honey's peculiar disease had called attention to the family, and stories, like one about their big white dog "which can't bark because it's had its larynx removed," followed them in their mostly-Italian bedroom town. Few here had gone to college and almost nobody to prep school, and the flamboyant newcomers were considered "the wealthy ones."

"Dr. Wolfe's wife is one of the Cheney silk people."

"No, she was married to a Cheney, that's all, and he was only related way back to the ones with the mills in Manchester."

"Well, there's a lot of money there somewhere; the doc drives a Jag."

"A patient gave it to him."

"He must have done a lot for her." (This last with a "Ho, ho, ho.")

"And what about all those fancy schools?"

"Cheney pays for that, they say."

This last was true—at least for Ben and Charlie, who remained behind at Yale and Taft when the Wolfes went to Puerto Rico.

In his forties, Pete had rented their house to others and took a leave from the Utica hospital to go as an anesthesiologist to a hospital in Puerto Rico for his second year's residency, "which wasn't the best year of our marriage, I think we would both agree." But Honey simply says that San Juan was hot and muggy and not as much fun as Cuba, "where we lived when Pete was in the Navy. In that year, we had the use of somebody's yacht, which was heaven. Still Puerto Rico was an experience, and the kids had a great time."

In their year away, Peter and Roxie went to an accredited combination junior high and high school, run by Methodists, and did well. Willy and John had what amounted to individual tutoring at Miss Clark's four-boy private school, which had a beach for its schoolyard. When Willy finished his lessons at one o'clock, he headed for the ocean, where he surfed and swam. He got a report card with all A's, turned as brown as the natives, became an excellent swimmer and learned fluent Spanish.

Mike, who was as much a part of the family as ever, flew down to see the Wolfes on the island and came away thinking that Willy, who was a wonderful-looking boy at eleven, "was the smartest kid I ever saw in my life." Some way, he says, Willy had taught himself the Morse code and could rap out messages as well as any telegrapher. "And he knew the name of every rock and shell on the beach and could read anything." To Mike, Willy and all the rest seemed to be leading an idyllic life, but the Wolfes preferred Utica to the island and were glad at the end of their year to go back to northern New York State, where they sold the home in Frankfort and moved to nearby

New Hartford to Honey's dream house. "I had driven by it many times, a lovely place with many trees, and when it came on the market, I wanted it very much."

In the ensuing years and through ninth grade, which in New Hartford was the first year of high school, Willy's grades, with only occasional one-semester lapses, stayed in the B-plus-to-A range, and he had little trouble making the honor roll. And because he was good-looking and had extracurricular interests that were classier than those of the average student, he was a child whom teachers found attractive and would turn to for special information. They urged him to tell the class about traveling on a trawler with fishermen who knew his dad; let him demonstrate fly-tying, which he had learned from his father, with whom he had fished in many rivers; asked him to show his collection of rocks, which he had decorated with engravings made with a dentist's drill brought home to him by his father. And they talked to him privately about his brothers and sister and friends, who went to the fanciest schools in the East. To them, something always seemed to be happening with the Wolfes.

What had been happening for some time was that Pete and Honey's marriage was coming apart, which was something Willy couldn't admit to himself even in his sleep and which had an immediate effect on his behavior. He had less patience than usual, demanded small attentions, argued more with John. But at school his grades stayed up, and his science teachers were sure that he would go far.

At this time, Willy's interest in earth science came to the attention of Dr. Harold Cahn, a professor of biology at Utica College who was doing special research with Dr. Wolfe in hypnotherapy. And as a result, Willy was invited to go to a ranch in Wyoming with Dr. Cahn and his wife, who saw that the boy had a home life that was making him anxious. So off went Willy with the Cahns and their small boy and girl for an unforgettable summer out west.

"Willy was a nervous boy in that period," says Dr. Cahn, who moved soon after that summer from New York State to Arizona, where he is now a consultant with the Potential Research Foundation at Glendale, "and he was too much of a loner for his age and a little bit spoiled. But he calmed down a lot on that trip and learned that he couldn't automatically get whatever he wanted and would have to give and take."

As he learned about himself during the vacation, Willy also learned about fossils. With the help of Dr. Cahn, he made a paleoecological study near the ranch of the Cretaceous remains of reptiles and other creatures that lived 70 to 135 million years ago. As a result, he had his first taste of fame. Asked to give a report of his Mesozoic findings to the Rock Hounds Society's meeting in the town of Thermopolis, which was twenty-five miles from the ranch, he later read an account of what he said in that town's newspaper. Now he would be a scientist for sure! "And he went on thinking this way," says Dr. Cahn, "when he returned home." First thing, he worked his report into a Science Fair project and gave a talk at school about his Wyoming research. "And that brought him further attention," remembers Dr. Cahn, who is Scandinavian but whose eyes have an Oriental slant which has occasioned a lot of kidding about his being a Lapp. "That was a standing joke between Willy and me," says Dr. Cahn now. "We talked a lot about how he had gone off on a trip with a Laplander."

After the Wyoming exploration, Willy's interest in science was regarded at school and at home, where his mother believed "This one will be an archaeologist," and his father said, "A scientist for sure, but the field will be medicine," and his teachers told one another, "He'll go to the top because everybody wants him to." "Things happen to Willy," Honey told a friend, who laughed. "So how is that different from your other kids?"

Ben, who had graduated from Yale, was by then an officer in the Navy and was stationed at Brunswick, Georgia. There he had fallen in love with an Alabama belle whose best friend would marry George Wallace. And Charlie was at Yale, headed for a career in anthropology that shortly took him to the University of the Americas in Mexico, and Roxie was rollicking along at her mother's old school, Abbot. Even Peter, who wasn't much of a student, was now ensconced at Parsons College in Fairfield, Iowa.

But Willy, above all, seemed to be riding high. "All the children know people in the news," said Honey, "but with Willy, he's in the news himself. Whether that's lucky or unlucky, we'll just have to see."

"Willy, too, thought of himself as lucky until Sharon came along," says Roxie, "because up till then, he was the apple of my father's eye, which he probably was afterward, but he never could be sure."

About the time Willy entered eighth grade, a lean, unsophisticated student nurse, who was a year younger than Honey's son Charlie, signed up with Dr. Wolfe at the hospital for a course in anesthesiology. Soon afterward she moved with a roommate to an apartment near the Wolfes' New Hartford house. From the first, the girl went in and out of the big house like other friends of the family, but in no time at all the children could sense a difference. Sharon listened with more attention than anyone else to everything their father had to say, and she smiled at his timeworn jokes, and sometimes she went to concerts or the opera without their mother, who did not like the girl.

Throughout the next painful year, as their parents confronted each other nightly with guilt and recrimination, the children could hear the pair shouting in the night, when one or both might have drunk more than either had done before. Still, only Willy's older brother, Peter, who had found a letter that his father had written to Sharon that convinced him the two were in love, had begun to see that his father and mother's marriage was damaged beyond repair. Until then, he and Roxie and John had felt that their parents were just going through a bad time and that things would soon change for the better. And Willy was even less able to face the truth. All people have fights, he had said, so that really doesn't mean anything. And what about Christmas when his mother and father had kissed each other? If you don't look too closely, this will pass; the marriage won't end.

Finally Honey told Roxie, Willy and John that she was going to get a divorce. In the days that followed, Roxie and John were sad. But Willy was devastated. Loyal now to his mother, whose husband he knew to be in the wrong, he couldn't stop loving the man who had been his hero and champion—his dad, who was rejecting his mother and sister and brothers and him. And now at last Willy didn't duck the old question that troubled his mind. If someone really loved you, would he bring on so much pain? In his four-poster bed Willy found his answer and felt sad.

Chapter Nine

Divorce is an event that affects family members in different ways. To Dr. Wolfe's credit, he anticipated emotional upsets in various forms, but he was personally involved, so objectivity was undone. Still, he couldn't leave the situation alone; he would play the dual role of leading man and supportive analyst, two parts he knew how to perform.

Most of the time he stayed inside the central character, who was hurting the ones he loved and felt guilty and grieved. But periodically he played Freud. As the therapist, he worked to ameliorate long-term harm and in this he took pride.

"Your mother and I loved each other more than any two people in the world," he told the boys and Roxie. (Let them know they were born in love.) "But we are not in love now." (Give it to them straight.) "But our falling out of love has nothing to do with you or with anything that you might have done." (Take away any feeling of guilt.) "And both of us will love each one of you just the same as always." (Don't let them feel rejected.)

"I adored him," said Roxie, "and while I'm sure there was nothing Oedipal in my feelings (I wasn't thinking 'if he wants somebody young, why not me?'), I was terribly hurt. And the boys had a tough time because they loved their mother—as I did too—yet they would

miss their father, so they hated him and loved him at the same time."
She said that all four of the children were in puberty and "mixed up
about our own sex feelings, and that didn't help."

"The Wolfes were out in Hohokus, New Jersey, that June for
Charlie's marriage to Susan Armstrong," says Mike, who had
graduated from City College by 1966 and was an officer in the Navy.
"The wedding was a big affair with a roving band and all kinds of food
and drink under a canopy and lots of flowers and people. And the
entire family was there.

"Charlie's real father, Dr. Cheney, and his wife and two children,
who were about Willy's age, were there, and so were Ben and his wife
who had little kids, and so was Honey, of course, and along with her
the doc and all the Wolfes, who knew by this time that a divorce was
coming. And I felt bad, because they all looked so sad."

Roxie says that Charlie's wedding was an emotional day for
everyone "but must have been terrible for my mother." Honey, she
knew, was glad for Charlie, who by then was through with his military
(he'd been a "swabby" in the Navy) and was marrying a super girl
(Susan had a master's degree from Northwestern, where she majored
in political science). "But still my mother must have felt embarrassed
because everyone knew that her husband was leaving her to marry
somebody else." She says that Honey sat straight and didn't cry during
the ceremony and talked to the others after the toasts about what a
good time the newlyweds would have in Mexico, "but my father cried
like a baby." She says that she told Willy, "Dad's a real slob," and that
Willy said he felt sorry for his father, who probably felt sad too that
things hadn't turned out right.

One of Dr. Wolfe's functions in Utica, which he had taken
seriously, was to talk to professional and civic groups about the
depression that can hit middle-aged men who have achieved what
they thought they wanted in life and whose children are growing and
going. "And, suddenly, they find themselves wondering 'Is this all?'
and go off on a tangent." Roxie says Pete could have been talking
about himself. "Here he had work that was easy for him and a chance
to do research, which he loved, and enough money." (Honey by then
had received a small inheritance—as had Pete, who was due to receive
an even more substantial sum from his mother's brother, who had
bought IBM stock early on.) "And he had a beautiful home and
healthy children who were doing well in school, and all kinds of

outside interests; he was even a doctor for the Clinton Comets hockey team." She shrugs. "But all of that wasn't enough, so he shook things up."

At the time of the divorce Dr. Wolfe and the hospital in Utica agreed that he and Sharon should resign. So shortly after Pete and Honey sold their home, the doctor moved with his new wife to Boonton, New Jersey, a dull little town with an opening for an anesthesiologist. In Boonton with Sharon, as in New Milford with Honey, Dr. Wolfe bought a large, comfortable house at the edge of town, with a brook, berry bushes and apple trees. There two more children would have kittens and puppies to play with and grown-up stepbrothers to make life interesting the way his and Honey's children had had the Cheney boys years before. The only problem: Willy and John would not come into his house.

"They were unhappy with the divorce, so they wouldn't have anything to do with their stepmother," says Pete, who remembers that when Willy and John first came to visit they put up a tent out back. "They wouldn't come in to eat, so Sharon fixed their meals on trays which she put on the back steps." Pete laughs. "The first night, a swarm of black flies got in the tent, and the boys came rushing into the house and went to bed, and we heard no more about their not staying inside."

The elements in Pete's life were about the same as those of twenty years before, but time had changed certain things. Gone was the young man with dash who had arrived in New Milford fresh from the Navy; in his place was a battle-scarred veteran with alimony, tuitions and child support he had agreed to pay who is rememberd by young women in the Boonton Hospital (from which Pete moved on in the sixties to a larger hospital in Allentown) as "pretty much of a square." Gone was the doctor who wanted to set the world on fire, replaced by an anesthesiologist bored with his specialty. Gone was the visionary with big dreams for himself. Let Willy carry on.

In the fall of '66, at age fifteen, Willy moved with John and his mother to Litchfield, where they occupied a rented three-story house on Main Street across from their Uncle Pete and Aunt Kate, as always, Honey's mentor. Honey got a job selling ads for the *Foot Hills Trader,* a giveaway newspaper with a big Litchfield County following that she still sells ads for today. And Willy and John started high school, where Willy got B grades in tenth-grade English, Spanish, algebra and trig, modern European history and chemistry, maintaining an 85 average in the first three, 82 and 80 in the last two. He knew, as did his mother, that although he made the honor roll, his work in math and science was not up to his old standard in New York state, where his grades in accelerated math and earth science and biology had been 12 to 17 points higher. So maybe he needed a boarding school.

Like his father and stepbrothers and their father, Dr. Cheney, who lives weekends in Litchfield on a gentleman farm where he raises Guernsey cattle that win prizes at nearby fairs, Willy had always expected to go to Yale. So maybe he needed a good preparatory school to insure his getting in. "Dad," he told Pete, "I want to go to prep school." And his father, who wanted this son to go to Yale, gave an immediate okay. "Better apply at Exeter."

Willy did so after applying first to Andover, where he was turned down, as he was at Exeter (where his father says he forgot to fill out two pages in his application). Then, with the help of his teachers at Litchfield High, where he was a favorite, he applied and was accepted at Mount Hermon.

"And, oh, how I hated to see him go," says Jacqueline Moreno, a Mexican divorcee who taught Willy Spanish in Litchfield. "Willy was a tall, beautiful boy, with nice eyes and clear skin and freckles, who knew Spanish. In class, you knew he was there, but he didn't talk much because he was shy—the last person in the world you would expect to be a terrorist. When I read his name in *Time*, I couldn't believe my eyes. Thinking back, Willy was the conventional one; John was far more the type to get caught up in a movement."

"John was more devilish than Willy," continues Ms. Moreno, who says that both boys loved their mother (John made her an acrostic that spelled MOTHER in Spanish) but John teased her a lot. "When she would come to school for Parents' Day, he would have the teachers and their room numbers switched around so his mother never knew whom she was seeing about what." Ms. Moreno says she can see John now directing traffic in front of the school in an opera cape or a tux or army suit he wore to classes. "He was the dramatic one; Willy was conservative." She said that while John would get a job as a cook in a traveling circus in the summertime, Willy would mow lawns for people or go off to visit relatives.

"But he would always have an adventure," says his mother, "and he was a good reporter." She remembers that the summer before he went to Mount Hermon Willy went to Mexico City "and had the craziest things happen to him." In a letter typed from Charlie's place he told of arriving by plane in Houston, where he could find no bus to Mexico City. "So I went to Laredo, Texas, and waited five hours for my bus and then was stopped at the border by a bony Mexican customs officer, who looked like the crooked cop in a movie version of some Latin American Hicksville who informed me I had to have a birth certificate (to prove I wasn't a Russian spy) and a signed permission from home to make sure I wasn't a runaway." So Willy got a notary to call his dad, who said to let him cross over, "which I did with the help of American greenbacks, which I see are valued world wide."

Twenty-four hours later, "after an enjoyable trip through Mexican villages and mountains," Willy got to Mexico City, where Charlie had moved to an address the university could not find. "So, suffering from Montezuma's Revenge which would have killed me if I hadn't been nursed by a friendly Mexican who got me back on my feet and even took me to a bullfight, I wandered around to see how other people live." Here, Willy's observations are pretty much "aren't they nuts?" comments. "Garbage collectors pile garbage on platforms on rollerskate wheels and drag it out of town." And after he found Charlie's apartment, where his half brother was "wandering around in his undertrou," Willy said "anthropologists are also nuts. One here the other day got high on drugs and booze and thought his Polish love was in a tree. So he jumped off a roof of a building to be with her and woke up without an ear, an eyebrow and a piece of his forehead—all this at age 42." In this same letter he reminded his mother to tell John to let his dad know when he could go trout fishing.

"The boys left with their dad for the St. Lawrence River right after Willy got back from Mexico," says his stepmother. "And after they left, I found a little tin box of Willy's that I thought contained fishhooks. But when I looked inside I found artifacts and little stone charms he had brought back from Mexico."

In the information he sent ahead to Mount Hermon, Willy listed "Episcopal" as his church, although his principal recommendation came from a Congregational minister who knew his mother and answered "Yes, indeed" to the question "Would you consider this boy a suitable companion for your son?" Willy reported "a severely cut left foot at age six" in his list of illnesses and/or accidents and mentioned that he belonged to "Troop 30, BSA, and a special explorer post for boys interested in medicine" and wrote this reason for asking for admission: "I want sports and advanced courses in Mathematics, Biology, Chemistry and Physics which Litchfield High School does not offer. Also, I feel that I can get into a good college much easier from your school than from a public high school." Then, with his dad's old duffel bag in hand, he entered Mount Hermon.

The school's name was selected by its founder, the revivalist Dwight Moody, when a wealthy clockmaker and Moody convert who had given Moody $25,000 to start "an earnestly Christian" school for poor boys remembered that Hermon (Psalm 133:3) was where the Lord promised "life for evermore." Located across the Connecticut River from Moody's farm birthplace, where in 1879 the evangelist had founded Northfield Seminary for Young Ladies (now combined with the boys' school), Mount Hermon had three postulates: 1) low cost; 2) a work program; 3) Christian commitment.

But today, far from being a low-cost school (in Moody's day each boy paid one hundred dollars a year), Mount Hermon is one of the most expensive. No longer a place where boys dig potatoes, tend cows, pigs and chickens, and do dishes and laundry in appreciation for a low entrance fee, the school urges students to concentrate on academic assignments and sports. And Mount Hermon's specific Christian commitment is no more. By Willy's time, both students and faculty had moved away from the old-time religion for which Moody was spokesman, and compulsory chapel was on its way out. Still, with several rich graduates, who include DeWitt Wallace, co-founder and longtime publisher of the *Reader's Digest* (Mount Hermon '07), who has donated more than $1.5 million to the Fund Committee, this is still an "opportunity school." Its scholarship fund is larger in proportion to its budget than that of any other school, so it can afford more than a token number of blacks, Indians and others who might be blocked from higher education by poverty, prejudice or lack of training.

Willy entered Mount Hermon as a junior with a secondary school admission test score of 317, which placed him in the top 1 percent of all tenth grade students who took Secondary School Admission Tests that year. Once in school, he quickly joined the staff of the *Hermonite*, where his ability to express himself (which was considered above average by four of his five day-to-day instructors) came into play. Before long the originality and independence of his thinking (which was marked "truly outstanding" by one of his advisers) and natural wit made his column on the sports page a good read, and he soon became sports editor. "Because I be so smart, I now be Junior Editor of the *Hermonite*," he wrote to his mother, who he believed was disappointed that he had not been accepted at a more fashionable school, like the ones attended by her first sons and Roxie.* "And Saturday, I made the varsity swimming team, and we've won two meets so far. (I swim the 100 meter backstroke and the 200 meter freestroke.) When the headmaster saw me and all of my 125 pounds in my sweat suit, his only comment was 'be sure and swim in this direction.' (I guess he thought he would lose sight of me.) That guy's a natural born confidence-builder."

In the same letter, Willy asked his mother to send him a golfing cap, "a houndstooth or something equally neat," and his fly-tying stuff "from my sacred chamber in the attic," and told her that he had only unmatched socks at school "so send me some and I'll send you some back" and finally, "everyone want to know how to tie a bow tie; I've started a fad."

This was 1967, a year of student riots when a Gallup poll reported that 81 percent of American students were dissatisfied with college administrations, and even at the secondary level, undergraduates insisted on a piece of the action. (Here's where Mount Hermon's compulsory chapel, voted down by 95 percent of the students, saw its end.) For a brief time, an underground newspaper, *Bulwarks*, appeared on campus, but Willy didn't write for it. Noted for his bow tie, he asked his mother in his next letter to send a huge, clip-on black tie "that is really wide at the ends" for a dance he was going to the following weekend. And in the next, he thanked his mother for the

---

* In the year following the divorce, Virginia Wolfe visited the school, where she talked with Frederick McVeigh, the director of admissions, who noted: "Mother a bundle of nerves—obviously, a little too good for Mount Hermon but can live with it. Daughter at Abbot—other sons at Andover, Taft. Our plant looks better when you see it than it does in pictures. Boy wants Yale, is probably O.K. Dr. Wolfe will pay."

tie, "which was the widest tie there, what a dude I am."

Willy liked playing with words, but the ideas and images that were new to him harked back to another time. "You wouldn't believe how wintery it is up here," he wrote to Aunt Kate and Uncle Pete when he thanked them for a camera and an antique English pub chair they had sent. "The wind is howling as if a raven was about to visit." And in another to his mother, "We rowed early this morning and the river was like a sheet of glass. Our first big race is next week against Tabor, quite often the best in the world! . . . It is now 24 hours later, and I had a great date last night, but now it is Easter Sunday and there has been a white dove flying around. (It's hard to believe but that really happened today in the apartment of our crew coach.) I guess somebody has great plans for us next Saturday."

Always Willy laughed about his skinniness ("from your muscle-bound son—bound to have muscle"). And, like all the kids in the school, he constantly asked for Care packages. "Send sundry cheeses, sardines, sundry crackers, peanut butter, jelly, filet mignon, artichoke hearts." And when he was going home, he announced his coming with a one-liner: "Make it frog legs instead of bacon on Saturday morning."

In this year when Lyndon Johnson was criticized by hawks for restricting bombing in North Vietnam and by doves for not ending the bombing altogether, Willy was not caught up. "My roommate has been arguing with some kids next door over Vietnam for about an hour now," he typed during the winter to Aunt Kate, "and it's not much for getting homework done." He said it would be stimulating if someone would bring in a new issue "dissimilar from the one which has been argued since September." Finally, "the talking has stopped now, but the room rings with shouts and dissension."

In the spring, which saw the assassination of Dr. Martin Luther King, a few students, in imitation of rioting college students, set fire to the school post office, pillaged dormitories, stomped on recordings, and tore up shirts in the school store and smashed Coke machines, photographic equipment, and the organ pipes in Memorial Chapel. Teachers, shaken by this strange new hostility, feared loss of control and an impaired educational process, but the disturbance (caused by a "handful of crazies," in the minds of Willy and his friends) had calmed down by the end of the school year, when commencement came off on schedule just three days after the murder of Robert Kennedy.

At meetings of the *Hermonite* staff, violence in or away from the school was not talked about much, and the paper took no position on the war. This was fine with Willy, who turned out stories about hockey, football, crew and track events. Were he to write about anything other than sports, he would have to do some digging, and research at this time was not Willy's strong point, but still he was making a name for himself.

"Willy knew people," says Michael Aisenberg, an honor student who wrote for the *Hermonite* along with Willy. "And he liked working with words and knew sports, so he was really good." He says that Willy didn't simply describe an event "but like a young Tom Wicker, told us the 'why' behind a win or a loss." Aisenberg, who went on to the universities of Pennsylvania and Georgetown after Mount Hermon and is now a lawyer with the FCC in Washington, D.C., says Willy also had "what I think of as a writer's personality . . . someone who gets along with people around him but still is kind of a recluse."

This private side of Willy was appealing to his athletic coach, who reported during Willy's first year, "I find his style of life rather engaging; there is a lack of over-sophistication in Wolfie.* Coupled with a freedom from crowd-following and conformity, this approach is positively refreshing among adolescents." He said that he thought of Bill as a growing adolescent. "He tires easily yet sticks to practice tenaciously," he said, "and for sheer doggedness you can hardly beat him." He said Bill spoke remarkably well on his feet and "he has a little showmanship and enough integrity to find me pleased with him as a person."

During his first year, Willy had talked with his college counselor, who was also approving: "Bill is as refreshing and genuine a young man as can be found on this campus of 650 teen-agers." But in this same period, Willy's day-to-day teachers were beginning to fear that he was a classic underachiever and that his charm, wit and laid-backness could be his undoing. One after another reported that he was

---

*While Willy signed his letters, papers and work on the *Hermonite* with his familiar nickname, he was called Wolfie by this coach and Bill in the classroom, where his teachers undoubtedly were encouraging him to mature.

imprecise, made little effort to refine his approach to a subject, lacked motivation and self-discipline, and "hasn't learned that he has something to learn from others." And when his grades went down on his permanent record at the end of his junior year, few on the faculty believed he would be accepted at Yale despite his CEEB* and SAT** scores, which again placed him above 99 percent of the test takers in the nation who took these particular exams. Finally, in the summer before he was to return for his senior year, his college counselor sent this report to his mother:

July 16, 1968

DEAR MRS. WOLFE:

Bill finished his junior year with an average of 72.5 which places him in the seventh decile of his class. His College Board scores were: on the Aptitude Test, Verbal 669, Math 720; and on the Achievement Tests, English 694, Physics 715, and Math Level II 736. Bill's verbal aptitude score is nearly 100 points above the median for his class, his math aptitude score 120 points above the median, his English achievement score approximately 90 points above the median, his Physics score approximately 50 points above the median, and his math achievement about 120 points above the median.* It is an understatement to say that Bill has been working far below his potential, and it is unfortunately true that a boy with this type of record usually ends up in a college which is far below his ability.

Bill has expressed interest in Yale and Cornell as possible college choices, but his chance for admission to either one is extremely remote. Other colleges for his consideration: Boston University, Drew, Fairleigh Dickinson, American University, Knox, Lawrence, Miami University (Ohio), Northeastern, University of Connecticut, Rutgers, University of California at Berkeley and at Los Angeles, University of Denver, Syracuse, University of the Pacific, Whitman, Whittier, the University of Southern California, Macalester, Grinnell, and Monmouth.

We hope this information is helpful for you in discussing Bill's

---

*College Entrance Examination Board.

**Scholastic Aptitude Test.

*Of special importance here are the *achievement* scores, which show that Willy had understood far more about every subject in every classroom than most of his classmates but had not had the desire or self-discipline to complete the notebooks, hand in the lab experiments and/or do the book reports that were required.

college plans with him and we will want to talk with Bill in more detail when he returns to school this fall.

Sincerely,

JAMES R. KELLEY
College Counselor

cc: Dr. L. S. Wolfe

In answer, Honey said she knew only too well what Willy's potential was compared to his performance but hoped that his National Merit Scholarship semifinals plus his work on the *Hermonite* might change the picture. "But in any case, please encourage him to apply to Yale. (He has been interviewed there as well as at other colleges.)" She said she was urging Yale because his one ambition since he was small had been Yale. It was not the end but it was a family affair. "As for the other colleges, I respect your judgment."

Willy's father, who appeared to be paying for one college, two preparatory schools, plus child support for John and alimony for Honey, should get little credit for largesse, according to Roxie, who says money often came late and was not enough for her mother to do what she had to do. "She's the one who busted her butt to get us all through school. My Dad's fatherly interest in this period consisted mostly of criticism."

"My son is aware," he scrawled in one note to Willy's school, "that I will *not* send him to a 3rd rate institution (Drew, Fairleigh Dickinson). Are Knox, Lawrence, Miami, Grinnell any better? His brother Peter has already wasted three years at Parsons—and I am rather bitter. Willy should be headed for Medical School. His College Board scores achievement ratio suggest a lack of incentive and maturity. If he should not apply for admission this year, but does well at M.H. in '68-'69, what happens?"

The school immediately urged Dr. Wolfe not to compare Knox, Lawrence, Miami (Ohio) and Grinnell, which in its opinion were topnotch institutions, with Parsons, and suggested again that it would be unwise for Willy to be unrealistic about his college plans. "However," the letter concluded, "we are all convinced Willy can achieve anything to which he sets mind and efforts, including admission to a first rate college, if he *works up to his potential in his*

107

senior year. But the hour is late, so we hope you and he will look at the schools we suggest. They are all good."

At the beginning of his senior year, when Willy still wanted Yale, his adviser suggested that he might take an extra year at Mount Hermon but wrote this into his record: "I am not sure than an extra year is a good idea, but I tried to make Bill see that the idea of going to Yale based on an excellent record this fall is unrealistic. I don't think he's mature enough for Yale a year from now—but possibly in 2 years. But I made it clear that an extra year was no guarantee; he might just sit back and drift. I gather there might be finance difficulties, too. But I don't think he should come back next year and then decide after a few months, the decision should be made ahead of time."

Willy and his mother and father decided soon after this against another year in prep school, and in his senior year, when he applied late to Yale, he was rejected in December. And after that he seemed to lose interest in what to do next even though his counselor wrote comprehensive reports about him to colleges where he might be accepted. "Before coming to Mount Hermon," says his recommendation, "Bill was able to slide along with a minimum of effort while receiving honor grades. It took him some time to respond to his new academic environment, and his overall performance was far below what might be expected. His lack of self-discipline was probably also a reflection of the fact that his parents were divorced a year or so before which was apparently unexpected by Bill, and so he found it difficult to concentrate on his academic responsibilities to the degree necessary to insure the academic success of which he is capable. There is no doubt that Bill Wolfe has exceptional ability and talent."

Still, Willy dreamed. When he didn't make Yale, he made a trip to Boston and wrote to his mother that he might apply to Harvard "on the million to one chance I might get in," which eventually he didn't risk. He did apply to Franklin and Marshall College in Lancaster, Pennsylvania, where he was rejected, and saw several representatives of colleges (Lafayette, Vanderbilt, Rollins, Penn) who wrote some version of "good-looking, friendly kid but shaky candidate due to difference between boards and performance." He filled out no more applications and finally, when his counselor had set up several appointments only to get a no-show, he said, "I'm just not interested in academics." Certainly at this time his classroom work reflected this. By the spring of his last year he was in danger of flunking Bible IV, which would make him ineligible for a diploma, and was getting discouraging reports from all teachers.

"He refuses to work at more than half throttle."

"Wish that he would try for more than a gentleman's C."

"Here is an honors capability boy with a low 60's achievement."

"Bill has been a lazy boy."

Now, looking back at his performance, some of the staff at the school wonder if he could have been involved with drugs, which invaded the school for the first time during Willy's senior year, when eight boys and two girls had to be dismissed. "The students were smuggling in LSD on postage stamps which they licked," said Richard Kellom, then dean of students, "and smoking marijuana and experimenting with mescaline and you name it." He says the teachers were scared and at the time didn't know what to expect, "but we brought in films and counselors and rode out the storm." He says that marijuana could account for the tiredness that Willy sometimes complained of, but that Willy wasn't really the hard-drugs type. "But if he were smoking much pot, the person who would know is his old roommate, Nick Monjo."

Today, Nick (whose father was the children's book author Ferdinand Monjo) is a cool, sharp-looking New Yorker who gave his impressions of Willy at a chic Manhattan restaurant where he sent back the spinach salad "because the leaves are sandy." He is a graduate of Columbia University and editor and publisher of the East Side's successful new magazine *Shop*. "Like most of us, Willy tried drugs," says Nick, "but he wasn't into anything heavy, because he lived within the rules, didn't take risks and wasn't a big spender. If somebody came to school with pot or alcohol, he might sample a little, but he wasn't setting anything up for anybody or buying for himself."

In his senior year Nick asked to live with Willy, "who was an easy person to share a room." He remembers that Willy was self-mocking on the surface and in any conversation half liked being the goat. "But he didn't want you to miss the fact he was playacting. You couldn't buy the buffoon for real."

Nick feels that Willy wasn't too upset by his parents' divorce ("although he was embarrassed that his stepmother was so young"), wasn't desolate that he didn't get into Yale, and wanted to travel, he believes, before settling into any college. He thinks that Willy wasn't challenged at Mount Hermon, "which is cut off up there from the rest of the world." He says that he and Willy had talked about the way students, teachers, everyone in the school was controlled by somebody else, and that both knew that neither of them would live like that. "You've got to be hypocritical to live as a surrogate." He says Willy was probably a virgin in his senior year ("most of us were"), was not a homosexual, was not interested in national politics and was probably bored, "so he just went floating along."

"A sweet guy," says the school's old Student Council president, Kirk Johnson, who took his premed work at Tufts and at Vermont and is now in Boston, where he is on his way to being an orthopedic surgeon. "Some fellows would invite me into a room where everybody was smoking pot and dare me to turn them in. But not Willy; putting somebody on the spot like that wasn't his style."

"The only one he ever hurt was himself," says a teacher who tried to help Willy "get his act together" but couldn't make it. And certainly she is right about Willy's tendency to hurt himself physically as well as emotionally. In his last spring at Mount Hermon, he sprained two fingers, a toe and an ankle and told his mother he averaged "only about five hours of sleep a night."

He didn't study even though he knew he was jeopardizing his chances for college, but he did read *The Turn of the Screw, Daisy Miller, The Red Badge of Courage, Hiroshima, Brave New World, Tom Jones* and *Walden*, which were required, and *In Cold Blood*, which was not. "And he read *Lolita*, which was our sex manual," reminds Nick Manjo, whose lasting image of the school is one of a line of what looked like black-and-white stick figures of males and females standing in a line in the snow waiting for the sun to go down "because we had a rule that we couldn't kiss a girl in the daytime." Another old classmate says Willy often chose to stand in the snow with a girl in the dusk because he had seen Bette Davis in *Dangerous* on TV and found out right afterward that she had gone to Northfield back in the twenties. "That did it! He would close his eyes when the sun went down and dream he was with a movie star. Besides, by that last winter he liked the kissing."

In his last spring, when every mail brought college acceptances to his classmates, Willy had no college to look ahead to, even though his high CEEB scores had brought him word from the National Merit Scholarship program telling him that he was a finalist. All this time he was still playing kid games and one day wrote to his mother for his dad's old dress suit and a cape. On "Parents' Weekend please bring my tails (stored in a box in the cellar by the garbage cans) and any other 'stud' wears and the dracula cape, boy would I be dynamite with that cape!"

When his mother came with the costumes, Willy wore the cape from class to class as he played the part of Count Dracula, Zorro or an archbishop. But dramatic as he must have been, he didn't try out for the senior class play, which that year was *Charley's Aunt*. Willy just wafted around the campus in a cape because, as Nick has said, this was not a fellow to take risks.

Toward the end of the year, when Willy's grades did not improve, he found a way to feel adequate in the classroom without digging into the basic problem behind his lack of drive. Instead of looking to the instructor for information, he looked for personality flaws. "I'm doing well except in Math," he wrote to his mother. "Just out of curiosity, I counted how many times the illiterate fool said 'okay.' 175 times. Needless to say I broke out in laughter once or twice. I've found that teachers don't really like kids to laugh in their classes when they haven't made jokes." But usually he let others be and was his merry, hungry self. "All the kids up here get huge boxes of cookies from their mothers who are diligent bakers," he wrote home. "You wouldn't want me to be a mooch, would you?"

So the days went by, and Willy's time at Mount Hermon ended in June 1969, when he finished 148 in a class of 194. On graduation day he sat on a wooden chair on a grassy hill in front of his mother and Roxie and John and down and across from his dad, who half blamed the school for Willy's not being accepted at Yale and muttered later to Honey, "This place stinks." And what Willy was thinking nobody knows. Was he embarrassed that he had no college to go to when Dana Cotton, the speaker from the Harvard School of Education, sent off the others to the colleges of their choice? Was he basking in the knowledge that his College Board scores had been just about the best of all? Or was he counting the number of times the speaker cleared his throat?

Other than having gained fifteen pounds, "which fill me out when I remember to wear three shirts," Willy, who listed his nickname as "Wee Willy Wolfe" in his yearbook and is described by more than one faculty member as "a boy who went his merry way" seemed little changed. He was a witty kid with good looks, a good mind and poor study habits. He didn't smoke or drink to any extent or smoke much pot (unless it was handed to him as a gift). And as far as sex went, he was drawn to girls, not boys, although as John was quick to remind him, he hadn't been too successful with either, so how did he know?

Unlike Nick and Kirk and Eric and the others in his row, he didn't know where he was headed now other than to Litchfield, which he mocked for its prejudices, not knowing that he shared the same. ("Don't let it get out in Litchfield that I am visiting a Jew school," he had written as a little joke to his mother when he was on his way to see a friend at Brandeis; "I have a reputation to uphold, you know.") But then what? He had the theatrical disposition of an actor, but he didn't want to act; the verbal skills of a writer, but he didn't like research; the scientific mind of a doctor, but he didn't want his dad's life; an aptitude for archaeology, but he was finished with that. So what now? Probably on this day he didn't know or care, because coming up this summer was a trip to California that he had worked out just that morning with Roxie and John.

A month later, they set out in his dad's car to drive across the country to visit Charlie, who was doing work in the graduate school at Berkeley. And who knew what might happen on the Coast? Maybe he would find that the school Charlie was attending was the one for him. Yes, if he couldn't get into Yale, Berkeley just might be the place.

Chapter Ten

The previous April, when the trees were coming into bud, fifty or more Berkeley students and street kids threw off their sweaters and shawls and set out to transform a muddy 3-acre parking lot into a park. They planned a covering of thick grass, a brick walk, apple trees, a fishpond, swings for children and a fire pit with a giant garbage can to be filled with vegetables in bubbling broth for visitors who wanted free soup. The concept took hold and by May hundreds of young people came every Sunday to work, watch or loll in the square, now called People's Park. Members of UC's conservative Board of Regents, one of whom was Patty Hearst's mother, feared trouble from congregating hippies.

Finally, one day in mid-May, after the board had met with Berkeley's chancellor, Roger Heyns, the school announced that a fence was going up around the flowering three acres "to re-establish the forgotten fact that this land belongs to the university and to exclude unwanted people." And at dawn a few days later groundmen encircled the field with an eight-foot steel-mesh fence.

By noon of that day, young people began arriving in waves at Sproul Plaza for a giant rally. There, student body president-elect Dan Siegel shouted the battle cry, "Let's go down and take the park." After that the war between the kids and the police, who were waiting on the corner of Telegraph and Haste, was on.

For three hours the would-be park beautifiers set fire to squad cars and stoned police, who retaliated with clubs and tear gas and finally fired directly into the crowd with shotguns loaded with bird shot. Student medics came in white coats to carry away their injured buddies and maimed policemen. At the first-aid station in Priestly Hall more than nine hundred persons were treated.

In the late afternoon, during an eerie cease-fire calm, Governor Ronald Reagan called up two thousand National Guardsmen and declared a 10 P.M. curfew. That night, when the bell rang, fifty-four persons had been arrested and policemen with guns were rattling their night sticks against the steel links of the barricade. All was quiet, but no one felt that much was settled. "The day of the Rhinoceros has not ended," said one graduate student, and in July, not long before Willy arrived on the Coast with his brother and sister, she was proved right.

The fight started on a midsummer morning when four guards tried to stop a group of activists from breaking the fence with knives and wire cutters brought to the park in loaves of home-baked bread. Next came a push from students, who were backed up by more and more of the same who arrived with bricks and rocks and hacksaws. Pushing back the hastily assembled army of local policemen with a blast of water from an opened hydrant and pounding at the law with any weapon they could lay their hands on, from a crust of bread to cherry-bomb firecrackers dipped in glue and tacks, they gained more and more recruits as the day went on, eventually becoming an army of one thousand. Not until nightfall was the mob subdued with the help of patrolmen who arrived with billy clubs and tear gas in screeching police cars. Eighteen demonstrators were taken to the hospital and the fence of steel contained fifty-seven medium-sized and walk-through holes, which Willy went to see on his first afternoon in Berkeley and which he found fascinating.

"This is where it's at," he told Charlie, who had a couple of years to go for his Ph.D. in Anthropology. As they stood in the sun in sprawling Sproul Plaza, singers with guitars strolled by, serious students trod earnestly to and from class, stoned street girls handed out limp carnations and intense believers in People's Park talked grimly about the conflict. "Dad's right; this place is the right one."

During the previous year, when Mount Hermon advisers had sent home suggested alternatives to Yale, Dr. Wolfe had disdained the small schools for Willy but rather approved when he saw Berkeley on the list. "That's the only one that's worthwhile."

"But not for you now," said Willy's adviser, who knew when Willy reported for his last talk before graduation that it was too late to apply that year. "Maybe later." At that conference Willy said a two-year stint with the Navy might be good, and his adviser said, "Or a year of work. Then I'd suggest a small school until you know what you want to do, and then, maybe, Berkeley."

But in California, when he and Roxie stopped for a drink at Fruity Rudy's stand at the edge of the campus on their last morning there, Willy knew no small school would do for him. "The vibes are right for me here," he said to his sister as one person after another who bought orange juice had something to say to Willy about People's Park.

"We got a guy on the moon last week, but we can't plant a flower in a mudhole," muttered a big bushy-haired woman of twenty-seven or twenty-eight who saw Willy as a sympathizer. "Sure, that rich Ted Kennedy can dump a dame in the drink," argued a boy with fuzz on his face, "but if we give out soup, we get thrown in jail." And a pretty girl in a long, crumpled skirt said to Willy, "That's right," as a limping student on crutches who thought Willy had been a fellow fighter in the PP war said confidently, "We're going to win this one yet." Then, as Willy answered, "Right on," the boy leaned heavily on one crutch and raised his right hand in an orange-juice salute.

Being part of something that everyone believed in was heady stuff for Willy, who told his sister, "I mean it, Roxie, I'm going to try to get in here."

A year and a half later he did this, but in the meantime he found out more about his world, his country and himself. This came in part from traveling, in part from girls and also from certain courses that he took. But mostly his new awareness stemmed from reading *The New York Times* in the office of the Metropolitan Life Insurance Company at 23rd Street and Madison Avenue in New York during one newsworthy winter and spring when he was living on New York's upper West Side at the edge of Harlem with Mike.

One is inclined to speculate about the privileged East Coast boy in the SLA and how he must have been affected by the plight of the poor blacks and Puerto Ricans around him when he lived at 788 Columbus Avenue. And a good many commentators have done so. But in reality, Willy felt at home in the neighborhood, and certainly, to the casual observer, looked less prosperous than nine out of ten of the whites on welfare whom he met on the way to the subway. Day after day, he flapped around in scarecrow hippie clothes, which were a step down from the basic clothes he had worn at Mount Hermon, where, like his friends of the period, he had been no fashion plate. ("In Willy's last spring here," said one MH faculty member "as I can remember, we worked our way to the close of the most disquieting year, the tone of the school slipped somewhat, and I said one day that our student body looked more like Coxey's army than like boys in a preparatory student body.") Completely at home in scroungy clothes, which took little thought and no cash to maintain—and which were acceptable at that time to fair-minded members of the Establishment, who considered long hair and strange-looking clothes a badge of the wearer's independence—Willy walked unself-consciously in and out of Mike's apartment, which was "just a pad" according to Mike, who by then had a glamour job and was eating out most nights and staying often at the apartment of the girl he was planning to marry.

In 1967, after college and four years in the Navy, Mike had passed a civil service exam that enabled him to work as a counselor in a job-training program for economically deprived New Yorkers, "which turned out to be a PR job for Rockefeller." Mike says that in the program "people who mopped floors to begin with ended up mopping floors afterward" and "once Rockefeller was re-elected governor, the whole deal was abolished anyway." By then, however, Mike was not affected because he had gone from his social service job to a good job in the personnel department of Celanese, "where everyone wore three button vests and ate steaks on expense accounts at Top of the Sixes."

"That year Willy was the one who looked deprived," says a friend who thinks back to the scruffy boy who lived with tall, slim, well-dressed Mike. And Mike tells about the day that Willy was to meet him for lunch and came to the office in a flopping hat and sixty-cent shoes and a shirt he had picked out of a rubbish barrel: "And I couldn't face going into a restaurant with him, so I sent out for sandwiches." He said that people in the office looked down their noses at this weird-looking kid whose sweater was full of holes "who, I explained, was saving his money to travel before going to college and, really that was true."

The year that Willy stayed with Mike, he spent little other than for subways and ten dollars weekly for a kitty, which paid for eating and sleeping in the apartment. "Yet, he saw everything there was to see in New York, and all for free." Willy went to museums on free days, wormed himself into rehearsals for plays and rock concerts and films, dropped into glass-blowing, weaving and pottery-making expositions, sampled tea, cheese, wine and anything else that was around at tourist offices, auto and boat shows and furniture markets, book and toy fairs and flower shows, and at galleries and outdoor art exhibits.

"He loved grocery-store bargains and would come home with chicken wings or turkey legs and fix up a pretty good meal of poultry and scalloped potatoes." Mike cooked too, but says that both he and Willy were glad for a good meal at his sister's house in Brooklyn, "where Socarro cooked spicy Caribbean dishes and had a daughter who was Willy's first love."

Willy had become aware of Mike's niece Mercedes when he was in prep school and she in Brooklyn High and within months had proposed marriage. This was not something that Mercedes, who was studying to be a secretary, could agree to, but she did want to go to Willy's Mount Hermon prom. So everytime Willy said "marriage," she said "prom," which he backed away from, telling Mike, who wondered what the fuss was all about, "I'd have to rent a tux." But when Mike offered to pay the rental, Willy did more back-shuffling, which was certainly not because the girl in his life was not good-looking.

Mercedes is slim, smooth-skinned and fashion-conscious. She is also black, which (if Willy had taken her to the party) would not have raised faculty eyebrows, as for decades Mount Hermon has not only admitted but recruited blacks (as well as American Indians and Asians). And the interracial socializing probably would have brought a salute from girls at Northfield, MH's sister school, where Bette Davis remembers that back in 1924 "a wonderful Negro girl was valedictorian of my class" and where students had insisted only the year before that the school's practice of asking parental permission before letting white and black girls room together be stopped. But inviting a black girl from New York to his school prom would have subjected him to questioning by his close friends, who had never heard about Mercedes at that time.

"Willy's feeling for Mercedes was deeply personal and tied up in his mind with Socarro's home," says Mike, "where you could feel love when you walked in." He says that when he heard on his car radio about Willy's death, "I kept thinking, 'If he could have stayed for a while with Socarro and been kind of a brother to Mercedes, he could have gone on from there okay.'" *

According to several persons in the Personnel Department and in the Statistical Bureau of the actuarial branch of Metropolitan Life, where Willy had a clerical job from November through May, the Mount Hermon graduate's assignment was to go through daily newspapers for accounts of fires and accidents, but this has not been confirmed by Nancy McCann, the company's press relations contact, who will simply give the dates of Willy's employment. So whether Willy read *The New York Times* as part of his job or picked up an employee's copy during a coffee break to find out what was going on around town is not clear, but certainly when he left the office each night he had read the nation's most influential newspaper from front to back. Never having been much of a follower of the news other than what was printed in the *Hermonite*, he soon found something of interest on page after page.

In the beginning he went directly to the sports section, where he followed the football and around-the-town activities of Jets quarterback, old "Broadway Joe" Namath, star of the '69 Super Bowl game at Miami's Orange Bowl, named MVP passer of all time. And he checked up on Gordie Howe, with the Detroit Red Wings, going now into his twenty-third hockey season with more goals credited to him than to any other player. And he read about the New York Knicks, slated to be that year's NBA champions in the Eastern Division. Always, he whipped back through the paper for news of freebies and action around town, and thus, in his first week in the city, learned of a peace rally in Times Square where on a Friday noon he joined a crowd of thousands screaming applause while Dr. Benjamin Spock

---

* On the same day, Honey was wondering if Willy's year with Mike had filled him with anger at America for its treatment of blacks. And Dr. Wolfe, who saw two "Negroes" raise clenched fists in salute when they received their diplomas from Mount Hermon, believes that Willy told him "they had a hard time here." Considering that Mount Hermon had formed a committee the year before to support black protest nationally, this would seem to indicate a misunderstanding on the part of either the father or son. Probably the black graduates were expressing a personal commitment to the black struggle nationally or simply saying, "Now I've got my diploma, *right on* to what comes next."

condemned President Nixon for not being able to end the war.

In November, the coming court-martial of First Lieutenant William Calley, Jr., accused by the Army of murdering civilians in South Vietnam, where he had been an infantry combat officer, was big news. So was the trial of the Chicago Seven, charged with conspiracy to incite to riot during the previous year's Democratic National Convention. So were Cesar Chavez and his United Farm Workers Organizing Committee and "don't eat grapes" marchers. So were Nixon's pledge of continuing support to South Vietnam's President Nguyen Van Thieu and George Wallace's insistence that war protestors should be sent to jail for treason and a rally in Washington of thousands wearing American flags who supported the President's Vietnam policy. So were the results of a Gallup poll that showed that, in spite of all the protesting, 74 percent of the American people opposed an immediate pullout of American troops from Vietnam.

"The people better look at all sides of the war question while they have a chance," Willy said to Mike a few nights later. This followed a speech by Vice President Agnew in which he accused TV commentators of manipulating the news when they analyzed Nixon's plea to the American people to see the Vietnam conflict through. "If we're not careful," Willy said, "reporters aren't going to be able to say anything about anyone in power."

Mike agreed. "I'm with you on this one, Willy," he said, "but the kids aren't helping with bombs."

Willy thought that was probably right, and he told Mike, "Since the bomb went off at Rockefeller Center, you ought to see the way women in our office dive under their desks whenever the elevator stops." He added, "Bombs are no good, but still, you can't keep going along with the Establishment no matter what." He reminded Mike of the Chicago police raid on Fred Hampton's apartment earlier that month in which the Illinois chairman of the Black Panther Party and another Panther were killed. "You can't let the police get by with things like that."

"But you've got to have policemen to round up creeps like Manson and those crazy girls of his out in California," Mike said about another story that he and Willy had followed since October. "You can't let freaks like that run around loose." Then he and Willy shrugged a resigned good night and moved off to their beds, where

Mike called out as he turned off his light, "What the hell, Agnew's going to Vietnam next week with a bunch of moon rocks, and all's right with the world." Both young men laughed, and the next morning Willy went home to Litchfield for Christmas, where he and John had a holiday party for the Zimmerman boys, who were over from England.

"And I was there," says Susan Hamlin, daughter of the former rector of New Milford's St. John's Episcopal Church, who was a student at Miss Hall's School at Pittsfield, Massachusetts, at the time and doesn't remember much about Willy other than "he had a lot of hair and was drunk." Then she laughs. "Anyway, I was—we all were." She remembers that her brother and sister, who were home from Penn, took along a little bottle of rum "in case the Wolfes wouldn't have anything but Coke in the house" and that she drank beer at the party "where a lot of Zimmermans with English accents were running around."

A couple of summers before, Susan's mother had said, "Pay attention to the Zimmerman boys; they have a lot to offer." And going home from meeting them, Susan had said, "They'll be the first to agree." Nevertheless, she had seen Michael Zimmerman often that summer, "when he kept wanting to take me to drive-in movies because he had heard in England that's where all American kids made out." And she saw him in this holiday time, too. She says, "He was very nice, really; it was probably the accent, which was natural but seemed affected, that put me off."

Susan doesn't remember that many of the guests at the Wolfes' party were smoking pot, "but maybe that's because I wasn't into it then," so she can't say whether Willy was into marijuana. But Mike says that when Willy lived with him, he often noticed a peculiar sweetish smell in the bathroom which he thought might be marijuana, "although one doctor told me the smell might have been coming from blood from Willy's rectum—that is, coming down from his ulcer, which bothered him a lot that spring." He says that sometimes the bathroom had blood all over the place.* "But Willy didn't do much about the problem, as far as I know—just lived with it."

* Red blood in the bathroom probably was vomited; blood from an ulcer that comes through the rectum is black. Or the blood came through the rectum as the result of diverticulitis in the lower intestine, which is what Roxie believes.

After Christmas, when Willy came back from the country, subway fares went up (from twenty to thirty cents), hemlines on the street went up and down, and the opinion of most students in large universities about Nixon went down and stayed there as the President vetoed aid to education, applauded his Vice President's attacks on "supercilious sophisticates" who advocated "open admissions" for universities, claimed credit for bringing Lieutenant Calley to trial (which three high Army officers denied), dolled up his White House police in operetta-type uniforms and talked with pride about ending the war through Vietnamization as negotiations between Saigon and Hanoi got no place. And, now, watching the passing scene from the sidelines had begun to depress Willy, who could see that an American campus was the place to be that spring, not trudging day after day into an insurance office.

"And then he read about an eighty-seven-year old philosopher who had been a defender of Sacco and Vanzetti back in the twenties who was retiring at the end of January after fifty years of nighttime teaching at New York's New School for Social Research." Mike says, "The story got Willy interested in taking an evening class at the school," which, according to that spring's Bulletin, is "America's only university to maintain a major commitment to meeting the intellectual and cultural needs of mature citizens." Down he went to 12th Street, where he signed up for five experimental evenings, each of which would focus on a different art form or experience—music, cinema, religion, sex and art, with a finale that would be a mixed-media presentation. Each Tuesday from 8:10 to 9:50, from February 3 through March 3, Willy sat in the school's lecture hall as an expert in one of the art forms attempted to transform the hall's 1930's environment through the presentation of his or her work. For this Willy was glad to pay a fee of fifteen dollars.* After the last night he talked to Mike about the multi-media presentation, which he thought everyone should see.

"What's happening to Vietnam soldiers and ordinary citizens in Vietnam is no worse than what's happened on any battlefield or to

*That year Willy read *Everything You Always Wanted to Know About Sex But Were Afraid to Ask*, which he borrowed from a girl in the office, and saw *Easy Rider* on his own before six o'clock one night. Outside of his classes and the movie, he paid nothing more for entertainment or edification, as far as Mike can tell.

people in any country where there was a war, probably, but when we see men dying and mothers and babies crying on TV, what's wrong about the whole thing comes home to us." He told Mike he thought that was good and "God help us if the government ever gets control of what we see and hear; then it's 1984 for sure." He said he was going down to the school the next week to see what sessions from then on were available on a single-admission ($3.50) basis, but he didn't do so because that same week a house blew up in the neighborhood of the school and presented a continuing drama that was more exciting and informative than anything he had seen in the lecture hall.

On Friday, March 6, word seeped into Willy's office that a fancy house in Greenwich Village, near the New School, had blown up. Willy slipped out and padded down to 11th Street a little west of Fifth Avenue, where he found the street filled with firemen, reporters and cameramen, and onlookers and neighbors. On that first afternoon everyone was saying the explosion had been caused by leaking gas, but mystery was in the air. It was said that two naked, screaming girls, all cut up, had run from the house to a neighbor's place, where they were given clean clothes and then promptly vanished. Willy was interested.

All that weekend the TV and newspapers sent out news about the $200,000 four-story house, now rubble, which belonged to James Wilkerson, a well-known adman and owner of five radio stations, whose daughter Cathy, from his first marriage, was known to be seriously committed to New Left politics and had worked in Chicago as editor of the newsletter put out by SDS.*

By Monday one body found in the ruins had been identified as that of twenty-three-year-old Theodore Gold, a member of SDS and a leader of the 1968 student strike at Columbia. After work on Tuesday, when Willy had been in the habit of heading downtown for a sandwich and a look at Greenwich Village before going for his session at the New School, he went again to the demolished house, where he found the street roped off and neighbors being evacuated. "We found fifty-seven sticks of dynamite in there, enough to blow up the block," the inspector in charge told reporters, who were pressing in to find out about a second body, this one of a young woman. And after that Willy watched every day for new developments.

* Students for a Democratic Society.

Shortly, the neighbor who had given clothes to the girls, who had not been seen since, identified one of them as Miss Wilkerson, and thereafter police found credit cards in the ruins belonging to Kathy Boudin, daughter of Leonard Boudin, a nationally known New York attorney active in antiwar and civil rights cases. Both girls, along with Bernardine Dohrn, one-time national secretary of SDS, and seven other young women, had been due to appear at the Chicago criminal court the week after the New York explosion. Free on bail, they had been charged in Chicago with assault and mob action the previous October when they took part in a "Days of Rage" protest marking the second anniversary of the death of Che Guevara, the Cuban revolutionary leader. Staged in Grant Park, the protest had been organized by the most violent faction of the SDS, known as the Weathermen.* The girls had not shown up as ordered.

The body of the girl found in the demolished house, believed from the first not to be that of Miss Boudin, was identified on March 17 as that of Diana Oughton, daughter of James Oughton, Jr., an Illinois legislator and banker. Like Cathy Wilkerson, Diana had been arrested in Chicago during a brief "kick ass" clash with police staged by Weathermen women during the larger demonstration. For some time she had been active in SDS, had organized radical education projects (i.e., sit-ins at schools like Michigan State University, distribution of SDS pamphlets at high schools, etc.) and had made arrangements for the Weathermen convention in Flint, Michigan, the preceding December.

Evidence that the house on 11th Street was being used as a "bomb factory" surfaced during the search for more bodies when a power shovel brought up dynamite sticks taped together to form packages, each of which had a fuse, along with thirty blasting caps, four lead pipes packed with dynamite with wires leading from them, and two crude alarm-clock timing devices. As the bombs tumbled into view so did the body of Terry Robbins, fellow Weatherman and friend of Diana Oughton's, and with that discovery the news story peaked, but many who had followed the events on 11th Street found themselves wondering why privileged rich kids would want to make bombs,

---

*The splinter group's name came from a line in a Bob Dylan song: "You don't need to be a weatherman to know which way the wind blows."

which is something that Willy probably found himself thinking about too.

Diana Oughton, Cathy Wilkerson and Kathy Boudin had been educated at top colleges (Diana and Kathy at Bryn Mawr; Cathy, who was raised a Quaker, at Swarthmore), as had Ted, who went to Columbia, and Terry, who went to Kent State. But just as interesting to Willy, now out of prep school, must have been the boarding-school backgrounds of Diana and Cathy. (Diana had gone with the daughters of other conservative Republican parents to The Madeira School in Greenway, Virginia, and Cathy, like Roxie and Honey Wolfe, had been a student at Abbot.) Why would girls who were pretty, rich and smart tie up sticks of dynamite to blow up buildings? What were they so mad about? Willy, who had looked for the "why" when writing about sports at Mount Hermon, began to look for the "why" in feature stories about students on the march and found a variety of opinions.

"Children of the rich feel guilty about having had so much," said one writer, "when all around them are others, especially the blacks, who have so little."

"Rejecting materialism, which they see as the source of many evils, activists are devoting themselves to society's destruction."

"Rich kids are used to getting whatever they want, so when they see a need for change, they think it should come right now and they are damn well going to blow up the world to get things done."

"Many involved in far Left politics have upset families behind them and are getting back at their parents in the most dramatic way they know for hurting them as children."

"The whole Movement is being manipulated by Communists, everybody knows that."

"It's TV again. Students who see the blah, blah, blah hypocrisy of the country's leaders want to tear down the Establishment so they can start fresh."

"All the kids are on drugs."

"Activists had some good ideas to begin with, but now they've exchanged the end for the means."

"The kids don't want to get their asses shot off in a war, that's all there is to this."

"They're living out the fantasies of their bored parents."

"The violence of the United States against Vietnam justifies violence in return."

"The Revolution is going to be world-wide, so America should be first, young people think, or we will be ruled by Revolutionaries who take over in other countries."

"Idealists are trying to help all human beings know what it means to be free."

Willy, who hadn't heard much about politics at home and hadn't been interested in them in school, now read as much about Mark Rudd, SDS leader of the Columbia revolt and dedicated Weatherman who had been arrested in the Guevera demonstration in Chicago, as he did about fast-balling Tom Seaver, top-winning pitcher of the New York Mets, and Joe Frazier, the new heavyweight boxing champion.

For any kid just catching up with what campus unrest was all about, this was the spring to get with it. Even the national news was dominated by youth. Girls were protesting in co-ed schools like Yale against the dominance of "male chauvinist pigs," a new epithet. Young middle-class prisoners (arrested in riots and for other crimes) were registering complaints against overcrowded jails and prisons. Student sympathizers with Black Panthers charged with conspiring to blow up public buildings in New York were marching in protest.

At the same time national news pointed up a seeming decadence in every stratum of society. Narcotics dealers, gamblers and businessmen were making illicit payments of millions of dollars a year to New York policemen, a *Times* survey reported. Pathologists gave conflicting opinions at the autopsy of Chicago's slain Black Panthers and reporters urged exhumation. Senator Edward Kennedy's veracity was questioned by Judge James Boyle after the inquest into the death of Mary Jo Kopechne. The murderers of Joseph A. Yablonski, reform leader in the United Mine Workers, who had opposed W.A. Boyle for the UMW presidency, and of Yablonski's wife and daughter, known to be insiders, remained unconvicted. And in Detroit, three policemen and a guard went on trial (finally) for beating eight Negro youths and two young white women in a motel annex during the riots of '67. While in New York, close to 1,000 heroin-related deaths a year (more than 225 of children) were being recorded in the City Medical Examiner's office.

A mail strike resulted in a call to the Army to deliver the mail; the New York City Transit Authority admitted it had discouraged arrests in subways to show a decrease in subway crime; a switch of funds in a New York suburb by an antibusing faction effectively postponed school integration. A memo to President Nixon from his counselor Daniel Patrick Moynihan suggested "benign neglect" as a way of handling the plight of black Americans; the Army reported racial tension at military bases. When a Maryland judge at the trial of Rap Brown for arson and riot questioned whether the black militant had been singled out because he was a national figure, without an effort made to identify other rioters, a police chief said that he had told a Senate Judiciary Committee nine days after the riot that he had six persons under arrest. A nine-year-old defoliation program in Vietnam (designed to destroy crops that might yield food in enemy-occupied areas) resulted in hardship and disease for innocent neighbors. About this time, Spiro Agnew gave credit to Attorney General John Mitchell for sharply reducing the rate of increase in street crime, and even as corruption seemed to be everywhere, the Vice President continued to pit the public against the press that reported examples. And all the time campus protests were on the rise.

At Yale, police fired tear gas at seven thousand students who massed to protest the jailing for contempt of court of two Panthers at the trial of Bobby Seale, co-founder with Huey Newton of the Black Panther organization, who was being tried for ordering the "offing" of Alex Rackley, a suspected informer. (Another issue at Yale was the relationship between students who urged the university to force the city to improve the treatment of its poorer classes, particularly blacks, and the city of New Haven itself, but the big draw for the rallies was Seale.) At Ohio State, where seven persons were wounded by shotgun pellets in a struggle between pro-and anti-ROTC students, the National Guard was called in. At New York's Hunter College, students protested against the fees of various kinds in a tuition-free institution, and at City College, night students did the same and went on to protest their exclusion from the university's open-admissions policy.

At the University of Illinois, five thousand students were dispersed by National Guardsmen and the local police when anti-war students protested recruitment by the General Electric Company. At Isla Vista, (a community that borders the University of California's Santa Barbara campus) after UC students had burned down a bank, helicopters dropped tear-gas grenades on unruly students to enforce a Reagan-proclaimed curfew. Seemingly senseless destruction by students and hardline retaliation by police separated the over-thirty from the young, and at Harvard, 19 percent of the alumni said they would give less than usual to the school as a protest against protesters. But finally, in April, when the Nixon Administration sent American troops to help South Vietnamese militarists clean out North Vietnamese and Vietcong sanctuaries inside Cambodia, many war-weary oldsters were as turned off as the kids. Thinking "Here we go again," as they saw that 43 Americans had been killed and 148 wounded in the first week of the surprise push, they too protested. (Not only did they disagree with the President's gamble that he could end the war by widening it; they were also bitter about the nature of his decision, which smacked of haste and deception.) Seldom in American history has a Presidential action resulted in a greater domestic outcry.

Willy followed with excitement everything that was happening on campuses. He read about the hit-and-run attack on the ROTC headquarters at the University of Maryland's College Park, the rock-throwing demonstration between Temple demonstrators and police in Philadelphia, a bitter antiwar rally at Wayne University in Detroit and a protest by upset students at Michigan State. He and Mike watched on the evening news as one campus after another across the country erupted with violence. And he joined at least one protest march through the garment district, listened to speeches at rallies that sprang up all over the city, and, on the Thursday night that Nixon was to give his televised explanation of his lurch into Cambodia, he went over to Penn Central and took a train out to Princeton, where there was to be a rally. There, after listening in a filling station to the President's speech, he went to a meeting of indignant professors and students in the chapel. And never in his life had he had such an experience. The small church was crammed with human beings with the same purpose, and their synchronized brain waves enveloped Willy. He felt internally full, whole, lifted up, loved.

As one person after another in the chapel had risen to protest U.S. military intevention in Cambodia and the group had voted to curtail spring house parties over the weekend and had made plans to meet at Jadwin Gym on Monday, Willy called John, who was a senior then at Litchfield High. "Man," he said to his brother, "you gotta get down here Monday; this is where it's at." Then, when John said he had finals that day, Willy told him, "This is where I'm going to be," and, according to Mike, that is where he was.

"I thought he might lose his job when he took off early Monday morning without calling in, but nothing happened afterward, so I guess they liked him down there."

Over the weekend, the presidents of thirty-seven presitigious colleges and universities had sent a letter to Nixon imploring him "to consider the incalculable dangers of an unprecedented alienation of America's youth," who were apprehensive about the invasion of Cambodia and new bombing in North Vietnam. The signers, who urged the President "to take immediate action to demonstrate unequivocally your determination to end the war quickly," included Dr. James M. Hester of New York University, who drafted the letter, and President Robert F. Goheen of Princeton.

At Monday's meeting a spokesman for Goheen announced that end-of-term procedures would be modified so that those individuals who believed that they must suspend their normal activities could do so without prejudice and that others could go on to class as usual. About this time someone interrupted to announce that four students at Kent State University had been shot and killed and eight others on the campus wounded by National Guardsmen (in fact, nine had been wounded). Minutes later, 2,300 Princetonians filed silently out of the gym, as did Willy, who returned to New York to listen to President Nixon's statement, read by a spokesman, placing the blame on the Kent State victims: "This should remind us all once again that when dissent turns to violence it invites tragedy." Then, for the rest of that week, Willy and Mike stayed close to the TV awaiting news of riots, which they were sure would follow.

They were not mistaken. In Boston, officials closed Boston University for the rest of the school term. At Columbus, Ohio, students and National Guardsmen confronted one another on the Ohio State campus. In Madison, Wisconsin, 2,800 students battled local policemen for a full day, until evening, when the campus was sealed off from outsiders. In Austin, Texas, police used tear gas to drive student antiwar demonstrators from the State Capitol. And in New York, all schools were closed for a day to honor the Kent State dead, while out in California, Governor Reagan closed the campuses of nineteen state colleges and nine universities and asked the state's private colleges to close after violence had taken place on UC campuses in Los Angeles and Berkeley.

On the Thursday following the Kent State tragedy, President Nixon, who had lumped all campus dissenters as "bums," met with college and university presidents, who told him that the majority of students and faculty members who opposed the Cambodia operation and indeed any extension of the war were not bums and that all resented the hostile comments of Agnew, who went after the campus dissenters with the same gleeful vitriol with which he had attacked the press.

The next night on TV, Nixon said that he and his critics wanted the same thing, peace, and that U.S. troop movement into Cambodia was the best way to get it; they would see. Then the following Monday, he met with the nation's governor's to seek advice on the student rebellion, which was duly reported and dismissed by the students, who by then were organizing for political action.

Notwithstanding his fitful involvements, Willy quit his job on May 29 to take the summer off, which Nick remarked on as odd "when half the people up here are looking for summer work." But Willy had done his winter stint and was ready for some hacking around. "After which he wanted to go to Stanford, where nine of his graduating class at Mount Hermon were in school," says Nick, "or to Berkeley, where he had just applied."

Nick recalls that Willy made arrangements to go to London, to stay with his cousins, and then on to Lapland and that "he was all hyped up about a special student travel deal he had maneuvered himself into to get overseas." Nick smiles. "When I go someplace, I take some money I've earned and buy a ticket. But not Willy. He always scrounged around until he got something off the price, which was as much fun for him as the trip."

This time Willy came out ahead two ways. According to Nick, he returned to the United States after working his way through Europe as a ditchdigger, dishwasher or anything else he could find without spending any money, "and then through some fluke mistake got a refund from the airline that was more than he paid out." And Willy's dad says he gave Willy ninety dollars when he took off and nine months later got back three ten-dollar bills, "and you can't fault a boy like that."

According to Mike, Willy saved $1,500 while he was living on the upper West Side, which he did not dip into for summer vacationing. "His plan was to work his way through Europe, which both he and I knew he could do." Mike says that Willy was "adaptable," so he was never going to have trouble getting a job, a hitch or a handout. "And he wasn't averse to ripping somebody off, either, especially if that somebody was an airline, a railroad or a company."

At the end of his stay with Mike, Willy brought him a place setting of silver every night for a week. "I was very much in love at the time and was thinking about getting married, but I didn't need silverware from an insurance company's cafeteria for a wedding gift," Mike says. "So I told Willy that his bringing home knives and forks from work was a nice thought, but I didn't need any more."

Owing to her having had six children over a period of almost twenty years, Honey hit the empty-nest stage more than ten years later than the average mother. But finally, as Willy prepared to leave for Europe, she was taking the best of what she had inherited from her parents and salvaged from her two marriages to a handsome three-bedroom apartment with balconies and foyers in Litchfield's snazzy new Woodlawn Court, where she would be living alone, "which I have now learned to love." John had departed after his graduation from Litchfield High to work with a circus and, at the end of that summer, to live with his father in his new house in Emmaus, Pennsylvania, and work at the Allentown Hospital.

Accordingly, Willy postponed his departure for a month to help his mother move. Roxie joined them in Litchfield, and Peter, who was preparing to move to Mexico, where he lives today, came east from Iowa for a final farewell.

"And it was at that time," says Roxie, "that Willy got to know Lydia, who was the most beautiful girl I had ever seen in my life."

"And Willy was the nicest boy," says Lydia, who manipulated her way past Honey's bird into Willy's old room, "where we looked at the clippings about his fossil findings and his year book and his artifacts from Mexico." She went home from the Wolfes' thinking that Willy, who was four years her senior, knew more about the world than anyone she had ever known, "but, of course, everyone didn't agree with me."

Dick Reventlow saw Willy five or six times and thought he was "pretty strange." Probably it was Willy's appearance as much as anything that put Dick off. "He was a hippie, and my life style was different. I had nothing to say to the guy."

"And we never got said all we wanted to say," says Lydia, who looks back to lazy sunny days when she and Willy packed a picnic lunch and went down along the Naugatuck River near Torrington "and sat by the water and fantasized." Neither she nor Willy could think of a marriage that they knew that was really happy "but we knew if we got married we would never hurt each other or our children, no matter what."

Lydia in her twenties is lovely. "I was very young when I knew Willy," she says now, "and he was kind. We didn't have a heavy sex relationship, but I felt sad when he went to Europe and saved up things to tell him when he came back."

"And when he did," his mother adds, "he was more grown up than when he went away."

"His first stop was with us," says Michael Zimmerman, who was living with his publisher father and his mother and two brothers in a home south of London at the time. Now at Amherst, where he is getting a doctorate, he recalls that Willy stayed with the family about a week "and then got ready to go up to Scotland, and I decided to hitch along."

The cousins bought fruit and sandwich makings along the way and ate and slept outdoors. "And on the road Willy would talk to workingmen who always wanted to know about John Kennedy, whom they had liked, and Vietnam, which they had not. And it didn't take Willy long to see that Americans weren't loved away from home the way he had thought."

After a week, Michael turned back and Willy pushed on. A few days later, in the East Highlands, he met a young traveler from Sweden who was about his age but not his sex. And thereafter they traveled together.

From Honey, who knows with a mother's instinct that "Willy became a man with Eva," a picture emerges of two healthy young people taking a holiday from constraint as they explored the pine-scented hills of northern Scotland. And from Dr. Wolfe, who spent time with Eva later in California (where the friends she made are no longer in contact), comes a portrait of Miss Olsson, who was blond like Lydia and "as hardy as a winter apple."

Eva knew the outdoors and taught Willy about mountain climbing, at which he later excelled. And certainly Willy delighted in the fearless young Scandinavian woman with whom he lay at night beneath rustling trees in a strange, rugged land, because when Eva left to go home, Willy took the boat with her to Sweden.

There the trail becomes indistinct. According to Dr. Wolfe, his son visited Arctic Scandinavia after visiting Eva and her family in Sonetunsa, but as far as Honey can recall, Willy indicated that he did not. Whatever the case, Willy returned soon to Eva and thereafter flew to France and worked his way south into Italy.

"And then he came home and got that refund," Nick Monjo remembers, laughing again, "and that made his summer. But it was his acceptance at Berkeley that made the whole year worthwhile. After working and traveling for a year and a half, Willy was ready for college."

"He was so happy to be going," remembers Lydia, who saw the old year out and the new year in with Willy just before he left for California. "At that time I was terribly unhappy at boarding school." She says Willy told her the time at Westover would go faster than she knew, "and all I needed to do was to keep my grades up so that I could get into a good school like the one he was going to. Of course, this made me want to go too."

Lydia, who has lived for several years with Michael Besteda, a composer of electronic music on the West Coast, doesn't think of Willy as a love object as she looks back. "He was more of a big brother—or even a father (which is what I wanted at the time)." The pull to that kind of boy, as Lydia realizes, can be more attractive to a young, inexperienced girl who is eager for life than anything she might find in a rollicking kid in her own peer group.

"Back in 1971," she says, "Willy was much younger than I am now, but I thought he was wise because he had lived in New York and supported himself, had traveled all through Europe on his own and was going to a school that most kids I knew would have been afraid to go to." Now she believes that, even though Willy was born four years before she was, she and he were moving through life at about the same emotional level. "Then, because of so much that happened in my life, I grew up fast."

Lydia is no soothsayer and does not pretend that in 1971 she could foretell the horror that lay ahead. "And certainly Willy had no premonition." She says that other than being sympathetic toward her having to go back to a school she despised, Willy didn't have a bigger concern in his life than to get out to Berkeley and get registered. "And this time," he told her, "I'm going to get someplace in school . . . no cape, no jokes, no fiddling around."

In the next year and a half Willy kept his pledge, and later, when he dropped out of Berkeley, he did not go back to the costumes and fiddling. This time, when again he let others in his class pass him by, he felt no apology because he was involved in something he felt was far more important. By then, like the dead Che Guevara, who had become his hero, Willy was into the revolution that he was sure would come.

PART THREE

*In the Coils
of the Cobra*

Chapter Eleven

Willy's two half brothers belonged at Yale to Delta Kappa Epsilon fraternity, but they did not call the chapter house at Berkeley to suggest that Willy be rushed because, suggests Ben, "fraternities weren't as important in the '60s as they were in my day and, anyway, Willy didn't have the money to pledge." And as Ben knows, Willy wasn't the type.

Apparently old family friends didn't think of Willy as fraternity material, because he wasn't called to come around to Kappa Sigma, Phi Delta Theta, Phi Gamma Delta, Sigma Chi, Sigma Nu or any of Berkeley's other Greek houses. "No, Willy wasn't invited to pledge," says his father, "and he wouldn't have known what to do about a fraternity, anyway." In thinking back over what might have been, Dr. Wolfe shakes his head no to fraternity row. "That wasn't his style." *

And certainly when he arrived at the University of California campus, Willy looked more beatnik than Greek, which he accepted with his usual rue. "I was just named best dressed on the Berkeley campus for January '71," he wrote in his first letter to his mother, in which he reported that his roommate in the college dormitory

* In his day, Dr. Wolfe arrived at Yale with top honors from a good prep school but was not a fraternity man, says Ben "because his Dad had lost most of his money in the crash of '29, and Pete was working his way through school."

"doesn't seem to be an ass," modifying this with "though it's hard to know, since he's spent only about three nights here in two weeks."

Alone a lot, he looked twice a day in his postbox for a letter from Eva, or from Lydia. And, as in boarding school, he wrote home often. "But I'm not bored," he assured his mother when he reported that he wouldn't be taking Swedish, as planned, but was taking required English, which must have been old hat stuff, and courses in zoology and cultural anthropology "where we have 500 people at each lecture." Dreaming a little as always, for which he apologized, he said that he was applying for a job on *The Daily Californian,* "which will pay $50 a week if I'm good enough to get on the regular staff, which I kind of doubt," and that he had signed up for lacrosse "just for laughs." * For this sport, he asked for "my black football shoes with cleats, stored behind the wood box," explaining, "I can't wear sneakers, we play in a swamp." In the same letter he said that, beginning the next day, he would be tutoring fifth and sixth graders "in whatever they want, be it reading or sex education" for which he would get credit.

As in New York, Willy found plenty of no-cost entertainment ("lectures, rock and classical concerts and movies going on here every night for nearly free"), but he missed the Northeast. "The temperature today is in the seventies," he wrote in late January. "Frankly, I miss the snow and skiing and skating."

Quite by chance, it was this homesickness for winter sports rather than any political conviction that attracted Willy to the boarding-house-style commune in Oakland's Chabot Road where night after night residents and sympathetic visitors discussed the revolution. What appealed to Willy about the place was that David Gunnell, overseer of the group, was an experienced mountain climber.

Climbing exhilarated Willy. In one of his letters to Connecticut, he told of finding a hill behind the dorm "where I can walk straight up and back for thirty miles without seeing a house once I get high enough." And in this period he subconsciously was drawn to others who gained strength, as he did, "from the earth and the trees and the sky."

One girl who became friends with Willy at this time was Nancy

---

* The job on the *Californian* did not come through, but Willy's performance in lacrosse earned him an A, for which he again apologized with "I must be a jock."

Boehm, a healthy UC freshman from nearby Fremont, whose vitality, blond good looks and ecological know-how reminded him of Eva. And one boy in the dorm became his special friend after Willy saw him start off for the Palisades with a backpack one weekend. Through this kid down the hall, who happened to be Chinese, Willy met Jean Wah Chan, owner of the Peking Man vending cart, which provides egg rolls and other Oriental delicacies to students and visitors to the Berkeley campus. And through Jean, who has lived for many years with Dave Gunnell, Willy found his way to the loosely organized commune at 5939 Chabot Road, known to the press during the SLA rampage as Peking Man House, a nickname that came from Jean's food stand but at the same time suggested Mao's early revolutionary theories discussed around the table.

What Willy hoped for after his first visit to the commune was to be invited on a mountain-climbing trip with Gunnell. "In spring vacation, I may be going back-packing in the Sierras," he told his mother. "Friends of a friend will be rock climbing with ropes, skiing across glaciers, the whole bit." In another few weeks, when he thanked Honey for a February birthday check, the expedition was set. "I was able to buy a pair of $45 mountaineering boots (scorched in a warehouse fire) for a fabulous $20," he wrote as he went on to whet Honey's interest in his coming trek with a little scare copy. "We'll beat our asses skiing up for six days with fifty pound packs for one glorious day down. Don't worry about my health, I'll be with veteran climbers, two of them have been going at it ten years and neither has died yet." In the same letter, he alluded to a telephone call in which he had told Honey he would be getting out of his dorm, which was being taken over for other university business. "So I'll be moving in with my mountain climbing friends who are also musicians," he announced. Then, in a quick postscript, he asked for recipes for spaghetti, lasagna, chili and turkey divan, which Honey sent to his new address.

So it was that Willy took up residence in the sprawling Victorian house near the Berkeley campus which is known today as the spawning place for the SLA. That he was taking a step that would lead to his death in the most spectacular shootout ever shown on TV he could not have anticipated nor would he have believed. What in the world for?

Clearly from the day he moved his few belongings into his narrow single room in Gunnell's house, Willy felt at home. Like the boy far from his family who pledges Deke and gratefully finds someone to connect with in every room of his fraternity house, he must have sensed immediately that he had made a happy choice. This was just like the Wolfe house in the old days. With people coming and going for jam sessions or to find a food cooperative or to show slides of Vietnam or to plan another trip to the mountains, something exciting was always going on. And with girls like Roxie to tell him to straighten up the kitchen or pick up his clothes, somebody was always making a fuss over him. And, to make his environment even more familiar, there was a head man, Dave, who ran a tight ship, had a big ego and was every bit as arrogant as his dad. Not since before his parents' divorce had Willy felt so right about his life.

And, as in years past, his "family" was a shade different from others. (Not only did Willy have Chinese housemates; he lived in the room next to Chris Thompson, a onetime New York Black Panther who had helped to edit Eldridge Cleaver's newspaper, *Right On*, and who was a romantic figure in Berkeley, where he operated a food stand called Harlem on My Mind.) And in the group itself, just as back home, Willy was a little different. The fact that he was from a well-heeled family with a doctor for a father and a prep school in his background put a little space between him and the others, who tended to let him off a little easy when there was a job to do. All in all, Willy must have felt completely comfortable, and his feeling of well-being resulted in good work at UC, both in and outside the classroom.

At the end of his first quarter, Willy had a B-plus average, had taken up skiing and was looking forward to a trip to Oregon with his lacrosse team. Obviously happy, he wrote in high spirits about his recent climb in the Sierras. "One member of our expedition was killed when he fell off a peak in a drunken stupor, another was buried in an avalanche caused by his loud yell of 'Fuck you, Reagan,' and I have to undergo a lobotomy to relieve frostbite, but I am alive." Living now with an accomplished rock musician (Dave Gunnell is a talented jazz drummer) and seven or eight others who were into gardening, potting and painting, he had taken to playing the recorder and was thinking about taking an art course in basic drawing "if it does not conflict with calculus." As a gesture to his politically oriented housemates, he was reading *The Rise and Fall of the Third Reich* and was considering taking Sociology 103 (Power and Conflict). But when he registered, he signed for calculus, astronomy, archaeology and lacrosse, going on to end his second quarter with two B's, a C and an A.

In another letter to his mother he laughed at himself for celebrating the second anniversary of the People's Park "massacre" by driving down Telegraph Avenue to "dodge tear gas and shot gun pellets and rant and rave at the pigs." He scribbled more seriously, "Why worry about Vietnam, the War's come home and it's escalating all the time!" But he went quickly on to tell of his lacrosse team's playing for the West Coast championship. Then, apologizing for seeming to claim that he was on a par with athletes on his undefeated team who were stars (which he was not), he concluded with "but the beer parties are fun." So far no parent could have been much concerned about Willy's radicalism.

Whenever possible that spring, Willy headed for the beach or the mountains over the weekend, and many times he had Nancy by his side. And gradually, as he became more and more attached to this vital, laughing California classmate, the memory of his girl in Europe appeared to fade, until he was telling others at the house that Nancy was the love of his life.

"He was like one of those romantic dudes from back in the fifties," remembers a friend who knew Willy in that period, and another recalls telling the kid from the East, "She's not the only chick in the world; at your age, you ought to be looking around." Eventually Nancy, who could feel Willy's deepening interest, conveyed the same message to her intense young suitor and backed away, whereupon Willy suffered. "By the time he went home to visit his family late that summer," reports another who knew him, "his ulcer was giving him fits."

"If he was carrying a torch that September, I didn't know about it," Roxie says. "The girl I thought he liked was Lydia."

That Willy could suffer from Nancy's rejection on one coast and happily take up where he left off with Lydia on the other was not a denial of the emotion aroused in him by either girl, which in each case was different. With Nancy, who was handsome, hardy and his own age, he was challenged and excited both physically and mentally; with Lydia, who was unhappy, intelligent and four years younger, he could be comforter and mentor. In one role, the masculine, competitive side of his personality revealed itself; in the other, the gentler, more compassionate side came out.

"Willy knew how much I hated my school," says Lydia, remembering how that fall she hadn't wanted to return to Westover, from which she soon ran away, "but he did not encourage me to come to California, even though I suggested this." She says that Willy was gentle but firm about her finishing high school. "Then maybe you can come to Peking Man House, where everyone does his own thing but cares about everyone else." She says she had begun making plans to go to Willy before he even got back to the Coast.

"Made it out here in three days," Willy wrote after hitchhiking west, "faster than if I'd been driving myself." He told his mother he was safe "in the comforting womb of my commune" and was enthusiastic about the courses he would be taking that quarter—Chinese ("with which the Chinese people in the house will help me"), Communist societies ("for which I have to write a 15-page paper on a cultural revolution"), history of architecture ("doesn't turn me on much, but the lecturer is flamboyant"), and calculus ("my favorite course last year, but now a complete bust, because the lecturer is an idiot and the organization of the class is very poor"). He said he was taking nineteen units, "well above average."

Willy's focus was changing from science to politics, which with hindsight his mother recognizes but which at the time she skimmed over as she made mental notes of Willy's requests, which poured in with every letter just as they had done when he was in prep school. "Send my tuxedo pants, if that's not too much bother," "my hammock, unless it costs more than about a buck," "my corduroy riding pants which I haven't seen in years," "the turntable which is under my bed." When he had an accident with his car or motorcycle, or was robbed of his wallet, he asked Honey to find out if the loss was covered by insurance, and when he lost his driver's license, he asked if she'd mind checking in Torrington about the procedure and cost of getting a new one. "Also, I've lost my draft card," he said in one letter, asking his mother if she wouldn't like to visit Eleanor Scully (her friend on the draft board) "and while reminiscing over the good old days, find out why I've never gotten anything but a 1A classification, even though I filled out forms for a student's classification. (After all, you wouldn't want your little boy dead, would you?)"

Sometimes at the bridge table Honey threw up her hands over the constant pigtailing she had to do for Willy, only to get complaints from other mothers in the same boat. Then, just before Thanksgiving, she got two requests of a new nature. "The County Welfare food stamp office will be sending you forms to verify my position of non-support," Willy wrote. "If you can't lie a little, don't send the forms back lest they throw me in the lock up." The letter continued, "I'll take care of Dad" and ended with "and if you'll be cool about it, I can call you with a telephone credit card number. Afterward, if the phone company asks if you received a call from a pay phone in Oakland, you can feign ignorance."

Honey had been embarrassed one Christmas when Willy had given Ben place settings from Metropolitan Life, and if she had not been hurrying around town to find recording equipment and some clothes Willy had asked her to send out to California with his half-brother Charlie, who was driving across country, she probably would have seen that this was the same kind of ripoff. As it was, she did not fill out the welfare form (but Willy got food stamps anyway) and she didn't look closely at the telephone business, because when Willy's calls became more frequent, she got no follow-up call from the telephone company. She did tell Willy he was nuts, however, when he began insisting "the old order of things is dying because it is impractical, immoral, genocidal and just downright sickening." "You're the one who's nuts," Willy wrote in January 1972, "and I don't like to see you going along with the colossal rip-off of our brothers and sisters around the world. Please stop kidding yourself, America is heading for either Communism or 1984. I hope you won't be a passive enemy of the people in the struggle for a decent life, and if 1984 does come, I'm a dead man." Dismissing this as rather muddled rhetoric, Honey nevertheless could see that Willy's interests were changing. For his fourth quarter, he had signed up for English, German, Chinese and a political course, "no math," and he suggested that come March, "I am planning to drop out of school, as I have about two dozen possible things that I'm thinking of doing." He assured Honey he would leave all doors open so that he could get back into college whenever he wanted and asked her to send two hundred dollars of his money from some stock that had been left him by a grandparent "because things are getting tight."

In his fourth quarter at UC, which was to be his last, Willy focused his attention on the Black Cultural Association at California's Vacaville prison, which turned out to be the most interesting project of his academic career. In the aftermath of the Los Angeles shoot-out and fire, commentators speculated about how Willy came to get involved with black prisoners. Had his humanitarian instincts led him to Vacaville, California's way-station prison for male convicts who are physically or mentally disturbed? Or did he get acquainted with the convicted robbers, arsonists, rapists and murderers who became his friends through a UC black studies course? The answer is neither. Willy got interested in black prisoners when he went to Vacaville to do a story about a new prison program designed to give black convicts pride in their blackness and hope and help for making it on the outside.

The idea for the prison project came to Willy from a neighbor at Peking Man House who suggested that he undertake the assignment as a study of cultural revolution for his political science course. "You ought to go to one of Vacaville's cultural nights," said the housemate, who suggested he go talk to a teaching assistant in the Afro-American division of Berkeley's ethnic studies department who was signing up tutors for a new self-help educational deal in the prison library. "The guy's name is Westbrook, and he's working with black cons who give a 'right on' salute to the Republic of New Africa and chant Swahili at their meetings. You might get a story there." Far more than a story, Willy found a culture that was to fascinate him for life. Whether he finished his paper, no one can remember, but two things are sure: Willy's future was radically altered the night he walked into a meeting of the BCA, and its outside coordinator, Colston Westbrook, became, as a result of his relationship with Willy, as famous as any black man on campus.

A stout man with large eyes and the extreme facial expressions of a stand-up comic, Colston Westbrook drops his entertainer's act when the name Willy Wolfe comes up. Under the fancy knit cap he wears like a clown's when teaching his adult education class in San Francisco, Westbrook's eyes lose their sparkle. Unknown to him, the folds in his face loosen and drop. "Poor Willy," he says, looking down, "he was just a kid."

Willy had just turned twenty-one when he got in Westbrook's car one afternoon late in March 1972 and rode with him about forty miles up Highway 80 to Vacaville (which means Cowtown). There, at the base of Mount Vaca, Willy paused to survey the long, gray, sterile-looking prison that has housed some of the country's sickest, most despised criminals, including Charles Manson. Then, without speaking, he followed Westbrook into the cold, fence-enclosed building, which holds more than 1,300 men at an annual cost to taxpayers of $16,000 a head. Advised beforehand not to wear denim lest it be confused with the prisoners' uniforms, Willy passed in front of an electronic eye, submitted to an invisible-ink branding at the admittance desk and followed the others to the library, where close to seventy black cons and thirty or so black and white visitors (mostly female) were assembled for the "cultural" meeting he had come to observe.

The meeting began, as billed, with a clenched-fist salute to the flag of New Africa and a Swahili chant. Then two or three of the imprisoned brothers announced their "reborn" names taken to replace "slave" names given to their families by white Americans. Thereafter a couple of convicts debated the economics awaiting them on the outside; somebody stood up and read a poem he had written in his cell; and somebody else sat back and played a guitar. The meeting concluded with a social hour with cake, coffee and head-to-head rap sessions between the black inmates and their visitors, who then went out to mail prisoners' letters, contact relatives and possible employers, obtain books at the library, solicit foundation money for BCA projects and in some cases arrange for beds for prospective parolees.

For Willy, the rapping must have been a real high. In this room were men who had lived at Soledad prison when George Jackson, John Clutchette and Fleeta Drumgo (known later as the Soledad Brothers) were charged with beating a guard and hurling him to his death. Others had been at San Quentin when word came that Jackson's seventeen-year-old brother, Jonathan, had been killed in a shoot-out at the Marin County Courthouse in a vain attempt to secure release of the Soledad Brothers. Still others had lived through the bloody San Quentin uprising in which George Jackson, who had loved Angela Davis, was killed.

Some of those who talked with Willy were Black Muslims who had known Malcolm X; others were Black Panthers who had worked with Huey Newton; still others were members of the Black Liberation Army founded by Eldridge Cleaver. Most had read the books that Willy himself was then reading—Frantz Fanon's *Wretched of the Earth*, which foretells a black revolution that will change the world; George Jackson's *Blood in My Eye*, which indicts the Hearsts (along with George Wallace and Lester Maddox) as right-wing enemies of the people and has become a primer for black revolutionaries; and *The Autobiography of Malcolm X*, in which he correctly prophesied he would die violently before the work was finished (it was finished by Alex Haley). Like animals in the wild, these convicts lived close to death, which could come from a suspicious inmate with a bar up his sleeve, a racist guard with his hand on a trigger or from a weirdo like Edmond Kemper, who had killed his mother and set her head on the mantle. Powerless and frustrated, a black at Vacaville in 1972 could fight with his fists and get his head bashed in, submit apathetically to whatever was dished up by the authorities or work with others in the BCA to improve his lot through political action.

"This last appealed to men about to be paroled, who didn't want to be ripped off when they hit the streets," says Thomas Charleston, then Vacaville's Information Officer, a black who says this was BCA's purpose. That the organization brought in not only black nationalists who were into black awareness but also dedicated revolutionaries and manipulators, did not bother the prison psychologists, "who know," says Charleston, "that convicts who talk things out aren't going to be stabbing and killing." But he smiles when he recalls Willy, "who was a friendly kid with good manners who came walking in here one night with his flyaway hair in a pigtail." Like Colston Westbrook, Charleston remembers Willy's enthusiasm, which moved others to come to teach English, math and political science.

More than one at Dave Gunnell's place followed Willy to Vacaville and signed up to be tutors shortly after Willy talked about the BCA at a rap session at Peking Man House, where his black friend Chris Thompson showed up with a film.

"I remember the night because it was the first time I met Mizmoon," says JoAnn Little, younger sister of Russ, who lived with her little boy and husband at Peking Man House. A pretty, feminine-looking woman with nice eyes, JoAnn says the white girl named Patricia Soltysik (who had recently changed her first name to Mizmoon) was twenty-two at the time but seemed much older. "She was well put together and very sure of herself at the showing of the film when she came with Chris, who lived with us but was her lover."

JoAnn remembers that Mizmoon was interested in the prisoners at BCA, who, like herself, were taking reborn names. And as JoAnn listened to Willy, she says, she got interested too, and soon was going with the others to Vacaville where the prisoners' terrible stories about what went on inside deeply upset her.

That they upset Willy too is confirmed in a letter he wrote to his mother in March 1972, which after some introductory family talk was devoted to his three passions—mountain climbing, the Movement and Vacaville.

Dear Mother:

Please send me another $200 from the Litchfield Savings Bank. Soon as possible, I'm getting a down sleeping bag, down mountaineering parka, a down vest and a glazier tent—all at ½ price, oh, joy.

14 hours later . . . I've spent the evening rapping with some folks and watching a movie entitled "The Murder of Fred Hampton" which is about the 21-year-old chairman of the Ill. Black Panther Party who was murdered while he slept in 1969 by 14 cops who raided his house in the early dawn. The cops claimed to have been attacked with guns by the Panthers in the house which is in total contradiction to all physical evidence. One example . . . the cops claim the Panters [sic] opened fire and that they (the cops) called for a cease fire three times but didn't get it. It was proved that of the 100 bullet holes in the walls, 99 were from bullets from the police while only one could possibly have come from a Panther gun (pretty definitely determined to have been fired by a man who had just been shot through the heart while in bed). This is only a fraction of the evidence against the cops, who are free; the police commissioner who was responsible is running for office. If you would see this, you would begin to question the bullshit you generally trust as the truth.

Last night, I went to the Vacaville Medical Treatment Center of California's Department of Corrections. This place is known for its lobotomies and terrifying drug treatments (which I've had described to me, second hand) which are used to vegetable-ize those who are troublesome in their political fervor. I sure wish you would step out of wonderland to see what the real world is like.

What did you think about the news coverage of Nixon's crusade to the UN-FREE world?

Umbilically yours,
Willy

That Honey gave up arguing with his politics that spring Willy may not have noticed, because by early summer he had become fast friends with Russ Little, who read the books that he read, saw the world as he saw it and believed, as he was coming to believe, that anarchy is preferable to a corrupt government.

Chapter Twelve

Today, at San Quentin, Russell Little moves with the grace of a college athlete when he is brought in handcuffs from his isolated upper-floor cell to the concrete cage where he sees visitors. Lithe, smooth-skinned, with a smile remembered as "dazzling" by one of the girls who slept with him in the year before he was imprisoned, Russ, whose IQ marks him as "gifted," should (it seems) be out with the people, not pacing away his life in a closet made of stone.

Born in 1949, a little more than a year before Willy, Russ seemed much the older when the two became friends in Berkeley during the summer of '72. Unlike Willy, who until recently had read few books more radical than *Walden*, Russ had switched his major from electrical engineering to philosophy at the University of Florida and was as familiar with Marx and Mao as Willy was with Thoreau. Also, during the years when Willy had been outside the fray at Mount Hermon, Russ had marched and protested in one city and on one campus after another until confrontation had become equated in his mind with achievement. And achievement was something Russ had been taking for granted for as along as he could remember.

In Florida, where O. J. Little, Russ's father, worked as a civilian electronics mechanic at the Pensacola Naval Air Station, Russ started off at an early age each morning to an all-white grade school not far from the government housing project where he and his parents and his little sister lived on the first floor of a duplex. From the beginning his good looks and curious mind made him a favorite with teachers, who urged him along with the special attentions all teachers give without thinking to the best and the brightest. In school he was one of the privileged ones, but after school he went home to a workingman's rented flat, where his father did not talk, think or act like the doctor, lawyer, dentist, banker or military officer who headed the families of the others at the top of his class.

Both of Russ's parents migrated to Florida from Alabama, where his father, who is half Creek Indian and half French, grew up as a cracker-style farmer in the backwoods where he fished and shot small game for family eating. "He enlisted in World War II when he was underage," says JoAnn, his daughter, who is a year and a half younger than Russ, "and he's been working too hard ever since." She feels sorry for her father, and her mother too, "who had a sad life as a child."

Born to an English mother and an Irish father, who soon divorced, Wynell Little, Russ's mother, was shipped off to live with one relative, friend or foster parent after another when her mother became mentally ill. "She didn't see her father until she was thirty-five," says JoAnn, "and by that time, it didn't matter; her life was what it was going to be." With little education behind her, the way it was going to be for Wynell was to have breakfast, lunch and supper on the table when her husband and kids got ready to eat and to look for companionship to psalm-singing members of her Baptist church and to coffee klatch neighbor women in her same boat.

"She and I didn't get along," says JoAnn, "but I always half knew it wasn't her fault; she'd never had an easy time of it." She says her father picked on her mother all the time and was hard on Russ.

"He didn't want Russ to settle for what he'd settled for," JoAnn believes, "so nothing he did in school was ever enough, but, still, my father and Russ understood each other in a way—especially out in the woods."

When he was seven years old, Russ mowed lawns to pay for a bolt-action 410-gauge shotgun so that he could hunt with his father, who went out to the woods many mornings with his double-barreled 12-gauge gun.

"We'd go out about once a week before the sun came up and hunt for turkeys and rabbits and quail in a wooded section on the outskirts of town. Afterward, we moved out near there, and that was good."

Not living in a government duplex was a step up for the Littles, who put their beds and cupboards and sofa into a small three-bedroom tract house that was home to Russ from the time he was eight until he was nineteen. By then—the year was 1968—he had finished high school ninth in a class of six hundred and had amassed credits for a year's work at Pensacola Junior College.

"And in all that time my attitude toward my family, my classmates and my town didn't change. I knew I was from one class and the other kids on the honor roll were from another, and that was that. They went to ride horseback or play tennis after school and I went home to play sandlot baseball. But I didn't feel inferior, because I knew I could cross over if I ever wanted to. You know, the American dream shit."

Conditioned by his father, whose work in electronics supported the house (and influenced too by a high-paid chemical engineer whose comely daughter he was dating), Russ made up his mind during his last year at home to be an electrical engineer. So that fall he went to Gainesville to enroll in the engineering school at the University of Florida. The first on either side of his family to go to college, he felt confident of himself. He had money earned from odd jobs and along with it a partial scholarship awarded as a result of his high rank in his graduating class, his good grades in junior college, and a superior CEEB score in science and math.

Away from home for the first time, and at a state university with seventeen thousand students, he wenched and boozed his way through his first year, at the end of which he lost his scholarship. But by now he had the hang of things and made up his mind to return the next year with a loan, if necessary, which he worked out. It was in that year that he became politically aware. Until then Russ hadn't read many newspapers or magazines or watched much TV, so he knew little about the Vietnam War (other than that he didn't want to go) and even less about the problems of blacks.

In an interview with John Bryan, editor of *The Phoenix*, an underground San Francisco paper, Russ remembered the black shantytown with houses made of cardboard and tin that was "kind of hid off in the woods" about half a mile down the road from his house in Pensacola. He said he saw black kids at the corner store, "but we'd just look at each other; we didn't know what to say or do." Any news of the civil rights movement was systematically suppressed, he believes, "and the blacks didn't raise hell because the crackers would come down on them, guns blazing, and everyone knew it."

According to JoAnn, her southern Baptist mother was afraid of blacks, and her father, who held a top office in the AFL-CIO union at the base, would not have worked where there were blacks (or even, maybe, where there were Italians).* Although she believes her dad was not a member of the Ku Klux Klan, "he flirted at one time with the idea of the Klan, I'm sure." Her father was a dedicated supporter of George Wallace, she remembers, whom he saw as the little man's champion. "And, of course, that meant 'the little *white* man's champion.'"

Neither JoAnn nor Russ thought of confronting their parents with their racism when they were living at home "because we had grown up with this, and everyone around us felt exactly the same way." Besides, JoAnn's father could be violent when his political views were questioned. "The most scared I've ever been was a night in Pensacola when a gang of boys tried to steal a 'Vote for Wallace' sign that my dad had wired to a tree in the yard," JoAnn says. Awakened after midnight by shots, the young girl sat up in bed and looked out the window to where her father was shooting at dark figures trying to rip the picture of Wallace's head out of the sign. "I still don't know whether the boys were black or white, but I know we were all lucky that nobody was killed. I was terrified."

Memories of his family's relationship with blacks came back in a rush when in the fall of '69 Russ took an elective course in philosophy from a Marxist graduate student with a background much like his own. Coming at a time when he was moving steadily toward a degree in electrical engineering, which would lead him to life with the tennis players, this class gave him a shake. With all that was going on in the world, did he really want a job with IBM, life with the swimming-pool set, marriage to the girl back home (who was planning their engagement party for Christmas)? He didn't know, but as he talked with his instructor, a onetime member of the SDS in West Germany, who had helped to organize street gangs to protest government practices, his mind opened up. By Christmas, when his engagement

*With this Russ disagrees. "My father was not that prejudiced."

was announced on schedule, he was wondering sometimes if electrical engineering was the field for him and at the beginning of the spring semester he switched his major to philosophy. And by then he had also begun to see that the marriage as envisioned by "the young lady I was engaged to in Pensacola" was not for him either and he asked to be released from his commitment. Apparently Russ had moved away from his parents' way of life when he had worked out a way to go to the university, "and now," he says, "I was saying to hell with the Good American Life, which was my only alternative."

What else was there to do? Russ didn't know in the spring that saw the Kent State killings. But now that he was free of old influences he knew he had some catching up to do.

Late to the Movement, he rushed into Florida's Yippie culture with a convert's zeal. By fall he was organizing leftist political groups between classes by day and at night reading books by leaders in Russia, China, Cuba, Uruguay and Brazil who had come up from the masses to challenge (and in some cases, bring down) the fascist ruling class. By the following spring of '71, when hundreds of Vietnam veterans walked or were wheeled to the U.S. Capitol in Washington to toss their combat medals on the steps, Russ was rioting against the president of his university, who, in his opinion and that of others, was a racist. Having followed the careers and writings of Malcolm X, Eldridge Cleaver and Huey Newton, he was convinced that blacks, who had the biggest cause for discontent, would be among the forefront fighters in the revolution he was sure would come sooner or later in the United States. (In light of all the abuses he was beginning to see in the society in which he lived, how could this be otherwise?) On campus he fought for the cause of the blacks, as he and every other revolutionary believed they would be fighting side by side with them later. He enlisted hundreds of students in a fight that lasted until final-exam time, when, for those who wanted credit for the year, the fighting had to stop. But not for Russ. Disgusted, he left for Washington's May Day protest, the bloodiest street war of 1971.

Like many young radicals, Russ had come to believe that confrontation with the pigs was the protester's only way to demonstrate to the average citizen the brutality of the police. So in Washington he joined with thousands of others to invite conflict by impeding traffic and spitting at the bureaucrats. And they got conflict until, at the end of three days, seven thousand protesters were under arrest. Battered, frustrated and enraged, Russ committed himself then and there to fight to the finish.

And so did another young University student who is the daughter of the owner of a successful Florida automobile franchise, who was living at the time as a hippie. She was Robyn Steiner, whose grace and good looks matched Russ's. (At another time, the attractive pair might have earned social entree almost anywhere.) In this period, the two young people were committed activists who were intensely interested in what was going on in California and were following the case of the Soledad brothers.

As they understood it, racist guards at Soledad State Prison in California had deliberately set up a row when they sent eight whites and seven blacks to a caged yard that had always been segregated. Coming not long after two and maybe three black convicts had been clubbed or stabbed to death by Chicano and white inmates or guards, this peculiar recess quickly exploded into a fight that was ended by a guard in the gun tower. Without warning, the guard, who was from Texas, opened fire with his semiautomatic carbine, wounding one white man in the groin and killing three black men, one of whom was a declared revolutionary and a friend of George Jackson's. Three days later a Salinas County grand jury found the action justifiable homicide. Within thirty minutes of the radio announcement, the body of John Mills, a young guard who was not long married and had a new baby and had not been part of the yard scene, was hurled from a third-floor tier where he had been beaten to death in the maximum security center.

After that the prison was in an uproar and within a week George Jackson, Fleeta Drumgo and John Clutchette were accused of the murder. "Not because there was evidence against them," said their attorneys, "but because they were known black militants." And, said George Jackson, who was serving a one year to life sentence for robbing a filling station of seventy dollars ten years before, "This charge carries an automatic death penalty for me. I can't get life. I already have it." Then Eldridge Cleaver and the Black Liberation Army and Huey Newton and the Black Panthers and Angela Davis and the U.S. Communist Party and a score of lesser-known leftist groups stepped forward. Never fear, they said, the Soledad Brothers will not be forgotten. And in this they were right. On August 7, 1970,

Jackson's brother Jonathan, who had been urged in a letter from George to be "the new black man, in his highest revolutionary form," staged his shoot-out at the Marin County Courthouse and paid with his life. (He attempted to escape with three black convicts and several hostages, including Judge Harold J. Haley, planning to exchange the hostages for the Soledad Brothers, but his plan backfired and he and two of the convicts and the judge were killed.)

Two days later, George Jackson wrote a letter to a friend that Jackson would later use as the signature for his book *Soledad Brother.* It contains a reference to Jonathan, followed by the words the boy spoke minutes before he was shot.

Cold and calm through. "All right, gentlemen, I'm taking over now."
Revolution,
   George

Russ went back through the book and thought about the blacks in Folsom, San Quentin, Soledad. "Believe me . . ." George had written, "with the time and incentive that these brothers have to read, study, and think, you will find no class or category more aware, more embittered, desperate, or dedicated to the ultimate remedy—revolution." And on another page: "Anyone with my same interest must be embraced."

Not for the first time, Robyn and Russ considered going to California, where there would be hundreds and probably thousands of confrontation-oriented blacks and young whites whose views they could embrace. But this time, salvaging what credits they could from a badly disrupted year, they took off for Berkeley. There they moved into a commune on Channing Way that had a huge red papier-mâché fist in its front yard. And here they lived in the same block with Patricia Soltysik, who had completed her college junior year and was living in a two-room flat with a black undergraduate who had been her lover for two years.

The black man, who was into computers and ambitious for the good life, was from the Midwest and bored with Berkeley rhetoric. Moreover, he knew that his relationship with Pat was coming to an end. So more and more, he spent his evenings at the Computer Center, and Pat, who worked at a YMCA day camp during the day, drifted off at night to talk in one of the dingy nearby houses about the

Movement. (By then, toppling the government was losing its force as an idea, but in certain parts of Berkeley, the coming revolution was as real as the Mao posters that hung on every wall.) Half out of loneliness but also out of conviction that life for a lot of people wasn't good, Pat began going to feminist consciousness-raising meetings two or three nights a week, and other nights to pot parties with friends who were into boycotting grapes, lettuce and the products of outfits that discriminated against women. Soon she moved from her apartment to one belonging to a girl nearby, where she pondered the sense of going back to school that fall. She had wanted once to be a lawyer, but now she was following the story of the Pentagon Papers and thought the lawyers were snarling up the case "so that all we're talking about is whether *The New York Times* should have printed the story. . . ."

She told others, "We ought to talk less about Ellsberg and more about why the Government's been fucking up the American people for the last twenty years. . . ."

At this time, she said, "I get sick of all the dancing around that the lawyers do and think maybe it would be better for me to get a job as a worker someplace and fight the system from the inside out." She smiled. "My brother's been saying if I get any more liberal, I'll wind up scrubbing floors; maybe he's right." She laughed. "And me one of the smart Soltysiks."

Pat's older brother, Fred, who was serving in the Peace Corps when Pat was living on Channing Way, and her other brother and four sisters and she are all remembered at the schools they went to in the Santa Barbara area as "those bright Soltysik kids." Year after year these children with the odd Polish name went home with report cards filled with all A's or close to it. "And they had good manners, too," said one principal. Straight-backed and neat, the children drew approving smiles every Sunday when they entered San Roque Catholic Church with their tanned father, a prosperous pharmacist, and their pretty Belgian-born mother, who had married and moved away from her Nazi-occupied homeland toward the end of World War II. Wherever they went, the Soltysiks were envied for their modesty and picture-book good looks. But things at home didn't measure up.

According to Fred, their father was moody and given to long, sadistic silences (he would come home at night and slap out twenty-six games of solitaire behind a closed door rather than talk with his family). He was also brutal on occasion (he once pulled a stool from under his wife when she sought to get cotton for her son's bloody nose, which he had smashed). And he was contemptuous (when the children's mother went to Europe to visit her aging mother, their father threw the money for her passage on the air terminal floor). In their unpredictable home, mealtimes were silent and the evenings were tense, so school, far from being a chore, was a release. "And Pat was into everything," says her older brother, who is now a teacher in the Santa Barbara school system. "Along with the honor societies she got into automatically, she worked with kids in social service clubs and 4-H and at the same time was elected president of Usherettes, which had all the nifty girls."

Surfers, now businessmen, who went to high school with Pat Soltysik remember her as a sexy cheerleader and a good dancer, and pretty girls, now homemakers, say she was bright and bouncy. But Fred knows she was sad. "When my father ridiculed anything she said as dumb or cheap, she cried. But she didn't get mad and leave home the way I did in high school; she just kept telling herself that things had to get better. They didn't, of course, until my mother got a divorce, and by then Pat was at Berkeley."

The winner of three academic scholarships, one of which was the Berkeley Alumni award, Pat went off for her freshman year with eight hundred dollars in prize money plus a stipend from her father, who found it easier to give a check than to give love. And away from home and alone she soon fell in love and moved in with her computer friend, "who," she told Fred, "loves me and lets me be myself."

Her Berkeley life-style obviously agreed with her. She kept up her grades during her first year and had time after cooking and making a home for her man to get involved in the People's Park project. "I'm going every day to plant marigolds and help put up a fence to keep the dogs from trampling down the flowers," she wrote to Fred. But after the clash, when the park was closed, she became depressed. "It's heavy here," she wrote later, explaining that she was going to Europe for the summer. There, away from her lover, she had a brief affair, again with a black man, this one an artist from Africa, but returned for her second year to Berkeley and to her hardworking lover, with whom she would live until 1971.

"I'm terribly domestic," she told a neighbor when the long relationship ended. "I love cooking for a man and sleeping beside him spoon fashion, and helping him to do what he wants to do with his life." Still, Pat did not want to be humiliated by a man as her mother had been, and this may have been why she was attracted over and over to black men. Whatever the case, in the summer of 1971 she found herself torn. "I like puttering around with my pots and pans," she told a friend, "but I don't want to be fucked over by some man." She said, "Women have been settling for that for years, and that's got to change." By August, she had received word from the city library that she could be janitor, which would bring her in close contact with workers, whose problems she wanted to understand. "School's irrelevant." And Russ and Robyn, over in their Red Fist commune, were of the same mind. Still, by September 1, they were thinking seriously about going back to school in Florida. Unable to get jobs or to qualify for welfare, they had been stealing food in a big supermarket for their daily living and had recently been picked up for shoplifting. They did not want to face the charge and also, like many activists in Berkeley that summer, they were tiring of talk sessions of liberals, "who never got around to doing anything." And Russ says now, "We realized that Berkeley was the most militant community we had ever lived in but we had to go back to my old university, where I could get a loan." He also admits to being disappointed when there was no demonstration in Ho Chi Minh park after George Jackson was killed in prison on August 21.

It was on that day that Jackson, whose second book, *Blood in My Eye*, would be published posthumously, made a wild dash for freedom that ended in gore. Still standing trial for the murder of the guard whose body was hurled from Tier 3 at Soledad, he got out of his cell with the help of a smuggled gun and for the next half hour all was chaos. Then, with terrifying suddenness, calm came back to the blood-spattered Adjustment Center, where three guards were dead, as were Jackson and two other prisoners. (Not among the dead were Drumgo and Clutchette, who later were found not guilty of the murder that had led to one horror scene after another.) In the terrible quiet, few of the prisoners who stood mute in their cells could remember a more awful carnage.

That night, as Russ listened to radio reports of the San Quentin battle and Jackson's death, he remembered the convict-author's comparison of blacks with buffalo. "Of all the world's people, we blacks love the company of others most," he wrote. And the buffalo, Jackson went on to remind his readers, are social animals. "They need to rub shoulders and butt butts. They like to rub noses. We shake hands, slap backs and rub lips." It stands to reason, the dead prisoner had said, that if each herd of buffalo was going to eat, sleep and travel as a group, it had to produce a leader. ". . . and to these natural leaders fall the responsibility for coordination of the group's activity, organizing them for survival." He said the buffalo hunter knew that if he could kill the leader of the herd, the rest would be helpless, "at his mercy, to be killed off as he saw fit." And continuing the analogy, "We blacks have the same problem the buffalo had; we have the same weakness also, and predatory man understands this weakness well."

Jackson's book listed murdered black leaders. "Medgar Evers, Malcolm X, Bobby Hutton, . . . M. L. King, . . . Fred Hampton. . . ." And, sadly, the night that Jackson died, Russ added his name to the list. "But tomorrow," he told himself, "all of Berkeley will protest." The time to storm the Bastille had come. The radicals would do something.

"But the next day," Russ remembers, "there was nothing." And now the young radical from Florida was as disappointed in Berkeley's big talkers as he had been in his fellow rioters back home who had copped out at final-exam time. "When the chips are down, nobody acts."

So after two months in the West, Russ went back to Florida, where he got his loan and (due to the urging of an instructor who thought he was too bright to go down the drain) set about pulling together the credits he would need to graduate. However, that winter as he burrowed in again at the university, he kept thinking about the Bay Area, with its Black Panthers and prisoners, radicals and philosophers, creative crusaders and revolutionaries. Okay, so he and Robyn had not found the revolution of their imagining. But where else was there? They would go back. And this they did in the summer of '72, arriving in July at Oakland, where they rented a room at Dave Gunnell's house on Chabot Road and soon got involved with the Black Cultural Association through their new friend Willy Wolfe.

By the time Russ and Robyn moved into Peking Man House, Willy was no longer enrolled at Berkeley. He was deeply involved with blacks at Vacaville, where he had become fascinated by the convicted murderers, rapists and robbers he was getting to know. Before the end of the winter quarter he had managed to piece together a sketchy account of the superficial aims of members of the Black Cultural Association (they want to know how to talk and manage money so they can be self-sustaining on the outside), but his heart wasn't in his report or any other school project, and when registration time came around for the next quarter he did not sign up.

Had Willy been living at a fraternity house or in a dormitory when he left school, he would have had to move out, but here with paternalistic Dave Gunnell, who had other roomers not in school, he simply stayed on. Eking out money for rent and food stamps, which he contributed to the house, by baking bread for sandwich makers on Telegraph Avenue and typing an occasional paper for someone, he lived about the same as before. But now, instead of going to the campus, he rode up two nights a week to Vacaville, where he worked as a volunteer tutor, and went on another night to an adult education class for some quick instruction in shorthand, the better to take down notes from locked-up men who wanted messages delivered to girls and mothers and dedicated revolutionaries who showed their hatred for fascist pigs.

Never, even when he heard from his mother, who urged him to go back to Berkeley, did Willy think of himself as a dropout. Stimulated by black men who had managed not to get killed by sharpening their eyes, ears and minds like beasts in a jungle, he was more alive to what was going on around him than ever before. No adventure fantasy in his dreamiest days could match what these wary men had lived through day after day.

As he read one book after another by a misused black (or angry black who resented the misuse of his brothers), Willy saw why blacks in prison, like the scorned downtrodden in any colonialist society, were damn well going to get the Man's boot off their necks. And now when Russell Little asked him at Peking Man House if the revolutionary spirit of George Jackson was still alive in California prisons, Willy nodded and quoted Norman Mailer. "There's a shit storm coming." He said that Russ would see for himself when he got to Vacaville that "every black who's worth a shit knows there's got to be a revolution in this country just like there was in Russia and China."

"And in Cuba," reminded Russ, who went to his room and brought back a half-dozen books by or about the late Ernesto "Che" Guevara, Fidel Castro's revolutionary lieutenant and guerrilla-war planner, who, beginning that summer, became Willy's special hero. "For

Willy (with fish) and his sister and brother, Roxie and John, shared summers at their home in Connecticut with Mike Carrerras, a Fresh Air Fund kid from New York. Before divorce split the family (shown in a Christmas-card picture with Willy at lower right), Willy expected to follow his doctor father and half brothers to Yale; but at age 17 (in football helmet) he let his grades slide, and Yale eventually turned him down.

In Europe for a year after graduation from prep school (*top left*), Willy camped out and worked his way (*above*). Later, at Peking Man House in Berkeley, he met Russell Little (in striped shirt above Willy in commune group), who became a fellow member of SLA. On his last visit home, dressed like Che Guevara, Willy posed with his half sister, Diane.

Albert Morch

Miss Hearst, Steven Weed are engaged

This is a week of special family significance for the Randolph Apperson Hearsts of Hillsborough.

Today they are announcing the engagement of their daughter, Patricia Campbell Hearst, to Steven Andrew Weed.

And on Friday, another daughter, Anne, will be presented at the annual debutante Cotillion at the Sheraton Palace Hotel.

Patricia's father is president and editor of the San Francisco Examiner, chairman of the board of the Hearst Corporation and a trustee of the

—Examiner photo by John Gorman

ENGAGED . . . Patricia Campbell Hearst and Steven Andrew Weed

William Randolph Hearst Foundation. Her mother, Catherine, is a regent of the University of California.

The bride-elect is the granddaughter of Mrs. William Randolph Hearst of New York and the late Mr. Hearst, founder of the Hearst newspaper and magazine empire. Her maternal grandparents were the late Morton R. Campbells of Atlanta, Ga.

In addition to Anne, her other sisters are Catherine, Virginia (Mrs. Jay Bosworth) and Victoria.

Oakland School Superintendent Marcus Foster was shot and killed on November 6, 1973. Two months later, Willy's friends Joseph Remiro and Russell Little (in light and dark shirts, respectively, before cameras) were captured and charged with the murder. Patricia Hearst (shown in newspaper story announcing her engagement to Steven Weed) was then seized as a hostage by the SLA.

World

UNITED STATES DEPARTMENT OF JUSTICE

FEDERAL BUREAU OF INVESTIGATION

WASHINGTON, D.C. 20535

April 19, 1974

RE: **DONALD DAVID DE FREEZE**　　**PATRICIA MICHELLE SOLTYSIK**　　**PATRICIA CAMPBELL HEARST**
　　NANCY LING PERRY　　　　　　**CAMILLA CHRISTINE HALL**　　　　**MATERIAL WITNESS**

TO WHOM IT MAY CONCERN:

The FBI is conducting an investigation to determine the whereabouts of these individuals whose descriptions and photographs appear below. Federal warrants charging robbery of a San Francisco bank on April 15, 1974, have been issued at San Francisco, California, for Camilla Hall, Donald DeFreeze, Nancy Perry, and Patricia Soltysik. A material witness warrant in this robbery has been issued for Patricia Hearst, who was abducted from her Berkeley, California, residence on February 4, 1974, by a group which has identified itself as the Symbionese Liberation Army (SLA). The participants in the bank robbery also claim to be members of the SLA.

DONALD DAVID DE FREEZE
N/M, DOB 11/16/43, 5'9" to 5'11",
150-160, blk hair, br eyes

PATRICIA MICHELLE SOLTYSIK
W/F, DOB 5/17/50, 5'3" to 5'4",
116, dk br hair, br eyes

PATRICIA CAMPBELL HEARST
W/F, DOB 2/20/54, 5'3", 110,
lt br hair, br eyes

MATERIAL WITNESS

NANCY LING PERRY
W/F, DOB 9/19/47, 5', 95-105, red
br hair, haz eyes

CAMILLA CHRISTINE HALL
W/F, DOB 3/24/45, 5'6", 125,
blonde hair, blue eyes

If you have any information concerning these individuals, please notify your local FBI office, a telephone listing for which can be found on the first page of your directory. In view of the crimes for which these individuals are being sought, they should be considered armed and extremely dangerous, and no action should be taken which would endanger anyone's safety.

Very truly yours,

Clarence M. Kelley
Director

Caught by a hidden camera participating in a bank robbery with her captors, Patty Hearst was sought as a material witness to the crime committed by those shown with her on the FBI "wanted" poster (*left*). Bill and Emily Harris (shown together) and Angela Atwood were only later implicated, with Willy, as accomplices.

Tom Zimberoff/Contact

Hiding out after the robbery, SLA members appear clockwise from upper left (*above*): Emily Harris, Willy, Donald DeFreeze (Cinque), Bill Harris, Camilla Hall, Nancy Ling Perry, Angela Atwood and Patty Hearst. Patricia Soltysik, not shown, probably took the picture. Meanwhile, back East, Willy's father, seated in front of a portrait of Willy and John, refused to believe Willy was in the SLA.

Death to the FASCIST INSECT
That preys upon the life
of THE people!

In early May, police entered an abandoned hideout in San Francisco and found on the wall the "Death to the Fascist Insect" slogan that was the SLA trademark. Two weeks later, six SLA members, including Willy, died in a fiery police shoot-out in a Los Angeles slum.

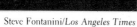
Steve Fontanini/*Los Angeles Times*

Jo

After the fire, Patty Hearst recognized Willy's watch (found still ticking on his body) and belt buckle in pictures printed by the *Los Angeles Times* and declared in her last, angry tape: "Cujo [Willy] and I loved each other so much." That spring, Willy's ashes were buried in his mother's family plot in Torrington, Connecticut.

Leslie Jacobs/*The*

sure," remembers Willy's brother John, who says that when Willy came home later that year "Che Guevara was all he could talk about."

According to Russ, Willy had enormous respect for Guevara's willingness to put his life on the line for the oppressed people in any country where an overthrow of an imperialistic government was overdue, but in Roxie's opinion there was more than admiration of a fighter in Willy's fascination. "He *identified* with him," she says. "With Che Guevara's shyness and with love for the outdoors and with the romantic life he led in the mountains with the girl he called Tania." She is quiet as she thinks of her dead brother and the dead Guevara. "Look at their pictures side by side. You'll see that Willy even looked like Che." And she adds, "He was like him in a lot of other ways too."

"He'll never be forgotten, that's for sure," Willy told his new friend, Russ, as they talked about Che on their first drive together up to Vacaville.

"Not as long as you're alive, that's for sure," Russ said, laughing at Willy, who was wearing a beret like Che's over his dark curly hair and was smoking what looked to be a big Cuban cigar.

"So I'm a fan."

"Who isn't?" Russ agreed, as he swerved off the highway in his "sweet little Chevy," painted this year in psychedelic colors. Talking animatedly like old-time college boys off on a spree, they wondered aloud about Guevara's failure to attract followers in Bolivia.

"Maybe he didn't convert any Indians," Willy said, "because he wasn't an Indian."

"You're talkin' bullshit."

"Well, what about here? Do you think a bunch of black dudes who want to do something about themselves are going to follow a guy who isn't black? They've been down the white leadership road before."

At the next crossroads he pointed in the direction of the prison. "What those guys in there don't need is Thomas Jefferson."

Russ laughed. "maybe one of his sons."

"A black Che Guevara."

Russ said that if there was going to be a change in the way this country is run, there would have to be more than blacks involved.

"But they've got the real gripe," Willy said. "And that's why Malcolm X and George Jackson and Martin Luther King made sense to them—and to a lot of other people too." He said Russ would see.

161

"Another black dude who's willing to give up everything he believes in will come along some day—and he'll make things happen." He said he would probably be someone like Mike.

"Who's Mike?" And then as they rattled their way to the end of their journey, Willy told Russ about the black Fresh Air kid who had come to stay with his family summer after summer when he was a kid. Of how Mike had worked his way through college and gone on to become an officer in the Navy. And of how, finally, he had fallen in love with a good-looking white girl and taken a big job with Celanese only to find that the dream he had been chasing all of his life was empty. "And now he's given the whole trip up."

"So what's he doing?"

"Going to Brazil."

"Brazil!"

"He's going to be a monk."

"A monk, for Chrissake? Why does he wanta do that?"

Willy shrugged. "He believes that's the way—used to go to Mass every day, even when we'd been out all night."

"Well, if that's what he wants."

By then Russ was parking the car and turning off the ignition but he didn't get out. Turning to Willy, he said he couldn't imagine any childhood as different from his as Willy's must have been. "Down there in Florida, I was in a real colonialist situation, believe me, and if anyone there had brought a black kid into the house, he would have been called a nigger lover and had a cross burned in his yard." Then Russ got out and walked thoughtfully into the prison, where he and Willy would be attending meetings of the Black Cultural Association for the next year. "Gotta get used to the feel of this place," he said to Willy as they followed a guard to the library. "Who knows? I may be checking in here on my own some time." Then he and Willy entered the room and encountered sixty or more inmates who had mugged, slugged and murdered their way into this place, but who thought of themselves that year as "political prisoners," victims of a racist society that had pushed them into crime. As the two from Berkeley walked in, the denim-clad men and about thirty black women visitors ("who want husbands," Willy said) and fifteen or twenty black and white tutors were finishing a clenched-fist salute to an upheld flag and were preparing to enjoy the hour-long program that preceded the work-shops and tutoring.

Leaving Russ with Westbrook, the coordinator of the tutoring program, to whom he had just been introduced, Willy went up to the front of the room to get two folding chairs for Russ and himself and was stopped by a tall, good-looking prisoner with an arresting face. The prisoner wore a bowl-shaped Afro, and he coolly surveyed the room through quiet, wide-apart eyes under arched eyebrows. But it was the nose with its flared nostrils separated from a sensual mouth by a small, neatly trimmed moustache that gave the face its drama. There was arrogance in this man and awareness of sex and, maybe, cruelty.

"The dude's got a new reborn name that I forget, but his real name is DeFreeze," Willy told Russ after they were seated and waiting for the program to get started. "Donald DeFreeze." He said that in the last election DeFreeze had tried to run for BCA's president but had had his name thrown out for a hokey reason when word went out that he might have been a snitch. "That's not true, and now the guy's talking about suing—through the state courts—because he shouldn't have been blocked.

As they waited for the others to settle down, Willy said that DeFreeze had started a spin-off group called Unisight, "which we're going to visit tonight because I've got to give a report." He said he'd be explaining to the group what jobs for black ex-cons might be available in the Bay Area and what agencies could be depended on to help a black man get back in the groove with his family. "Maybe you'd like to be a tutor for that group; you can see."

And Russ said, "Maybe. Anyway, I'd like to meet that DeFreeze."

"Except I've got to remember not to call him DeFreeze," said Willy, racking his brain for the adopted name of his black friend, which continued to elude him up to the minute he and Russ were joined by the twenty-two members of Unisight for their meeting at one end of the room. Then, just as he and Russ walked up to the leader, the reborn name of the black convict came to mind. And so it was, as he introduced the Unisight leader to Russ, Willy used a name that neither Russ nor any other survivor of the Movement will ever forget. "Russ," he said, "I'd like you to meet Cinque."

Chapter Thirteen

Willy was not a leader nor had he been trained along the way to think long term. Yet of all those who would eventually join up with the SLA, he was more important in the group's formation than any other. This had nothing to do with an ability to plan but, rather, to his affability.

In the past, in school and elsewhere, Willy's happy-go-lucky approach to life (at least on the surface) had put few people off but had attracted no followers either. And the reason was simple. Beyond his merry smile, Willy had nothing to trade. But this time around, things were different. One of the first tutors to go with Westbrook to Vacaville, Willy was the envy of romantic white visitors who followed him to the Black Cultural Association for his "in" with black prisoners, which they could not understand. What was there about this innocuous kid that made him a favorite with rough cons like Death Row Jeff, who had spent more than half of his forty-seven years in California prisons, where he had survived a hundred knife fights, homosexual encounters and at least one close call with death in San Quentin's gas chamber? (Later, after thirty years in prison, gnarled old Clifford Jefferson, who suffered a stroke after Willy's death, is not so befuddled that he does not remember the young white tutor he got to know at Vacaville, where he is now hospitalized. "Willy was like a son to me.") What was the attraction?

Again, Willy's natural friendliness was no drawback, but with every prison black who came in contact with Willy in this period, two other characteristics had a deeper appeal. Willy showed no trace of racism (because he had none), which counted for a lot with a black behind bars where every white guard, chaplain, social worker or curious female visitor looked on him with conscious or unconscious scorn, pity, fear or peculiar lust that marked him as different because of the color of his skin. Not so with Willy. That any man Willy was talking to happened to be black made no impression, and that the other was a prisoner enhanced him in Willy's eyes. "He admired a dude who could hold his head up after wadin' through a bunch of muck," said one who knew him at the time. And this came through to cons. But what really turned them on was Willy's willingness to run errands.* "Once Willy got to know DeFreeze, he worked his ass off for the dude, whose aim," he was telling people, "was to help black men and women be more understanding of each other, which is kind of strange, when you think of how DeFreeze pushed black women around before he hit Vacaville."

At age twenty-five, by which time he had been married for several years to an attractive black mother of six, two of them his own, DeFreeze checked into a downtown Los Angeles motel with a prostitute. There, after having sex, which included some fancy contortions and for which he had paid the woman ten dollars, he put a pistol to her head and took back his ten-spot and the rest of her day's earnings and rolled over content. He didn't think the girl would go to the police. But once her John had conked out, the prostitute slipped out and called the cops, who soon became more interested in a stash of stolen guns they found in the black man's car than in the robbery.

At this point DeFreeze made a deal, "a recommendation from the cops for leniency in exchange for a lead to more stolen guns stored in a friend's house." This was arranged and the young black would have come out all right if he had not done some more stealing (this time,

* "They were using Willy," says Mike Carrerras, "and pulling him down to their level in every way they knew how, so that he would stay involved." He makes the point that "men with little to lose want you to do what they've been doing so you won't be able to walk away." He tried to warn Willy, he says, that the cons "will try to get you to commit an act of violence."

he took a motorcycle). And then, when he got out after a few months, he played around some more with guns and bomb makings and had trouble from one end of the country to the other with his wife.

During 1968 and 1969, DeFreeze and his wife and her children moved from Los Angeles to Newark, where he had worked as a house painter in the early days of his marriage; from there to Cleveland, where he had been born in 1943 and where they lived with his mother, who was a recent widow and a registered nurse; and back to California, where he soon was under arrest for taking a thousand-dollar cashier's check at gunpoint from a dark-skinned Filipino woman who was parked downtown in her car. And now a long series of petty crimes he had committed as he had dashed—sometimes alone and sometimes with his family—back and forth across the country came to light.

In New Jersey, he had been mixed up in an attempted kidnapping of the black caretaker of a synagogue for whom (it was believed) he hoped to extort a ransom from the rabbi; in Cleveland, he had taken one hundred dollars from the cash drawer of a restaurant where he worked; in another part of that city, he had been sighted on top of a bank building, where he was captured with a knife, loaded guns, a bomb and burglary tools as he chopped a hole in the roof. Then, in California again, he burglarized a gun shop. And, finally, as he tried to cash a stolen cashier's check, he was shot in the hand and foot in a gun battle with police, which sent him to Vacaville, where two years later he met Willy and Russ. But by this time he had changed from the petty hood who had run through life catch-as-catch-can since his earliest days in Cleveland, where his hardworking toolmaker father had tried to direct his first-born toward a position of respectability by knocking him with a baseball bat.

A bright kid, Donald had reached ninth grade by age fourteen, but was unhappy in Cleveland, where three different times he had been hospitalized with hammer wounds inflicted by his father. Finally, he told psychiatrists at a later date, he bought (or stole) a gun "to kill my father" but took instead to the road, to go home only one more time before his father's death. Traveling east, he got to Buffalo, where he was taken on by a social worker who lodged him in the home of a black minister who had a lovely young daughter named Harriet. Later Donald told a counselor, "I dreamed that some day I would be a preacher and could marry Harriet."

Before he could do so, however, he was done in by his habit of stealing—in at least one case a car, for which he was sent up for two and a half years in a reformatory in Elmira, "where all the black kids hated me because I wouldn't fight in the black gang against the whites and was edging away from their homosexual scene too." Released at eighteen, he hitchhiked to the home of the preacher and asked for Harriet's hand, which was refused, then headed for Cleveland, where he moved back in with his mother and saw his father, ill by then, for the last time. Taking off after the funeral, he went to New Jersey, where he thought he could find work. And there he met Glory, the black twenty-five-year-old mother of three who became his partner in a love-hate relationship that was to keep him stirred up one way or another until the night of his death by fire a decade later.

Glory was six years older and more experienced in the ways of women and men than the loner who was just out of the reformatory. She was also a bourgeoise (which, in his prison years, when Cinque came to understand the word, was the most derisive description he could apply to a woman), reared in a middle-class home. So she looked down on her young husband, and in the five years before he went to prison she constantly whacked away at his manhood.

After encouraging her husband to adopt her children from a former marriage, which he discovered later had never been, Glory gave birth to three more who bore his name, although the last one, he told others, had not been conceived by him. Throwing him out one month and taking him back the next, Glory lived partly on welfare and partly on what Donald earned variously as a house painter, machinist, carpenter, short-order cook and illegal gunrunner. And always, he told a prisoner he rapped with, she pleaded for more and more things. "Finally, every room in our house had its own TV set, which I had managed to buy or steal, but still she wasn't satisfied."

Hardly a model spouse himself, DeFreeze still had a deep respect for the family. Unhappy with his father, he had wanted to do better, but in his mind his wife kept fucking him up, even after he was in prison. Her letters to correctional authorities appealed for her husband's release on one hand and brought up old abuses on the other. This confused and embarrassed him and eventually he no longer wanted to go back with her, although he continued to miss and talk about the children, whose world as grown-ups, he insisted, had to be better than his.

"And that is what the Unisight plan I'm organizing is going to be about," he declared.

"He doesn't want his kids to grow up in a police state, which this country could be," Willy whispered to Russ as they listened to Cinque tell his group what he wanted for them. Later, as they were having coffee and cake, Willy said the dude had balls, and Russ added, "He's been reading the stuff we've all been reading, but he can run it down so all the prisoners understand."

At Vacaville, DeFreeze had turned earnestly to books for the first time. And as he read Cleaver, Malcolm X and Jackson, he began to see that society had not dealt them or him much of a hand, which was something he hadn't thought about in the past as he was conning, cheating or shooting his way out of one back-against-the-wall situation after another. Now he began to look at himself in a new way.

Unlike blacks who grow up with contemptuous whites and are infected with their loathing for blackness, DeFreeze had not done much thinking about the color of his skin. Along the way, his immediate problems had given him little time to ponder the troubles that had come down to him as a result of someone's peddling black flesh way back when. And, anyway, any rejection that he had known had come from blacks—from his father in the ghetto, from black gangs in reform school, from the father of black Harriet in Buffalo, from black cops along the way who busted him, and from Glory, most of all from Glory. Never again would he let any black woman (or man, either) push him around. Every minute in prison he would be pulling himself up, learning things, toughening himself so that no one anywhere would dare to pour on the shit again.

In the beginning, he turned to the teachings of the fundamentalist black preacher in Buffalo. Either as a way of conning officials into giving him good marks for a speedy parole or because he was a true believer, he talked of a higher Power that would not let him down. "I am not alone," he told one judge.

In this period, he considered being a preacher himself, once he got back outside, who would tell the gospel as blacks had been taught by whites. But he soon relinquished this aim to follow the teachings of Islam as a Black Muslim. Along with other followers of the religion in prisons, he aimed to be temperate and neat and to work as a black nationalist to keep separate the blacks and the whites. Eventually, like

Malcom X, who at one time was black Islam's most effective ex-con minister and prison recruiter, he moved away from nationalism, but he took with him the belief that a black man, no matter what had gone before, could be reborn.

And so it was that about this time DeFreeze turned his guilt over to society. Then, like many black convicts, he could think of himself as a political prisoner (which was the teaching of the Muslims) rather than as a common hood. And now that he was as pure as on the day he was born, he was ready for a reborn name. His would be Cinque Mtume, which in the language of Africans means Fifth Prophet, but which, in the mind of DeFreeze himself, may have had meanings beyond that. Probably, as he searched for a new name, he had come across the name Cinque when he read the newspaper accounts of Jonathan Jackson's death. For one of the convicts whom Jonathan had helped to escape briefly had had the reborn name Cinque. Moreover, Cinque, as the dead convict probably knew, was the number given in the early 1800's to an enslaved African chief who broke out of his chains, killed his Portuguese captor, seized the slave vessel and sailed away. Also, when combined with Mtume, the name had an Islamic connotation that would be attractive to blacks. And, finally, with a little forward shift on the tongue, *Cin* could come out as *Sin*, which would work like a Halloween mask for this black man with prison politics on his mind. As Cinque Mtume, DeFreeze could go forth as a prophet; as Sin, he had a name to be paid attention to by the bourgeoise, should he decide later on to fight fascism as a guerrilla.

Little of what went on inside Cinque was revealed in 1972. At Vacaville he was a model prisoner, who spoke in a soft voice, looked to the system for justice and applied the precepts of the civil rights movement to the problems of blacks, which impressed Willy and Russ, who were supportive of his Unisight project.* They promised Cinque they would talk about Unisight back at Peking Man House, where one of the occasional visitors that summer was Pat Soltysik, who went now by the name Mizmoon.

"Is that a reborn name?" her brother asked her in the summer of '72 when he and his wife came home from a Peace Corps stint in Algeria.

"You might call it that." Pat said that she had been searching for a

---

* Russ says Unisight was "Definitely a front."

special me-name for a long time. "And then, one night, a dear friend was talking poems. And she came up with a name that has a rhythm and feeling that I can identify with."

"That's what she said: '*She*' came up with the name." Fred said he wondered when he heard this whether his sister was gay, which was not repulsive to him but which he couldn't believe. "Even though," he added, "I was just back from Algeria, where male homosexuality is so much a part of the culture that mothers there teach their daughters to masturbate, and a lesbian relationship for many women is almost mandatory." On the other hand, his sister had been popular with boys in high school and had introduced him to her black lover, so he did not see her as a homosexual. "But I worried about her politics because, by this time, she was talking *revolution* all the time."

"She was aggressive and working every day as a janitor and I got the impression she was gay," says George Martin, who lived next door to Peking Man House, "and I still thought she was gay when I saw later that year that she was into a thing with Chris Thompson."

Chris, the black man who had lived at Peking Man House when Willy had moved in the year before, had moved out by the time Russ and Robyn arrived, but he dropped by often to show antiwar films, and sometimes he brought along Mizmoon. "One night when he was showing a propaganda film from Hanoi," George remembers, "everybody stood up and cheered when a woman on the screen shot down an American bomber after her baby was blown up, and Mizmoon cheered the loudest of all and then she got very upset."

Once a film was finished—and on other nights too—everyone would traipse down to the music room in the basement and jam. "Dave and my girl played drums," says George, who was taking music as well as journalism at a junior college on Grove Street in the ghetto, "and I was playin' percussion and Russ Little had a soprano saxophone; and along with some others who would come around, we would let go with some real Oakland jazz." As he explains, "That's real ass-kicking, superintense music—an extension of bebop, really loud, knockout, hard-driving jazz."

According to JoAnn Little, Russ's sister, who had come from Florida with her husband and baby by this time, nobody was into hard drugs in Peking Man House. With this, George agrees. "Pot and psychedelics, that was about it. And," he says, "no firearms, either. As long as I was going in and out of the place, I never saw a gun or heard a shot." He says he did look out his window one morning and saw the folks from the next house going through a martial-arts exercise in the back yard. "Everybody in Berkeley was into Swan I Ching and doing Tai Chi or some Oriental group exercise that's supposed to release psychic and physical energy. But these people looked more serious and disciplined than I would have supposed, and I remember thinking I didn't know they were into that." He says that in 1972 the people next door, like others on the street, raised tomatoes and baked bread and earned a little money at odd jobs and took a class or two at the nearby junior college in the ghetto, "which was free but where every morning we thought we might get a knife stuck in our chest and end up on the front page." He says that in the late afternoons Russ and Willy would throw Frisbees out front, "and I'd go out and toss the disks around with them."

In George's mind, "Willy was a sweet, sensually oriented guy who you would have thought was a surfer maybe. While Russ was not so loose and would be someone you might see fixing a car in a commercial garage. But Robyn, who came with Russ from Florida, was something else." George remembers the girl who lived with Russ as "a little older than the rest of us and cool and really put together— with quiet eyes and light-brown hair."* He says she was someone "I used to think about taking for a long bike ride in the country, if she would go," but he never got around to asking. Still, he remembers Robyn fondly and is glad she left California "before the start of all that SLA business."

Today, when George hears Willy described as a possible kidnapper, murderer, car thief and bank bandit, he shakes his head. "I could see Willy in a revolution maybe, but not pushing people around or robbing." He remembers the day when he left some tools "worth a hundred and fifty dollars or so" on the curb out front and then drove off to class and forgot them. "And that night when I got home, I found that Willy and Russ had brought them inside so they wouldn't be stolen. They could have ripped me off that day, but they wouldn't have thought of it." He says the picture he carries in his mind of Willy and Russ "hasn't any relationship with what most people got from *Time* and *Newsweek*."

"We all carry contrasting pictures in our minds of the ones we knew

---

* Actually, Robyn was a few years younger than Russ.

best in the SLA," says Fred Soltysik, the brother of Mizmoon. "I remember one day in my sister's apartment when she was jiggling our daughter, who was about six months old at the time, on her foot. Her face was tender as she looked down at Natasha, yet above her head was a poster of a Vietnamese woman whose eyes under her cone-shaped hat were filled with hate as she aimed down at us with her automatic. Mizmoon was compassionate, but this feeling of pity could turn to rage like that of the peasant woman when she thought about injustice and exploitation." He said when the hatred became more than his sister could bear, "she picked up a gun, I guess, as later so did her friend Camilla."

Of all who eventually became members of the SLA, Camilla Hall, who lived with Mizmoon in the summer of '72, was the most sensitive. Deeply creative (she was a gifted poet and painter), she was not heavily into radical politics that year as she pushed to support herself as an artist. A graduate of the University of Minnesota, where her father when she went there was Lutheran chaplain, she painted at home and took her wares to open bazaars and stayed in touch with her church as she coped with her lesbianism and her passion for Mizmoon, who was less committed than Camilla to the relationship. "Most of us didn't even know Camilla," says Russ Little about the girl who was to die for the cause he believed in. When Mizmoon came to Peking Man House, she did not come with Camilla; she came with Chris Thompson, "who was the man she was having an affair with" says JoAnn Little, "or anyway, that's what most of us thought."

Apparently what they thought was true, because later in the year Camilla moved from Mizmoon's apartment because "she is involved with someone else," she told a friend, "which makes me jealous, which is something I am trying to work through." For the rest of her life, the possessiveness Camilla felt for Mizmoon would torment her as the woman she loved had one affair after another with black men.

Why Mizmoon usually turned to nonwhite men for sex and to nonblack women for companionship and love is not clear. But probably both penchants had to do with her particular relationship with her parents as well as with her politics. As a liberated white radical, she would have wanted to give generously to the systematically deprived, and what better way to do so than to live with

172

and care for a black man?* But also, she had bitter memories of life with her father, who had run the conventional route of a poor Polish white kid to a position of well-being in the community. So perhaps now she wanted to taunt him (and also avoid being hurt by another like him) by living as he would not have dared to live, with a black. At the same time, she loved her supportive mother, who had never expressed distaste for her daughter's life-style, and where better to look for the same unwavering loyalty than to Camilla?

Why Camilla was attracted to Mizmoon is somewhat clearer. As a well-educated woman, she surely appreciated Mizmoon's quick mind, and, as a quiet, oversized lesbian, she must have been drawn to Mizmoon's small, graceful body and slim good looks. But perhaps above all, it was Mizmoon's daring that would not let her go. As a timid girl, Camilla must have appreciated the smaller girl's courage.

As for the black men who lived with Mizmoon, their reason for being attracted may have had its start back in time. Now what was taboo for their fathers and grandfathers was handed to them on a platter. Moreover, the girl in this case was devoting her life to working against the forces that had held their families down. (They didn't have to apologize; she understood.) And, last, Mizmoon was less critical than the average matriarchal black woman. Whereas today's black mother, like others before her, can be steely and wants no nonsense from a man, Mizmoon took plenty of nonsense from her black lovers, or as her brother says, "let herself be fucked over in one relationship after another."

In this respect she was soul mate to Nancy Ling Perry, who came to Berkeley a few years before the others and had married a talented but moody and sometimes violent black jazz musician and then, after their separation, had been involved with other black men on the prowl (including Chris Thompson). So Nancy was no newcomer to the problems and hang-ups of black men in the fall of '72 when she got to know Willy, who talked to her much about Vacaville.

Not through design but through coincidence, she met Willy on Telegraph Avenue, where she hung out with street people and he sold

---

* "Many girls who called themselves liberals did the same in that period," says Steve Weed, who lived with Patty Hearst, "and many got ripped off." To this, Mike Carreras says, "And many black men found themselves involved with white girls who brought no honest emotion to the relationship. So who was ripping off who?"

home-baked bread, and then through him she met others who had taken to dropping in at Peking Man House, where she became friendly with Mizmoon.

The two girls were not lovers (Nancy was for men), but they had much in common. Both had been born into families with no financial problems. (Nancy's father, Hal Ling, owns a prosperous furniture store in Santa Rosa, north of San Francisco.) And both girls (like all the children in both of their families) were exceptionally bright. Nancy made a straight-A average in high school and, like her friend, was a high-spirited cheerleader, active in social clubs. She also had a concerned older brother, who stayed in touch after his parents had lost track.

Today, like Mizmoon's older brother, Nancy's brother, Gary, is a teacher in the Bay Area. As he thinks back to what happened to his sister, he does not blame his parents, who, he says, were supportive of their children and loving in their relationship with each other. ("And they became even closer in the weeks of horror they went through at the end of Nancy's life.") No, Gary cannot believe that Nancy's tragedy was the result of her upbringing. "We had no problems to speak of at home or at school."

As far as most outsiders can tell, Nancy was an exception in the army of peculiar soldiers. (All other members introduced so far—Willy, Mizmoon, Cinque and Russ—had families that were different from the ordinary.) She was also exceptional in another way. Of all the SLA members, this one was a true product of Berkeley in the sixties, where, says Tom Drake, who went to UC for a short time after graduating in Willy's class at Mount Hermon, "the pressure to get into the Movement was absolutely unbelievable." Now a teacher at Phillips Academy, Andover, Massachusetts, Tom says, "Even the toilets at Berkeley had posters urging you to get involved. Anybody would have had to be insensitive or incredibly self-reliant not to wonder whether he or she should be fighting the system."

Nancy, who had spent one year at Whittier, Richard Nixon's old school, before entering Berkeley in 1967, did not wonder long. In her first year at UC, she broke with her past. Much to the shock of her conservative father (he worked hard in town for the Republican Party) and the horror of her dignified grandparents, she married Gilbert Perry, a tormented black jazz pianist and composer whom many consider a genius. And thereafter she went to school in a climate that was far different from the one her mother had known when she and Nancy's father had gone to Berkeley in the forties.

After her marriage Nancy moved with her husband into a drab little cottage in which in the next few years she would worry, weep and fight with her man, who insisted on fidelity from her but "screwed around," as one neighbor put it, "all he wanted to himself." Finally, after three years, degraded and on drugs, she moved out, not to be divorced but not to live with her husband again for more than an occasional one-night stand. By then it was 1971 and Nancy, who had earned a degree in English literature while living as the poor wife of an incarnate storm, was greatly changed in both personality and looks.

Less than five feet tall, she had been a plump bride, but now her tiny body was pipe-stem thin. For years she had smoked more marijuana (moistened with hashish) than was good for her, but she managed not to look spaced-out, even after all the drugs and what she had been through with her husband, who could be cruel in a fancy way. (Once he painted a big red A on the door of their house to show that she had been unfaithful, which her friends denied.) Occasionally wan-looking, she could be beautiful too. Framed by dark hair, her face had the classic big-eyed appearance of a miniature Sophia Loren.

Not a sweet girl by any means, Nancy on graduation was no strident radical either. While she had run along with the pack to People's Park back in 1969 and had been picked up by police, she obviously had not been a leader and had easily talked her way out of being jailed. To support her drug habit, she had worked occasionally after school, but her husband hadn't approved and so more often than not she had picked up extra money by shoplifting. (On Telegraph Avenue she could hawk what she lifted in a hurry.) In school or out, she didn't go to rallies but was a pushover for Yoga and I Ching and astrology and every other movement with mystic overtones.

Once she had graduated and was on her own, Nancy took more schooling to qualify for a certificate to teach high school and did get a job for a while as a part-time grade-school teacher. But with her free-and-easy approach to life, she couldn't take the bureaucracy and backed off to become a blackjack dealer in a restaurant, where she wore a see-through blouse and the waitresses went topless. In the fall of '72, by which time she knew Willy, she went back to UC to become a paramedic (or maybe even go on to be a doctor, she told her parents, who were sending her occasional checks), but "she was burned out," said one instructor. "The drugs were getting to her; she couldn't concentrate." Also, she had a part-time job in a biology laboratory which depressed her. "I'm taking care of a bunch of horny toads that are doomed to destruction," she told an old friend. "What I'm thinking of doing is taking them up to the Russian River and setting them free."

In the spring and summer of '72, Nancy went up to the woods and hills (with or without the toads, nobody knows) and lived in an old camper with two cats, which she taught to be independent and set free. And in these woods she may have been a hostess to Willy, who used to go there with his mountain-climbing friends, one of whom this year was Russ Little. "I wasn't much of a climber at first," says Russ, thinking back at San Quentin, "but I loved being outdoors with Willy, who, clumsy as he was around the house, was like a goat in the mountains." Russ remembers trying to follow Willy on the side of a cliff one day when he fell "and damn near broke my neck."

Not in the woods but back on Telegraph Avenue, where Nancy worked part-time in Fruity Rudy's orange-juice stand, she was introduced by Willy to Mizmoon, who was living at the time with Camilla. And sometime that fall, at an art festival where the blond Camilla had a booth, Mizmoon introduced Nancy to her big-boned, motherly lover. Friends recall that it was the only meeting Nancy had with Camilla, who soon went off to Greece to try to get over her infatuation, until the following year, when both young women began going to the Chabot Gun Range in Oakland where they learned to shoot straight and true. And it was there that they met Vietnam veteran Joseph Michael Remiro, who by this time was a committed revolutionary, as was Willy.

Chapter Fourteen

Sent forth into the community by the prison's Black Cultural Association, Willy moved across the Bay Area like the cue ball on a pool table, bumping into one radical after another as he went rolling along. Intent on getting information for the prisoners, he paid little attention to many of the radicals he came up against, but he was stimulated and entertained by one wiry, hyperactive Vietnam graduate. The fellow was gun-savvy Joe Remiro, founder of the Oakland chapter of the Vietnam Veterans Against the War and member of Venceremos, a radical left organization that had a spin-off connection with the Students for a Democratic Society.

From his first contact with Willy in the spring of '72, Remiro had an immense effect on the younger man, although for many months Joe did not even know Willy's last name when he saw him around. Hopping around to meetings and parades in trousers that had a small American flag sewed to the seat (for which he would later be arrested), Joe was a taunt to cops but a sketch to Willy. Here was a fellow who went out of his way to defy the law. Yet for most of his life this one had been a superpatriot.

As a little kid, Joe Remiro hadn't felt dressed without his toy guns, which he strapped to his body in the morning before he got out of bed. Once this was attended to, he might run helter-skelter out front to defend the house from an attack by Indians. Later he went on to more derring-do, picked up from the John Wayne movies he went to with his Mexican-American father, who had entered the country as a migrant worker, obtained legal residence as a veteran of World War II and supported his family as a laundry truck driver.

To compare Joe with the kidnapped Patty Hearst would seem to be ludicrous. Other than Cinque, no one who joined the SLA had less in common with the heiress. And yet in curious ways their pasts were similar. Of all in the band, these two were the only native San Franciscans. And both went in their early years to Roman Catholic schools. Moreover, long before, when most kids their age were getting into schoolyard sports, these two were getting into sex. But once these comparisons are made, any further similarity ceases.

Unlike the parents of the privileged Patricia, Joe's Chicano father and dark-skinned mother, whose father was a Sicilian fisherman, were nonwhites—not "niggers," as some called them when Joe went to school, but not full-blooded Spaniards either, which Joe's father liked to suggest. And the Irish Catholic school in the Sunset district where Joe in his all-boy classroom learned a little about adding and subtracting and a lot about why it was sinful to touch himself was a far cry from the elegant convents where Patty and her sisters went to school.

In grade school in Saint Anne's parish, Joe, whose IQ has been reported by one newsman as 105, was no student, but still was "cool," says one girl who remembers that "Joe was a ladies' man before he was ten years old and into absolutely everything." She smiles as she thinks back to when this boy she thought she was in love with was an altar boy and the school traffic director and "a flashy dancer at our school mixers even before eighth grade."

At Sacred Heart High School, Joe's grades and his attendance at Sunday Mass went down as his interest in drinking, cars and girls went up. While he went from ninth grade to tenth and on up on schedule, he was a low man in his class, which didn't bother him because he knew that once school was over he would be going into the Army. In the meantime, he was a cheerleader at football games, which featured him for the girls he wanted to make out with, and he also had a job as a short-order cook, which brought in the money he had to have for gas for his car and dates.

Once he had his high-school diploma, Joe signed up for City

College, which was free but not much of a college. Again, this didn't matter much to Joe, who never went to a class. His reason for matriculating, says a friend who knew him then, "was not to learn stuff or get credits but to be a college man, which would get him better women than saying he was a fry cook." In conflict with his father, he didn't stay at home in his City College year but slept most nights in his car or at the Alpha Kappa Rho fraternity, which he had managed to pledge and where he distinguished himself with "actives" as "just about the most resourceful pledge we ever had." This accolade from upperclassmen came after hell week, when we was taken naked "and covered with tar, feathers and catsup" to the woods. Left to shiver until morning, he made his way through the underbrush to his car, which he had had the foresight to park nearby (after getting wind about where he would be taken), and was back in the house before his gleeful brothers got back. Soon thereafter he got the call he was waiting for. Enlisted in the Army, he was sent to Vietnam, where he served for a year and a half in the 1966–68 period as a combat grunt and, for eight of his overseas months, as a volunteer LRRP.

In volunteering for one of the six-man units in the Army's Long-Range Reconnaissance Patrols (shortened to LRRP's in everyday talk), Joe understood that he would be dropped repeatedly by helicopter, with only his teammates, into enemy territory. Camouflaged by natural and/or phony mud and foliage, they either collected information (through ears, eyes and noses) to send back to friendly forces or went out on search-and-destroy missions.

Later Joe said, "If any Vietnamese saw us, we were supposed to kill them or get out of the area." He said he had discusssions with his commanding officer about what to do if he came across a kid or an old lady. "Well, it was a standing order; we were supposed to kill." He said that "if we couldn't kill the person we saw, we were supposed to get out of the area, because everybody on the team knew that six people couldn't defend very well." Several times he had to be pulled out by rescue teams.

"When I went over," Joe recalls, "I'd been all for the war. But after a while I began to have questions. Like about seeing people murdered who weren't armed or any threat or anything. And sometimes I would think about this and sometimes I wouldn't, and then I would do what I was told and wouldn't think of this at all."

One time, when Joe had returned from a mission, he went to see a chaplain. "This was a Catholic priest, and I told him I wanted to go to confession—said I hadn't been to any confession for eight years and that I thought it would be a good idea. So I started telling this dude about the things we were doing and stuff, and he stopped me before I was finished and he said, 'Do you smoke marijuana?' And I said yeah. Then he said, 'Well you know you shouldn't smoke marijuana' and started giving me a lecture. So here I was telling this chaplain about killing people and he was talking about smoking marijuana, and I told him to get fucked or something and walked out. I decided that wasn't the way to deal with that, you know."

On the plane trip back to the United States from Vietnam, Joe tried to think what he believed in and found that he didn't believe in anything. "I just couldn't say whether I agreed or disagreed with anything; I was just an empty shell. Just, here I am, Joseph Remiro, and I'm nobody." Then, at Ford Ord, where he stayed for several months at the end of his military stint, he went heavy into drugs. "I smoked a lot of grass in Vietnam. And then, when I got back to this country, I started taking LSD and I kind of developed a dependency on it. And every weekend I'd pay to have someone take my duty so I could go into the city and get acid." And the drug habit stayed with Joe for some time after he got back to San Francisco, where he will never forget the day he arrived at the airport and got in a cab to go home.

"People were mowing their lawns and walking in the park and driving around, and I couldn't believe that everything was the same as when I went away when all of this stuff was going on in Vietnam." This was the start of Joe's deciding to become a pacifist, and soon after, when he tried to talk to his parents about Vietnam, he came to the conclusion that the only reason he had gone to Vietnam was because his father hadn't told him what he had experienced in World War II. "He forgot," Joe says. "And I was determined not to let myself forget."

At home, Joe told his parents that he'd been suckered into a war that was wrong, which upset his mother and infuriated his father, who threw him out of the house. So Joe turned to more drugs. And to hippies. And to Kathy, whom he had known before he went away and whom he now married "because she was the one person in the world I could talk to."

For two years thereafter Joe had difficulty relating to anyone.

Repeatedly he took a job—as a cabdriver, newspaper hawker, diaper clerk, delivery boy, short-order cook—only to leave in a couple of months when his employers didn't see things his way. Along the way he started and dropped courses at several schools; drove in and out of one drug deal or hippie commune after another in Washington, Oregon and California; had affairs with many women he didn't love and had a son, Joshua, whom he did.

By the spring of '72, when Willy met him in Oakland, Joe was twenty-six years old, no longer married and off drugs and pacifism. And through a fluke much like the one that had taken Willy to the Peking Man House, he was living with Communist sympathizers. He had simply wandered into a rooming house near a college on Alameda Street in which he had enrolled to take an auto mechanics course. And the three single women in the house just happened to be Marxist-Leninists.

"At first I didn't know what they were talking about," Joe says, "but after they asked me to go to a political study group, I said okay. Then, once I got there, I began finding answers to questions I didn't think had answers and began seeing the historical progression of events and things, and I got involved."

When the women in his house became members of Venceremos, which means "We shall overcome" and which was considered by the Senate Internal Security Committee to be the most dangerous organization in the country, Joe became a member of that too. And then, as he saw how the war was continuing, he looked up other veterans who were opposed to what was happening and soon was organizing the VVAW chapter in Oakland. "And about that time Willy came along."

Shortly after Russ had arrived at Peking Man House and both Willy and Russ were working with prisoners, someone in Joe's VVAW group or in Venceremos got hold of a film about the Attica rebellion to show in a community house and talked to Joe about getting someone who was into prison work to come and discuss what was going on behind bars in California. "And I looked up this dude who's name was Willy that I had seen around," says Joe, "and got him to come to the meeting. And I remembered afterward that Russ Little came along, although I didn't have a reason on that first night to talk to him much."

From the beginning Willy and Joe liked each other, and sometime that year, when Joe showed the film about the killing of Fred Hampton, "who never had a chance to give himself up because he wasn't armed to defend himself," he again asked Willy to come to the hall. "And by this time, after seeing how the Panthers were getting shot at around the country and after bein' harassed myself because of the Venceremos, I was beginning to see that some kind of personal self-defense was necessary for me and others like me to keep from getting killed.

"So I began going to a self-defense class. But that didn't last long because I knew more about weapons than the dude who was teaching the class. I was continually contradicting him. So people in the class began encouraging me to start teaching on my own. So I began studying laws about buying guns and transporting them and search warrants and seizure laws. And after that I started teaching a self-defense class.

"In class, we kept instruction down to shotguns, .30 caliber carbines and handguns—revolvers and automatics. And I began teaching the safe use of weapons too—how to clean them and store them. And after a while we got into emergency first aid, like how to stop bleeding.

"Before long Willy was coming to the classes, and then he began to want to be an instructor—with me there to help him in the beginning so that afterward he could go out on his own to teach self-defense classes the way I was doing. And about this same time, I got interested in the prison work he was doing. So with these two special interests, we had kind of a trade to make which brought us a closeness."

Later Joe and Willy lived together, and at that time Joe got to be good friends with Russ Little. But that was a year later. In the meantime, Joe, who was as sexy as a super Communist as he had been as a cheerleader, was going to bed with Angela Atwood.

Voluptuously good-looking and innately dramatic, "Angel" had arrived in the Bay Area with her husband, Gary, in 1972 about the time Joe was becoming heavily involved with Venceremos. And arriving with her and her mate were Bill and Emily Harris, who were destined for a wild kind of fame that even they could not possibly have anticipated when they were acting in college plays with the Atwoods back at Indiana University. And once again, it had been Willy, rolling along like the cue ball, who had touched one after another of the newcomers and sent them on to the others. And soon, because of Willy's connections, with a single exception, the Harrises' handsome likenesses would be adorning the covers of national magazines, as recognizable to celebrity watchers in the early seventies as the familiar faces of Richard and Liz.

Chapter Fifteen

Willy met Bill Harris shortly after the Atwoods and the Harrises arrived in the Bay Area in 1972. But in Bill's case, Joe Remiro was the first to connect.

"I met him in Oakland in front of a Safeway store at the time Bobby Seale was running for mayor," Joe told John Bryan, who has written a book about Joe.* "Bill was registering people to vote in the election." Joe says that on that day he himself was handing out leaflets in support of Cesar Chavez and his Farm Workers and he noticed Bill, who was wearing a Venceremos button. "So I asked him if he was a member, and he said 'No' but that he was interested in radical politics. So I asked him to come that night to a meeting of a coalition against racism at the Glide Memorial Church.

"Well, Bill came with Emily, but I was busy at the door and could only say hello. I think Russ was there and met them, and so did Willy, who talked to the coalition that night about the problems of black prisoners. Then, a few nights later, Bill and Emily came to a prison film and to hear Willy talk, but Bill and I didn't spent more than a few minutes together, so it wasn't until much later that I really

*This Soldier Still at War

184

got to know the Harrises and their friend Angela Atwood, who was also from Indiana." (Actually, Angela was from New Jersey, but attended Indiana University as an out-of-state student, as did Emily, who was from a suburb of Chicago. Only Bill had a family nearby—in Carmel, a suburb of Indianapolis.)

Older than the others who gained fame in the Hearst-SLA tragedies, Bill had been involved with the university in some way since the early sixties, when, as a longtime enthusiast of its football team, he entered the school as a freshman. ("He was on our high-school golf team and went out for track," says a friend from the old days, "but his real love was football, and he'd drive down to Bloomington on Saturday to see any home game he could get a ticket to. We all knew he'd go there to school; I don't think he looked at any other college.")

A hep kid with a socially aware family behind him, Bill pledged Sigma Alpha Epsilon, one of the best houses on campus, and moved into a jolly life of beer drinking, dates and Dylan. He had little time for study, which told in his grades, and at the end of his first semester, when he did not make the average required for initiation into the fraternity, he had to move out of the Sig Alph house.

Nevertheless, for the next year and a half, when he lived in a dormitory, he stayed in touch with his pals on fraternity row. He still was one of the boys and went right along making out with sorority girls at night and cheering for the Hoosiers on Saturday afternoons at the stadium. But Bill also had a cause. Living close to the Ku Klux Klan national headquarters, which were just outside his university town, he began to harangue for a better break for the blacks, and, while he did not go south to register voters, he impressed his friends with the seriousness of his concern.

As in his first semester, Bill did little studying at the library and most of the time he was on probation, a distinct disappointment to his conservative, hardworking father, who had been an Army career officer in Bill's early life and now was a success-oriented building-equipment salesman. Finally, in 1965, Mr. Harris told his son, "Enough is enough." There would be no money for school until Bill got hold of himself.

Lacking anything more constructive to do, Bill, in the fall of '65, like others before him, headed west to look around California, where at that time antiwar protests were tearing Berkeley and other UC campuses apart. "But Bill wasn't affected," says a friend who knew him in San Francisco. "He didn't get involved."

Instead, Bill went home after several weeks and stayed with his parents and sisters in their large, comfortable home near the Episcopal church where, as a boy, he had served as an acolyte. And while there, he looked up his old pledge class pal Larry Leach, who urged him to sign up with him in the Marines. "So late in the fall," says Leach, "off we went on the buddy system." With this plan, suggested by the military, they could take their training at the same camp in the United States and go overseas together. This pleased Bill's mother, who wanted her son to find himself, and satisfied his father, who felt that Bill hadn't appreciated his opportunities and that a stint with the military might straighten him out.

A competitive kid, Bill was attracted to the well-advertised toughness of life as a Marine. "That kind of turned Bill on," says Larry. "At the time we were both into that. Besides, he wanted to show his dad what he was made of." So the boy who hadn't done too well in school and his good friend went to boot camp, where Bill had a shock that affected his behavior from then on. Only days before he was to leave for Vietnam, he got word that his father had died of a heart attack. And after that Bill didn't seem to care what he did in the Marines.

"Neither Bill nor I wanted to be an officer, anyway," says Larry Leach. "I looked into it a couple of times, but as time went on it seemed ridiculous to go to officers' training when that would mean two more years in the service."

Together until they got to Vietnam, the friends were separated there and Bill went to DaNang, where, before he could see combat, he got into a touch football game and tore a ligament (for which disability he collects twenty-eight dollars a month). He was shipped off to Okinawa, where, while recuperating, he was detailed to staff the officers' club and where he saw race hatred even more appalling than the worst he had seen at home. "The islanders despise blacks," says one who was there, "and would attack black Marines on the street. And on base, the whites wouldn't go to the enlisted club at night when the blacks were there—the whole scene was the pits."

"When it came time to go home," says Larry, "Bill asked his company commander if he could go to Camp Lejeune in North Carolina, where I was being sent, and the orders came through. And

186

there we ran into more racism—which must have spread from overseas." He recalls Bill's running into a comrade Marine from Vietnam, only to have the Marine tell him, "You're fine, Bill, but I'm not going around with whites anymore, just blacks." He says the rebuff cut Bill terribly—"This man had been his friend."

Back at Indiana University, after having been away for two years, Bill was surprised at the strangeness of the place. Only later did he tell his roommate (who was Larry), "The change isn't in the place, I'm finding out. It's in me."

"And he was right," says a friend who knew him in his prewar days. "First, he became a theater major, which surprised me. I'd have taken him for a golf-pro type or maybe a newspaperman—he'd won a prize for writing something in high school. And, then, he'd been all for the Marines before he went to Vietnam and now he was pretty much of a pacifist, didn't even want to stay in a house where anyone had a gun. And, finally, a lot of the rah-rah had gone out of Bill."

"And he didn't understand the ones who were still into it," says Larry Leach, "when to him after Vietnam the whole scene seemed juvenile." He says the more Bill looked around the campus the more he wanted to do something meaningful. "So it wasn't long before he got involved in Vietnam Veterans Against the War." And at about the same time, he began to date Emily Schwartz, a junior-year English major from Clarendon Hills, Illinois, who was brighter than the average, socially deft (she was rush chairman at the Chi Omega house), and attracted to male students who were witty, irreverent and a little offbeat. Bill had no trouble getting a second and third audience with Emily after their first blind date. The tousled ex-Marine who was getting his name in the campus paper for his opposition to Lyndon Johnson's war and was a member of the backstage clique in the theater department had more in common with the glossy sorority girl than met the eye.

Emily, like Bill, came from a family that was used to good living. (Her father is a consulting engineer in his Chicago suburb, goes to his clients in his private plane, supports a handsome home and is extremely conservative politically.) At home, like Bill, she was one of a kind. (She has three brothers; Bill, two sisters.) She was a straight-A student in high school, a cheerleader and confidently popular. Bill got good grades in his early years, was an achiever in the sports he went out for, and was appealing to his teachers and to the other kids in his puckish way. Both had been members of what Russ Little called, with derision, the tennis set. Still, by the time they met, both had branched out a little from the norm.

Emily had chosen to go out of state to college; Bill had been to war. And both had lived briefly in California; the summer before they met, two years after Bill had lived for a short time in San Francisco, Emily had worked at Disneyland, south of Los Angeles. Now, in Indiana, these two were watching what was happening on the Coast and had much to talk about. Often they did this while dropping acid with two friends who were making names for themselves in college plays. The two new ones they tripped with were Gary Atwood and Angela DeAngelis, who in Indiana, as back home in New Jersey, was always called Angel.

Back in North Haledon, where in the fifties any grade-school kid who had crossed the George Washington Bridge (twenty miles away) was considered well traveled, Angel, for as long as anyone there can remember, was expected to go places. A dark-eyed beauty since babyhood, the oldest child of Lawrence DeAngelis, an official in Local 999 in the Teamsters Union, and his late wife, Elena, sincere Roman Catholics if there ever were two, was the town's darling. No one who had seen her play Kim in her high school's producton of *Bye Bye Birdie* or Tuptim in *The King and I* was surprised to read that she was playing Perdita in the university's production of *The Winter's Tale*. And most in town could have told you that Angel would be living in the best house at the university and would be a head-turner on campus. Back at Manchester High, where she was in the honor society and president of the Dramatic Club, Angel is remembered by former teachers as a stunner. "And in this way," say the town's old-timers, "Angel was like her mother."

In 1958, Elena DeAngelis moved with her husband and three children—Angela, Elena and Larry—from Paterson, one of the country's oldest manufacturing towns, with more than its share of blacks and Puerto Ricans, to North Haledon, which had no ghetto. "Elena didn't want her children to have any problems that she could prevent," says one old friend. Another says she was "a good wife and mother and a good athlete, and in no time at all became the town's recreation commissioner and one of the best-liked people around." Unfortunately, Elena did not live to enjoy her good life. She died of a heart attack in a bowling alley when Angel was fourteen, and after that the oldest DeAngelis child became the mainstay of the home.

But she was no poor little Cinderella. Angel had a convertible in high school and a French poodle named Demi-Tasse and could bring as many kids as she wanted to the big house that had one of the first swimming pools in town. "She looked beautiful in a bathing suit," says her sister, "but she worried that her thighs were too fat and she was always on a diet." "And," says one of her old crowd, "she wasn't a tramp by any means, but she was a luscious-looking kid who knew how to suggest sex." Author Michael Wolff, who went to Angel's high school, recalls that Angel startled a girl in her class by going up to their math teacher in the hall "and cutely straightening his belt."

There was no question in Angela's mind that she would be an actress, and from about eleventh grade on she knew where she would prepare. "One of her professors in high school told her that she ought to go out to Indiana University," says Elena, who is taller than Angel was but looks like her sister. "The theater department out there, he told her, was one of the best in the country, maybe in the world." So in the fall of '66, with the blessings of her father, Angel headed west—in her own car and with a goodly supply of the deceptively simple, easy-fitting expensive dresses that Jackie Kennedy made popular. And soon she was sending home letters (in which she signed her hallowed name with a halo) that told about the friendly people she was meeting through the church.

In her first year on campus Angel, with her gentle ways and quiet voice, went along at IU with the same light, sure-footed steps that had taken her to the top at Manchester High. In no time at all she was installed in the Kappa Kappa Gamma sorority house and acting in plays in the theater department. "And that's where she got to know Gary Atwood and Bill Harris," says Michael Bourn, film critic and music director of WFIU radio station in Bloomington, who was a graduate student in the theater department when Angel, Bill and Emily were on campus.

Michael remembers them all as attractive and serious. He says Bill was a good actor and a good guy, and adds that he likes to talk to people about his old friends "because when you hear the word 'terrorist' you think of someone who is evil, and that doesn't apply to Bill, who was a real person, as was Angel, whom I knew very well."

189

He says that Angel was short but slim and stood tall on stage. "Along with stage presence, she had energy that made up for any lack of talent." She was a member from the first of the elite backstage clique that was dominated by the university's prize actor, Gary Atwood, who was a far-left idealist. And, as Angel listened to Gary's dreams for his country, she fell in love. "Gary was a thinking man," Michael says, "and Angel was supportive. Soon she was selling Gary's socialist beliefs to anyone who would listen."

At the Kappa house, the political twist of the once-innocent Angel was a shocker to the careful girls who were her sisters, and when finally Angel, having become defensive and embittered, asked permission to move out into her own apartment (a move not usually approved by the chapter), her sorority sisters were glad to let her go. From that time on, even as Angel achieved respect on campus for her work in the theater (she played other heroines after Perdita), she changed her style. Behind the composed star, she was a new girl-woman who was one part hippie (she and Gary were as heavy into LSD as any on campus) and one part Italian mama (she spent a lot of time cooking for her man). Also, she was uncertain about her future as an actress. According to Michael Bourne, "Living with Gary, who was a far better actor than she would ever be, she began to wonder if she was kidding herself that any day now she would be getting a call from Hollywood or Broadway, which had been her dream."

Now, hoping to marry Gary, and knowing that her allowance from home would stop with graduation or her wedding, she worked in some courses in education and was soon doing student teaching at a nearby high school, where she was considered a radical. (She wore a black armband when Kent State was in the headlines and was critcized by the principal for stirring things up.) As she became more involved in the antiwar movement, she rarely went back to North Haledon, where she upset the peace at home as she had at the Kappa house, and by 1970 was in a standoff position with her father. And when she got married in the chapel on campus, her father, a good Catholic, wouldn't go to Indiana.

"I was a maid of honor," says Elena, "And Billy Harris was best man." She remembers how beautiful her sister looked in the Elizabethan costume she wore for a wedding gown and what a good time everybody had at the picnic on a nearby farm, "where Michael

Bourne came with his rock band and we roasted a pig." Before returning east, Elena talked to her sister about what she would do next and "even then, she was talking about going to California, where Gary, who was a conscientious objector, wanted to find some kind of job that would serve as an alternative to going to war." The plan didn't work out until later, by which time Bill and Emily also had their degrees and were married and decided to head west too.

Like Angel, Bill took courses in teaching while still an undergraduate, and afterward went on to get a master's degree in urban education. And Emily, who had been involved in the theater only on the periphery, finished college as an English major and, like Angel, got a job nearby as a teacher. "She was really into kids," says a girl who knew Emily when she was teaching French and English at Bloomington's junior high. "Lots of days, after her last class, she'd rap with the kids and help them see they didn't have to swallow everything that was handed down to them and that they should be looking for better ways to do things and should be thinking for themselves."

Both Emily and Angel were devotees of women's lib, but both took their husband's name when they married and thought of themselves from their wedding day on as Emily Harris and Angela Atwood. They lived next door to each other and often at night sat down with their husbands at the table as a foursome. Then the room would ring with political talk as propounded by Emily, Bill and Gary. (In the early days, Angel was pretty much a listener.) Usually, by the end of the evening, Bill and Gary would be arguing "the gun."

An admirer of Che Guevara and the French Marxist Régis Debray, who was Guevara's friend, Bill was coming to believe that armed struggle in the United States was the only way for blacks and other minorities to resist oppression. Gary, on the other hand, who called himself a Trotskyite, favored an organizational approach to change (as Trotsky and Lenin had organized the Bolshevik Revolution in Russia in 1917) and resisted the idea of violence by little men.

Friends who dropped by the apartment of one or the other gave credit to the Marines for fostering Bill's aggressive "armed struggle" dedication, but Michael Bourne, who spent a lot of time with Bill, says no. "Remember Bill was no LRRP in the war. He told me himself that all the time he was overseas he never fired a gun, not even for practice." He shakes his head. "No, Bill wasn't gun happy so much as he was an idealist who believed that black militancy was the way for blacks to get attention and that maybe violence for any cause was the only way to cut through apathy." He adds, "Long before he enlisted in the Marines, he felt deeply about the problems of colored people."

"He'd been reading Jackson and Cleaver and the others," reports a friend who knew Bill later, "so of course he was interested in getting to know black prisoners when he and Emily got to California a few months after the Atwoods had moved there."

In 1972, as he searched for a way to discharge his duties as a CO, Gary Atwood heard about an unpaid job he could do for credit for a government-funded theater in San Francisco and went west with Angela by his side. To put food on the table in their apartment, Angela got a job as a waitress in The Great Electric Underground on a subfloor in the Bank of America building. Bored by their grubby lives and nudged along by their yearnings for the theater, the Atwoods stayed in their jobs but moved to Berkeley, where Gary took courses at UC and Angela got a part in *Hedda Gabler* at the Town's Company Theater.

Playing in *Hedda* with Angel, who played Thea, was Kathy Soliah from Palmdale, California, who became Angel's friend. Soon, they both had jobs at the restaurant in the bank building in San Francisco, to which they commuted by day, returning to Berkeley for rehearsals at night. The two actresses talked of organizing a "Plays for Politics" acting company, signed up for a course at Berkeley in radical politics and worked to unionize waitresses in San Francisco. And as she moved around the Bay Area, Angel, who had willingly subjected herself to Gary's whims and put-downs in the first year of her marriage, began to resent her earlier dependency "and began telling Gary to shove it," said a friend, "if he asked her to pass the salt." Truth was Angel had manipulated her way into her marriage, and now that she was supporting her husband, who was dissatisfied with his life and could be waspish, she had begun to wonder why. Gaining confidence as she talked to waitresses about their rights as workers and as she worked at the theater with her new friend, Kathy, she was moving away from her old Italian mama role, which must have been immediately apparent to the Harrises, who moved in with the Atwoods when they first came to the Coast. "Emily saw the change," says someone who knew them well, "and was delighted."

Like Angel, both of the Harrises found jobs that would have classified them on any employment chart as "underemployed." Emily, the expert linguist and teacher, went to work as a typist at a university research center, and Bill, with his theatrical background and advanced degree in education, got a job sorting mail at the Post Office. Had they found work more to their liking, they might not have had the energy to plunge headlong into radical politics. As it was, their jobs, which brought in about $1,200 a month, took no more than 10 percent of their concentration, and their two-bedroom apartment in Oakland, which they soon moved into and which they furnished with taste and kept as neat as a stage setting, took less than 5 percent. So they had plenty of energy left for the United Farm Workers and Oakland's mayoralty race and Venceremos causes and films about revolutionists, like the Tupamaros of Uruguay, whose method for freeing a captured *compañero* was to kidnap someone and offer to swap.

Sometimes after a film seen with Willy, the Harrises stopped in to talk with the Atwoods at their apartment on Delaware Street, which is not far from the fourplex where Steven Weed, a new teaching assistant at Berkeley that year, was living with one of the richest girls in the world. (Pursued by Patty two years before when he was her math teacher at Crystal Springs School for Girls in the wealthy community of Hillsborough, he was living better than most as he worked for his Ph.D.) Whether the four from Indiana talked, as many in the neighborhood did, about the unprepossessing "Mr. Peepers" in the philosophy department who had lucked out with an adoring heiress in his first job out of college, no one is saying, but the answer is probably no. For the Harrises, this was a time for action, not gossip.

As the year 1972 neared December and the Harrises in their stopovers with the Atwoods talked more and more of violence, Gary Atwood became apprehensive. These people weren't kidding! At an emotional standstill with his wife, he could no longer discuss his fears with her, but he did argue with Bill far into the night. Armed struggle was no solution to this country's problems, he believed. And, as he presented his views, the arguments became more than a gentlemen's disagreement. The two men were deadlocked. Still, when Christmas lights twinkled in Berkeley and the sound of carols filled the air, the longtime friends lifted a glass to wish one another well as others were doing at the same time at Peking Man House, where Robyn Steiner and Russ Little's sister fixed a turkey dinner that night for everybody who hadn't gone home.

Chapter Sixteen

Now that Patty Hearst was living with her lover and clerking at Cap's ("because I've never worked before and it will be good experience") until time to enroll for UC's spring quarter as a science major, all who would become members of the SLA were in the Berkeley area. All, that is, but Camilla Hall. For more than three months Camilla had been absent in Greece, painting and contemplating her lesbian relationship with Patricia Soltysik, whom she had named Mizmoon.

In September and October, before Camilla had taken off for Europe, she and Mizmoon, who had decided previously not to live permanently together as a couple, had given themselves to each other for six weeks of lovemaking before each went her own way. But by January 1973 each was miserable. Sometimes in Spain, but most of the time in Greece, Camilla was writing to the younger woman to give up her job as a janitor and come live with her on an island in the sun. And in Berkeley, where Mizmoon was sleeping, shouting and suffering with Chris Thompson, the black friend of Willy's and Russ's who had stayed until recently at Peking Man House, she told Camilla by mail that she yearned for her embrace. Still, Mizmoon was not all sad-faced and teary. When her brother and his wife visited her that winter, she frightened them with her hard eyes and straight talk of "armed struggle as the only way to alter dehumanizing conditions in this country."

"I remember that she wrote to my mother that December and asked if it would be all right if she brought home a black man for Christmas," says Fred Soltysik about his sister. "And, of course, my mother said yes. But at the last minute, Mizmoon got sick and could not get up to Santa Barbara." According to others who knew Mizmoon in the Bay Area, her illness that winter was gonorrhea, which, coming as it did at Christmastime, left her listless and depressed. "For much of the month of December," says one who knew her well, "she stayed alone in her apartment where she had lots of time to think."

Not far away, Nancy Ling Perry was also doing some thinking as best she could in her strung-out condition. In the science courses she was taking for her second B.A., this one in chemistry, so that she could go on to be a paramedic, she was having a tough time with chemistry and felt outclassed, she told her brother, by younger students. (In her first quarter at Berkeley, Patty Hearst shortly had the same trouble with the biochemistry course she was taking in order to be a veterinarian and switched her major to art history.) And Nancy was also having a problem with her fingers, which had puffy knuckles by then, and her hands, which were red and swollen. "Maybe I have rheumatoid arthritis," she said, "or dope's getting to me." (At the time, she was smoking a per diem average of ten or more joints, which she moistened with hashish oil, and also she sometimes used cocaine.) By this time she knew that any more full-time schooling was not for her and had applied for and got a job at the Fruity Rudy cart owned by Rudy Henderson, a black man old enough to be her father, who became her occasional lover for a brief time and her friend.

"She was the best girl I ever had working for me," says Rudy, who owns five or six Fruity Rudy stands in the Bay Area today, "and the most generous person I ever knew." In the beginning, when Nancy was spending as much as fifty dollars a week for drugs, she had little money to give away, but she gave (and sometimes sold) her body, and she handed out little and big gifts that she shoplifted. Extremely nervous at this stage, she was claustrophobic and, according to Rudy, "had a tough time staying in the cart on a bad day, or in any room in a house with a door closed." But she wasn't completely spaced-out; she knew something was wrong with her and talked to friends and her

196

brother about turning over a leaf. She would give up drugs and "cleanse" herself with health foods. From then on, she would take care of herself physically and devote her life to something she believed in. And, even though she was still seeing her husband, she had to admit "it isn't any good anymore," and she was making up her mind to get a divorce at last. About this time she began working for the Movement in a serious way. And shortly she learned to shoot at the club with Joe Remiro, who was doing some serious thinking about this time about his own future as a radical.

Early in 1973, Joe and others in his radical Venceremos circle began putting all their money and energy into a plan to help California prisoners escape and go underground to form a vanguard of hardened cons ready to mount an all-out revolution in America when opportune. Some of Joe's Venceremos group (not Joe) had already pulled off their first coup on October 6, when they surrounded a prison convoy, murdered one surprised guard, wounded another and sped away with Ronald Beaty, an armed robbery convict and effective organizer of would-be revolutionaries at Chino prison.

Successful in their first ambush, all of the group were jubilant. More determined than ever, they made plans for a camp in the mountains to accommodate freed prisoners (released under fire from prison transport buses) to be trained to rob, assassinate and kidnap. But the euphoria was brief, because in early December, before their next commando push could take place, Ronald Beaty was picked up and turned canary. (As a result, four Venceremos guerrillas, including the woman who drove the car in which Beaty had escaped, were convicted of murder.) Afterward, Venceremos, which on the surface had seemed to be much more than a group of off-the-wall protesters and disillusioned Nam vets, was doomed. Watched constantly by police, it wobbled along as an organization for another ten months and then became extinct, to pop up again, some believe, as the SLA.

As Venceremos began to disintegrate, Joe lost faith in the Oakland VVAW chapter as well. (The other vets, who were into marching in groups and writing letters to editors, weren't as gung ho as he.) So, as he looked ahead in early 1973, Joe had some thinking to do about where to put his energy and his money, which he always seemed able to come up with. For even though the organizations he had believed in were not going to be important, the coming armed struggle still entailed recruiting prisoners for helpmates.

Determined at first to make a better world for his year-and-a-half-old son, he told the editor of San Francisco's underground *Phoenix*, "I began to expand this to all the helpless people oppressed by our military or through the funding we give other armies." To another friend, he said, "I can't get things done by trying to be some little turd who never swears, that greases his hair back and wears a suit and tap-dances around in the system. But I'm willing to go all the way if it's necessary and to teach others to handle weapons safely so they can protect themselves."

Joe's flashy talk and courage to commit himself 100 percent made him as attractive to women as to the disillusioned veterans at loose ends who admired his bantam rooster guts. On the range and at home, the women in the revolution laughed at his verbal antics, were challenged by his openness (he not only kept two or three affairs going at once but expected the involved girls to be friends) and delighted in his sexiness. (No sufferer for the Cause once he got in bed, Joe listed "fucking" as his favorite recreation on one questionnaire sent to him by a prosepctive employer.) Still, with all his busyness, Joe was something of a loner, not a party man, as was Willy, who still cared enough about old ties in 1973 to fill out and return an alumni questionnaire from Mount Hermon.

Married?	Yes in 1972.
Name?	Darlene from Dolce Vita Massage Parlor.
Children?	Reggie 2, and Opal, one year.

"Willy was half little boy and half grown-up," says Russ Little's sister. She remembers that he was sloppy in the kitchen, "where he would have four pots bubbling away and things flying all over the place and would never clean the place up when it was his turn to cook. And he was terribly clumsy and walked with such a heavy tramp he'd wake us all up in the morning. But he was romantic too." JoAnn recalls that one night Willy took off for a party on his bicycle and came home half drunk and all cut up and bleeding. "He got to thinking about the girl he thought he was in love with and went out and got a rose and put it on her windowsill. Then, afterward, he fell off his bike on his face and would have had to go to the emergency room if it hadn't been for Robyn Steiner, who knew something about medicine and washed and patched him up."

"To most girls Willy was like a brother," says Rayne Alexander, who lived in an apartment building next to Peking Man House. "Girls liked him, but he seemed innocent and kind of shy. Once I invited him over with a girl I thought he might like, but they just talked away the night and never did get it together."

"He looked like a big, loose, easygoing guy to me," says George Martin from the same house. "I can't imagine why he'd have had any trouble with girls if he'd put his mind to it."

But in the winter of 1972–73, Willy was putting his mind to his work with black prisoners, and getting closer every week to Cinque. Flattered to have been the first white member of Unisight, he worked hard to bring in radical speakers from the Bay Area and to sign up white tutors, who, it turned out, were resented by the BCA's black women for their assumption of knowledge about a world that they themselves knew better. After a visit or two, most of the black sisters avoided Unisight, where many who were there to get husbands objected to Cinque's criticism of the relationship between black men and women.

No one at Vacaville, on the staff or imprisoned, looks back on Cinque as a leader like George Jackson, but most say that he was dedicated, hardworking and well organized—and in every way a model prisoner. This last led to his being transferred in December to a lower-security unit at Soledad prison, and thus temporarily out of the picture.

His replacement as head of the Unisight program at Vacaville was a brilliant and sometimes suicidal convicted robber later suspected of being one of the kidnappers of Patricia Hearst. His name is Thero Wheeler, and he was to be important in the early days of the SLA, but that came later. No believer in the let's-all-learn-about-black-history-aim of the Black Cultural Association, Wheeler stayed away from the white tutors and their admiring black prisoner-students until the Venceremos organization (of which he was the first convict member) became interested, and then he got involved. And as Venceremos faded, he and old con-wise Death Row Jeff drew even closer to the white radicals who had worked with Cinque. Neither prisoner had been much taken with Cinque, but both liked Willy Wolfe and his friend Russ Little and approved of their way of helping prisoners, which was not always what their outside coordinator had in mind. (Colston Westbrook's plan was to help convicts prepare to live life pacifically on the outside; the white newcomers, on the other hand, were talking to the prisoners about Che and Mao and Marx.)

By early 1973, with Cinque in one prison and Thero and Death Row Jeff in another (and other BCA members in San Quentin and Chino), Willy and Russ had to find a way to see them all. With California's rule that visitors can go to only one prison in a six-month period, they had to figure out a way to get into different prisons with phony ID cards. This they managed to do by requesting cards in the names of dead persons to be sent to one or another of their addresses in the Bay Area or to the Berkeley Post Office, where Bill Harris had rented a box in the name of Jonathan Mark Salamone.

This last actually was a drop set up to receive mail from prisoners, who were prohibited from writing to inmates of other prisons. As the letters came in, they were rewritten and sent on by Emily Harris, who was serving at the time as a member of the "defense committee" for the alleged murderers of the guard of the prisoner Ronald Beaty. At the same time she was trying to put together a "prison collective" to take the place of the collapsing Venceremos organization, but it didn't get off the ground.

According to an article in the April 16, 1976, issue of *New Times* magazine, she and Bill were by the spring of '73 good friends with Joe, Russ and Willy—and, of course, with Angela (who was having an on-again, off-again relationship with her husband but was having occasional dates with both Russ and Joe). In the article Emily said, "We wanted to keep on working together. We started to feel each other out about some more clandestine types of activities. It started kind of slowly, with Willy asking if we had ever considered helping someone escape, even if it just meant hiding them out. All six of us had to consider what we were really committed to doing."

There has been speculation whether these six helped Cinque escape from Soledad, but Russ says no. ("Cinque was out before we six became close.") But there is no doubt that Willy helped to master-mind the escape, which must have been a ticklish business for him at the time because in January he heard from home that both his mother and father were coming to visit. In a letter written to Pennsylvania in January, after his dad had thanked him for his oyster sauce (a Christmas present) and said he'd be hitting the Bay Area for a medical convention in the fall, Willy wrote: "I can't possibly say what my situation will be in September. I might possibly own some sheets by then, but at any rate, I shall find a way to put you up in a way befitting the dean of hypnotists of the Lehigh Valley." Then, looking ahead to his twenty-second birthday in another couple of weeks, he added: "At the risk of stepping out of bounds, I would like to request that if you send me a birthday present that it be something for out-of-doors (like crampons, or a climbing rope or a woolrich shirt). Things continue here as usual—always getting better." And to his mother in Connecticut, who had written that in February she would be going to visit a friend in Guatemala and could, if he wanted, fly on to California to see him in March before heading back to Connecticut, he had said to come. Yet, at the same time, he knew that his friend Cinque at Soledad was plotting his escape, which the future leader of the SLA managed to pull off on the night of March 5.

In careful preparation for his getaway, Cinque had avoided fights, complained only through regular channels and kept his revolutionary planning undercover.

Now, on a moonless night (according to most accounts) Cinque slipped away and ran close to the brush at the side of the road for thirteen miles, until at daylight he got to a small home of some Mexican-Americans who took in the stranger and gave him food and a change of clothes. After that, all stories differ, but according to the Harrises, who knew him best, Willy picked up Cinque and took him to Peking Man House, where David Gunnell and Jean Wah Chan were understandably nervous to have the guy around. (So were others, according to another account, which maintains that not Willy but a black who knew Cinque at Vacaville took him from house to house in the Bay Area where black women who opened the door turned thumbs down on their old acquaintance. With all of his truck with white girls, say some reports, this one had not been one of their favorites.) However he got to Chabot Road, Cinque stayed until the next day, when Willy took him to live with Mizmoon, a safe place, as it turned out, that was arranged by Russ Little through Chris Thompson, whose name comes up time after time in the SLA story.

Always at the wrong place at the wrong time, Chris Thompson nevertheless had an uncanny Mack-the-Knife ability to sense danger and slither away without a nick, and even sometimes (as when the police and newspapers later offered rewards for news of the SLA) to end up with a bagful of dough. And so it was this time.

Sometime later, when Chris was going for the rewards offered for clues to the killers of Marcus Foster, he said that a couple of days before Cinque's escape he had met Russ on the street and that Russ had asked why they hadn't seen him lately at Peking Man House. "I don't like to show up," Chris said he told Russ, "because I owe Dave Gunnell sixty-five bucks." According to the black man's account, he had left a gun with Gunnell in lieu of the $65, saying he'd be back later to pay up and take the gun. So when he and Russ met, he reported, Russ said he'd pay off Gunnell and take the gun, which was a .38 Rossi (which would later be introduced as evidence in the trials of Russ and Joe Remiro for the killing of Foster).

The story told by Thompson was later contradicted by a half dozen witnesses, including Dave Gunnell, who said under oath that Thompson took the gun with him when he moved out of Peking Man House, and by friends of Nancy Ling Perry, who say the gun was given or sold to her.

But all of that was to come later. Certainly Russ and Chris did talk on the street. Moreover, a few days later, after Cinque escaped, Russ reportedly went to Chris, who was living no more than an easy jog from where Steve Weed lived with Patty Hearst, and told him about the escaped con he wanted a place for. And Thompson, who had just had a final blowup with Patricia Soltysik, suggested that Russ call Mizmoon.

To Russ (and to Willy, when he found out), Mizmoon's comfortable apartment was the ideal place for Cinque and one where the cops would not be inclined to look. Not in prison work as yet, Mizmoon wasn't someone the cops might expect to hide a con. At the same time, she was drawn to black men and could be counted on to make Cinque comfortable. This she did, which must have wrenched the heart of Camilla Hall, who had flown back to the United States from Greece in February.

Camilla had gone first to the home of her parents in Lincolnwood, Illinois, outside Chicago, where her Lutheran minister father was keeping her little blue VW and her cat. But she longed for Mizmoon and, according to Fred Soltysik, "would go down to do the laundry in her parents' basement and would drop acid." At length, she called Berkeley and persuaded Mizmoon to meet her in Denver.

In Colorado, the twosome, in love again, stopped for a day or two at Duck Lake Commune, a lesbian community high in the mountains.

Then they went on to Berkeley, where they unloaded Camilla's clothes and took off for Santa Barbara to see Mizmoon's Belgian-American mother, who was confused and worried by her daughter's uncertainties but who (of all the parents of the SLA members) tried with all her heart to understand.

Like everyone who met Camilla, Mrs. Soltysik was drawn to the big, laughing, well-mannered girl who played a guitar and told funny jokes and was generous to a fault. Obviously this outgoing girl from the Middle West had much to give her daughter and vice versa. But Mrs. Soltysik's security didn't last long because during Mizmoon's second day in Santa Barbara she called in tears from a nearby hotel to report that Camilla had gone back to Berkeley alone. Apparently the old problem—could Mizmoon commit herself to Camilla alone—had come up again.

For the next six months Camilla, who went to work for a park supervisor (who remembers her as "an incredible woman") as a grounds keeper and landscape artist, lived alone, and Mizmoon lived with the escapee from Soledad.

According to Fred Soltysik again, who visited his sister when Mizmoon was living with Cinque, Cin spoke in a quiet voice, chose his words carefully as he talked of his work with children back in New Jersey and cooked an excellent vegetarian dinner with which he drank only beer. Of course, Fred did not know that Mizmoon's friend, who soon became her lover, was on the lam, as did few others (besides Willy and Russ) who came to the cozy apartment, which was decorated with sketches and paintings by Camilla.

Much had been written about why Donald "Cinque" DeFreeze was not picked up. He had associated with radicals in Berkeley and was living with an unconventional white woman. Didn't anyone look for him? No, say the suspicious ones, who believe he was working for the CIA and was allowed to walk away from prison to infiltrate the radical group that befriended him. Yes, say the police, but he wasn't as visible as you might think in Berkeley, where many blacks and whites live together. And, anyway, Cinque had no need to go out much. All the books about revolutionaries and their methods were brought to him from the library via Mizmoon, who also bought the food that Cinque prepared. And all the messages that he wanted to send to prisoners (who were ready to go with a revolution once they could get out) were transported direct or through the Harris drop by Willy, who was having a nervous spring. In March, less than two weeks after he got Cinque located with Mizmoon, his mother came for her visit.

"Willy met me in Russ Little's car that was painted all over in jazzy colors," Honey remembers as she thinks about the morning she flew into the Oakland airport from Guatemala after a stopover in Los Angeles. "Russ was along and from the first I got the feeling he was leading Willy down the garden path." She recalls "what may seem like a little thing" that turned her off in the first half hour. "On the way to Berkeley, I gave Russ a bill to run in and get a case of beer. And when he came out, he had bought twenty-four of the large-size cans. Again, that isn't much . . ."

Like all parents, Honey wanted to be liked by her son's friends, and she laughed a lot and contributed generously to the table and to Willy in her stay of three days. And she was a winner. ("Everyone was amazed at the way you fit right in," Willy wrote to her later, "especially when they compared you to other parents—like the Littles—who have visited here.")*But she had a vague sense of foreboding in Peking Man House, with its food stamps and Mao posters and women who slept with men but wore no wedding rings and talked with obscenities. Once, when one of the girls went to the kitchen because "I forgot the fuckin' potatoes," Honey asked with all seriousness why a girl as pretty as she was wanted to talk that way, and the girl shrugged. She didn't know; it was just a habit, what's the difference?

Still smarting from her divorce, Honey tended to blame her husband's closeness with money for her son's living conditions. "If Willy had come here with just a few more dollars," she found herself thinking, "he wouldn't be living in such a sleazy place." Still, it didn't occur to her to call her husband ("I hate to call there") or to urge Willy to go back east with her now that he was no longer in school. But she did talk with him about what he was going to do next. "You were getting such good grades at Berkeley, I don't know why you dropped out."

Willy told her, as many others his age were telling their parents in

---

* The Littles, who the officer at the gate at San Quentin says "are just about the nicest people you'd ever want to know" may have been worried at the time about Russ, for whom they had had high hopes.

that period, that school wasn't relevant and that he believed in the work he was doing with prisoners. Honey wanted to hear more, but on two of the three nights of her stay Willy went out to meetings and during the days he worked as a laborer at a die-casting plant. "And I've been taking a course in electronics," he told his mother, "and I'm trying to get a civil service job."

"But you're better than all this," Honey said when Willy was driving her to the airport in a car he had borrowed from one of the unmarried couples at the house.

"Spoken like a true mother." Then Willy's voice was sympathetic. "You'd still want me to be an archaeologist."

"Or something."

"And work hard—and get married—and—"

"How's Eva?" his mother asked him.

"She may be coming over in August," Willy said.

"Maybe you'll bring her to Connecticut."

"I might at that."

But, of course, he didn't. For by the time August came around and his girl from three years earlier arrived in California, Willy was deeply involved in the new guerrilla group known as the Symbionese Liberation Army.

Chapter Seventeen

Like a talented adman who aims for the perfect umbrella words to explain the good points of the product or service he is selling, Cinque spent hours pouring over a dictionary, thesaurus and books by revolutionaries that Mizmoon brought from the library searching for a name for his revolutionary band.

Carefully, he analyzed what he wanted to convey. His group would be an army, certainly. His soldiers would fight with guns, if necessary. But, unlike the Black Panthers and other Afro-American protesters, his army would not be made up of blacks only or work for blacks only. Rather, the group he had in mind would fight for browns and whites (as well as blacks) who hadn't had a break and would push for social justice for women as well as men.

One day Cinque came upon the word "symbiosis," which delighted his eye and mind. Here was a word that described the living together of two dissimilar organisms, which was the exact description of the army of soldiers with dissimilar backgrounds that he hoped to put together. So, from that day on, Cinque began using the word "symbiosis" in the letters he wrote in Mizmoon's apartment to be taken around to known radicals who were possible recruits for his revolutionary project.

In August, Cinque made a presentation to the faithful, who

included Mizmoon, Nancy Ling Perry (by then having occasional dates with Russ Little, whose relationship with Robyn Steiner was strained) and Russ and Willy. Also present was Thero Wheeler, who had escaped early in the month from Vacaville with the help of Nancy Ling Perry and Cinque. And this time Cinque shared the name of his new army with his followers, who applauded both the name and the concept. All, that is, but the recent escapee, who declared that the whole idea of the army as a way of life was "shit." Nor was he impressed with Cinque's symbolic seven-headed cobra, which the General Field Marshal presented to the group in the form of a crude pen drawing and which he explained with a pointer.*

As Cinque told his friends, the seven heads of the cobra stood for cooperation, self-reliance, work for the good of all, personal responsibility, productivity, creativity and faith. Not a bad seven-way code for any group, and one that was not original with Cinque but was "borrowed" from a revolutionary group of blacks in the Bay Area. But then Cinque went on (and on and on some more, as he always did) with the words and theorizing that would amuse, puzzle and terrify readers of his communiqués later on.

The seven heads of the cobra, he said, could stand also for the many races and religions represented by members of his group. And the ancient snake with its many branches had occult significance from way back and would bring good fortune to the cause (as would the lucky number seven). This last was titillating to Nancy Ling Perry, an astrology freak, but turned off Thero Wheeler, which Cinque might have anticipated had he been a little less enthusiastic. (All the sevens along the way that had promised good times ahead for Thero had not paid off.) Still, Thero owed a debt for his escape to Cinque that he could not forget.

As a political heavy (he was a Venceremos comrade inside Folsom prison) and brilliant strategist in his confrontations with "the Man," Thero, who was in the Vacaville stress program when Cinque was in prison, was respected as a "jailhouse lawyer" and had more followers among his fellow convicts than Cinque would ever know. Still, in prison, Cinque and Thero had been good friends. "They did a lot of whistling in the wind about the revolution that would be led by

---

* Later, a wood carving of the cobra (which many attributed to Camilla) was made by Cinque, who, Russ says, "could do anything."

blacks," said someone who watched both in BCA, where they talked within earshot of smirking, disbelieving guards about the hour and the day when the push would start. "And after Cinque went to Soledad, he sent word by Willy Wolfe to Thero to take over his Unisight program."

Later, after Cinque had escaped without stirring up much of a fuss, Thero had determined to do the same. His first step was to write a letter denouncing his old friends in Venceremos, which was intercepted by authorities and put down in his record as a credit. Next, he asked to be transferred to an outside hospital for help for a severe stomach disorder, which was substantiated by a reputable doctor. Thereafter he requested a review by a judge, which was approved. But on the day before his scheduled hearing, Thero walked out of the prison orchard where he was working and was not seen again by the authorities until long after Patricia Hearst's kidnapping. Only later was his escape route determined.

Nancy Ling Perry and probably Mizmoon were waiting near the prison gate in a car. They opened the trunk and Thero climbed in. And in minutes they were speeding to Palo Alto to meet Cinque. Only when the time came for Thero to change cars did he learn that the mastermind behind his escape was his old prison associate Donald DeFreeze, known as Cinque.

At Mizmoon's apartment, where he was to hide, Thero met no blacks. Moreover, the few whites who came by did not look on him as their leader. Cinque, it appeared, had grabbed the top spot. Clearly, Thero's plan, which called for only a small band of protesting black revolutionaries, was not to be. Instead, Cinque was embarked on a project far more radical than anything Thero had dreamed, and called for a life-style that, in his opinion, could only lead to suicide.

At the outset, Cinque's group invited Thero to read the proposed communiqué in which the SLA would be introduced, and in which the SLA would take credit for Thero Wheeler's escape. Knowing that he would be picked up within days if the message went out, Thero said no thanks, and this refusal caused intense resentment in the group. After that, fearing he might be killed, Thero could not wait to get away, but he didn't manage his escape for another two months. (Thereafter he hid out with a woman friend out of state until after Cinque had burned to death in the Los Angeles fire.)

In July of '73, Willy made a commitment that would lead to his death. He was feeling low, he told his father by letter, and had considered taking off East "but have too many responsibilities so I better stay and struggle." Simultaneously, all principals who would move to center stage with the SLA were going through change. Mizmoon visited her family in Santa Barbara but left them no telephone number nor the address of the new Oakland hideaway where she was living with Thero, Nancy and Cinque. About this time, she also asked to be called Zoya, which was the name of a Russian saboteur woman hanged by Germans in 1941, rather than Mizmoon, but even in her immediate circle the name never quite took.

Like Mizmoon (now Zoya), Nancy (now Fahizah) was no longer in touch with her family. To her brother and to Rudy, for whom she worked until August in the Fruity Rudy stand, she said that she would be moving around and would have no telephone. Once she stopped working, Nancy had no paycheck to turn over to Cinque (who could not risk applying for a job, nor could Thero), so the foursome lived on the small salary Mizmoon brought home from the library, from Nancy's expert shoplifting and from money contributed by sympathizers in the Bay Area who were interested if not committed.

Two persons close to members of the SLA in its early days, watching with concern as their friends became more and more interested in guns, began to back away. In August Gary Atwood went home with his wife to New Jersey, where Angela's sister, Elena, was married. Afterward, in Indiana, as he and his wife drove west, he made a decision to re-enter the university at Bloomington as a law student and not to return to the Coast with his wife, who drove on alone to her doom. And Robyn Steiner, who after two years with Russ Little was pulling away from him and the others as she saw flaws in the propositions set forth by Cinque, moved out of Peking Man House and away from Russ. (This was before Thero Wheeler arrived from Vacaville in the trunk of Cinque's car.) Robyn lived for a time with the Harrises, but after the SLA's first headline-making "hit," she headed home to Florida, where she has been incommunicado for several years.

That same summer, as his relationship with Robyn was coming to an end, Russ slept sometimes with Rayne Alexander, who lived next to Peking Man House, and also with Angel, who was still then on the fence. He also was getting to know Nancy Ling Perry, who as time went on became his special "girl" in the SLA.

Then the busy revolutionaries moved out of Peking Man House. Rayne did not hear from Russ after he left the house next door in July 1973 and did not see Willy after he moved out in September. Only much later did she learn from newspaper reports that Russ, who paid rent at Peking Man House through September but did not come back, was dividing his time between the apartment shared by Cinque, Mizmoon and Nancy Ling Perry (Thero having left) and the Harrises, and that Willy and Joe Remiro had taken over a small bungalow in the 4600 block on Bond Street from a friend Willy had met in his work with Oakland's fighting-mad Coalition to Save Our Schools. That both of her friends were busy night and day with their revolutionary projects and that Russ had one or more new love interests Rayne might have surmised, and she would have been correct. The summer was as busy on a political and personal level as any either one had known.

Both Russ, who was on welfare, and Willy, still at work in the factory, where he would like to have organized laborers, were going as often as possible to see prisoners at Folsom, Vacaville, San Quentin and Chino prisons. They were called regularly by Cinque, Mizmoon and Nancy, who were formulating the introductory campaign for the Symbionese Liberation Army, which was by then a reality. And both were perfecting their marksmanship with guns with the help of Joe Remiro, who was also having a busy year.

In late April, Joe had left North Peralta Community College, where he was getting straight A's in auto mechanics, to go to Wounded Knee, South Dakota, to fight with the Indians in the first armed engagement he had known since Vietnam. He returned on crutches, but made up his work at college. However, he did not sign up for a new semester. By then the war was over (America's part in it, at least), and he cut all ties to the Vietnam Veterans but went heavy into guns. According to a former housemate, he bought guns, conducted gun classes, went to range practice with others with guns, talked guns, guns, guns with the men he lived with, who were becoming concerned about his intensity, and with the girls he slept with, who (like the ones who slept with Russ) were apparently fascinated.

In the summer of '73 both Russ and Joe were involved at one time or another with Nancy and Angela, eventually lining up with one for each (Nancy for Russ and Angela for Joe). But at the same time, Russ could not bring himself to break off his alliance with Robyn, who had then moved in with the Harrises. Often he went to Robyn from Angela, or from Nancy to Robyn, who, he maintains later, meant more to him in his life on the outside than any other woman. And Willy, too, was romantically involved. While not as peripatetic as the other two, he had a sexually active fall. Because in late August Eva arrived from Sweden.

Whether or not Eva's appearance was disturbing to Willy when he was so deeply involved with Cinque and the others in the new SLA is not known, but Willy's mother felt reassured by the fact that the girl Willy had known in Europe would be living close to her son in California. ("I believed from Willy's letters that he was in love with her.") And whether Eva was sympathetic toward the armed struggle that Willy and his friends were anticipating (or was even aware that urban guerrilla warfare was in the offing) is not known. A quiet girl who, according to Russ Little, "just sat there," she did not get seriously involved in the SLA because after a few months in this country, she was deported. (Having come in on an I–94 Visitors Visa for a two-month period, she was not allowed to work in the country, which was a ruling that she violated.) In the meantime, however, she slept repeatedly with Willy but at the same time—either through her own choice or because her lover so advised—lived away from him in a room close to the restaurant where, through the help of Angela Atwood, she had found a job as a waitress. And it was as a waitress that she was introduced to the third person close to Willy who came to the Bay Area from far away to stay with him in the year 1973. The newcomer was Willy's father, who visited Oakland for a week in October and went home to go over for the rest of his life the events of his stay with his son.

The day before he left for the Coast, Dr. Wolfe received a letter from Willy that assured him, "Got my pad, I'll be able to entertain in style." He had no phone, he said, but gave his father the number of the big house in front of his little one. ("They're my friends.") And five days later Dr. Wolfe made contact and moved into the bungalow, to sleep on an air mattress in one of the two small bedrooms that Willy shared with Joe. And there he met Eva.

"Was she pretty?" Willy's mother asked her divorced husband after he had returned from the Coast, and he replied, "Not to me, she wasn't." The reply was so quick Honey wondered if the man made an advance of some kind. (Later her hunch was halfway confirmed by Willy's half brother Ben, who says that Willy told him that his father "made a pass at one of the girls on the Coast," which was disappointing to him. To this, Ben had replied, "Don't let it get you down; he's been making passes at my wife for years.") Possibly because the family resents Dr. Wolfe's involvement with Sharon while he was wedded to Honey, all are suspicious of him now, which gets a "no comment" from the doctor. To reporters who have asked him about Eva, he has said she was "gorgeous" and that on the first night of his stay, when Eva left Willy's house to go her room, he said to his son, "Most guys have been looking for something like that all of their lives. Don't tell me you're going to let it walk out of here." According to him, on the other nights during his visit Eva stayed in one of the bedrooms with Willy, but at no time did he hear anything about a plan to marry. "That didn't come up until the following Christmas when Willy talked to others in the family about going to Sweden." He says that when he was in California, Willy and Joe and the others were so busy with prisoners and getting permission to march in the Veterans Day parade and doing all kinds of other things "that we didn't have time for a long, personal talk."

"Willy saw to that," says Russell Little, who says that everyone around Willy was concerned that the arrival of Willy's father, who was definitely "Establishment," would get in the way of plans for the SLA.

"Russ and Joe," says a reporter who followed the group, "and Cinque, Mizmoon and Nancy [as well as Willy and Camilla and the others who would come in later] were going off in all directions about this time." Yet Dr. Wolfe, who stayed nights in the little house that Willy had rented with Joe, saw nothing but a few books, like *The Autobiography of Malcolm X*, that seemed to him like "high-school stuff" and did not sense that lightning was about to strike.

Suspecting nothing, Dr. Wolfe found nothing. He lived innocently in the thunderous path of the SLA storm but saw and heard nothing to make him believe his son was involved in anything more than a protest against government corruption ("and wasn't he entitled to complain in this period of Watergate?") and post-Vietnam disillusionment. "In the week that I was with Willy, there wasn't a gun in the house—I know because I would have found it when I reached down in a box the boys had moved into the house to get a towel or something. Nor did I ever see a Negro with Willy and the others, which I remembered later when I read that the leadership of the SLA was black. Nor did I ever see evidence of drugs, which I would recognize." All true. Willy and the others weren't about to wave guns around in front of Dr. Wolfe in this formative period of the SLA. And they were not about to call attention to their bungalow by meeting in it with the only two blacks outside prison thought to be members of the SLA (after all, Cinque and Thero Wheeler were escaped convicts). And they had no drugs in the house because all in the group were into physical fitness, and all who had been on drugs (including heavy users like Joe Remiro and Nancy Ling Perry) had quit cold.

During his stay Dr. Wolfe, who, according to one of Willy's California friends, brought in "good booze" and argued his pro-capitalist views over meals that Willy stirred up in pots or a wok, may have wondered at the jobs that all in the group had settled for. ("Remiro was a mechanic, Eva was a waitress, Willy had been working in a factory.") And he probably sensed that the fathers and grandfathers of Willy's new pals weren't products of Yale. ("I got the feeling Ace thought of himself as slumming with Willy's low-class friends," says Russ Little.) But he could not know that most of the ones he met through Willy were moving out of their day-to-day jobs at this time to support themselves through crime.

On September 30, the day Willy wrote his "come on" letter to his father, Mizmoon and Nancy Ling Perry had robbed an Oakland florist at gunpoint of four hundred or six hundred dollars (depending on whether you believe the robbers or the police). After driving away from the shop on Piedmont Avenue, they went to a nearby park where they abandoned their van, which was picked up within the hour by police, who auctioned off the car a few months later.

By coincidence, on the same day, back in Berkeley, Camilla Hall tearfully left her job as a temporary gardener with the East Bay Regional Park District (which had been pressured by a women's group six months before to take on female groundskeepers for a trial period). Camilla had loved her job, and both she and her tough old supervisor were sorry to say goodbye. No one knows whether Camilla saw the love of her life between then and October 10, when Mizmoon quit

213

her janitor's job (taking the library's passkeys with her, which later worried employees there), but probably she made contact. Alone and without a job, she may have waited outside the library one night for Mizmoon, who had moved already from her cozy little house on Parker Street to go with Cinque and the others to recruit for the SLA. Probably Mizmoon did not talk about the robbery she had pulled off, but surely she challenged Camilla's "fight for what's right" beliefs with her commitment to Cinque's project.

Camilla, however, did not join up in the beginning. Like Angela Atwood, who had not committed herself to Venceremos and would not come into the SLA until later, she was a romantic. Only because she was in love would she be pulled into the army. In a way, so would Angela, who, after her separation from her husband and her brief affair with Russ Little, became seriously involved with Joe Remiro.

To Dr. Wolfe, as he thinks back to October 1973, Joe Remiro was "a little mechanic" who was unusually uptight the week he was around. There were good reasons for this. Today Russ Little denies that Cinque demanded an armed act of violence to underscore any new SLA member's commitment to the cause. But, if the truth is otherwise, as many reporters believe, this was a week in which Joe Remiro proved himself worthy of initiation.

Surely before this time Remiro had robbed and perhaps burglarized to obtain guns and ammunition. But he was not actually linked with armed robbery until after Friday, October 12 (the day before Dr. Wolfe flew home to Pennsylvania), when he is charged with having held up the owner of a van and driven off in the stolen vehicle, which he allegedly stripped down to remodel a Chevy van owned by SLA members.

After Mizmoon and Nancy had abandoned their "hot" van (and with new members who needed to get around), the SLA was desperate for fast getaway cars, one of which Dr. Wolfe unwittingly provided. "When I was in California, I gave Willy three hundred dollars to buy an Oldsmobile convertible, which was used later by Nancy Ling Perry as a getaway car when she tried to burn down a house," he says. "All I knew when I bought it was that I hadn't been giving Willy any money since he left school and that with all the rushing around he was doing he needed a car."

On the first night he had the beige Oldsmobile (which was to tie him later to the SLA), Willy left his father at the Convention Hall, where he was to give a lecture on hypnotism, and drove to a meeting of the Oakland school board at the request of friends he had met through his work with the Coalition to Save Our Schools. The October night was a tense one because at the meeting Marcus Foster, Oakland's superintendent of schools, was scheduled to propose a plan for ID cards for students in schools where there had been violence and vandalism to keep out truants, nonstudent criminals and outside dope peddlers. Sensing opposition from Panthers like Elaine Brown and Bobby Seale, who were in the room, and from others in the community who called the plan "fascist," Foster avoided discussion of the cards (which would provide the police with a computerized record of each schoolchild), but, even so, protesters, led by Vera Silverman, a black mother, marched menacingly to the front of the room, where Vera cut into slices an ID card belonging to one of her children—a card like those contemplated for all Oakland schoolchildren.

Later Willy reported what happened at the school-board meeting to BCA members at Vacaville and to Cinque and his SLA cadre in Oakland, but that night he said nothing to his father. "I didn't hear Foster's name until a month later when I was back home and heard on the radio that the black superintendent of schools out in Oakland had been killed, and then I certainly didn't suspect that anyone I had met in California through Willy would be tied in." Later he was to find out he was wrong.

For, as a result of Willy's report of the school-board meeting, Cinque made a decision that Foster, whom he thought of as an oreo type (black on the outside and white on the inside), would have to go. And soon after (within two weeks after Dr. Wolfe had flown home), Nancy Ling Perry rented two new hideouts. One was on Seventh Avenue in Oakland, within a quarter of a mile of the School Administration building where Foster had his office. The other was a small house in nearby Concord, which would be pointed out for years to come as the planning place for the Foster murder.

It was at the second place, at Christmastime, that Willy left his car while going home. By then he knew the little house well—because on many a night he had stayed there with Cinque, putting an old talent to work for the SLA. Using a drill, much like the dental drill his father had given him for lapidary work on the rocks he had brought home from his travels to western states, he hollowed out the tips of bullets to be fired from a .380 Walther automatic which others packed with cyanide. His careful workmanship got an appreciative nod from the black leader he had met at Vacaville, who by this time was as close to Willy as Ace.

Chapter Eighteen

On a dark, drizzly November evening, less than a month after Willy's father had gone home, Dr. Marcus Foster was killed by a German-made .380 caliber automatic pistol in the parking lot behind the Oakland School Administration building, where he had met with the city's Board of Education. With him was his deputy superintendent. Robert W. Blackburn, who was wounded but did not die in the explosion of gunfire that apparently came from three assailants. On the day after the shooting—as a numbed community asked itself *Why?*—a letter dropped into the mailbox of Berkeley radio station KPFA took credit for the slaying in the name of the Symbionese Liberation Army, which never before had been mentioned in print.

The message, labeled "Communiqué No. 1" under a drawing of a seven-headed cobra, called for the "execution by cyanide bullets of Dr. Foster and Mr. Blackburn." Because it was delivered after the fact as a "warrant order by the Court of the People," it was considered a crank letter by police and given little credence by the San Francisco *Chronicle* and the Oakland *Tribune*, which received photocopies of the original (written by Nancy Ling Perry). But later a bullet that had passed through Foster's chest was found in his shirt pocket by Alameda County Coroner's Chief Investigator Roland Prahl, who discovered the slug contained cyanide. And, with that, the SLA was a force in Oakland to be reckoned with. Along with a reward of $10,000 in state funds pledged by Governor Ronald Reagan for information leading to the arrest and conviction of the slayers, and another $10,000 pledged for the same cause by the city council, a third offer of $10,000 was made for help in the Foster case by the Oakland *Tribune* once the SLA came into the picture. Now, police believed, the case would break.

As the ante went up, however, no one stepped forward to talk and claim. Still, at the hideout Nancy Ling Perry had rented just outside the city of Concord, at 1560 Sutherland Court, all was not optimism. The mood of Oakland following Foster's death was not what Cinque had expected when at the end of September he is reported to have said to his followers, "This nigger's got to go." And no one understood better than Willy why his leader had suggested the hit. After all, Willy was the lieutenant who had reported back from a meeting of parents belonging to the Coalition to Save Our Schools that every black in town was enraged at "the white nigger" for urging the adoption of the ID cards and in-house police.

At Foster's funeral three thousand mourners crammed into the church and an even larger number followed the coffin to its burial place. And that evening another five thousand mourners, including many of the tough young blacks whose mothers had accused Foster of wanting to label them criminals, attended Foster's memorial service in the cavernous Oakland Coliseum and sang along with the thousand-voice choir in praise of their fallen school leader. A few shook their fists at the unseen murderers, but most bowed their heads when Dr. Foster's widow urged the mourners to "pray for Dr. Foster's assassins," whose identities even to this day are disputed.

According to Patty Hearst and Jack Scott, who heard the story from the Harrises, Zoya (Mizmoon) fired the handgun that pumped the cyanide-tipped bullets into Foster's body; then Fahizah (Nancy Ling Perry) fired with the Rossi .38 that was to incriminate Russ Little, while Cinque, standing back in the bushes, hit Blackburn with a shotgun blast. When Joe Remiro and Russell Little were picked up and jailed (and later imprisoned) for the murder, "Willy really felt bad," said Emily Harris. She has insisted that Patty made up her testimony that Russ and Joe were in a car near the shooting as a backup. "We had talked to her for over a year about how they were innocent," she has said. In the meantime, Russ in San Quentin and

Joe in Folsom have served years of time for a crime they and others say they did not commit. Like all who became associated in any way with the SLA, they were doomed once Foster was hit. "The assassination was an error," says Russ Little and agrees with Emily's opinion that "the SLA seriously misjudged the way the community would respond." He also believes the press exaggerated the grief.

Willy, who had passed along the feelings of the community about Foster's "fascist" programs as he had read them, had given misinformation to the Black Cultural Association at Vacaville as well as to Cinque and must have had squeamish moments as Oakland's mourning for the superintendent continued through November into December. For by this time, he, like his friends in and out of prison, had to know that he and others who brought news from the outside had made a serious two-way reportorial mistake. First, he had misread the emotions of the parents who opposed Foster, who were proving that they were not nearly as caught up in the school controversy as he had been. And second, and even more important, Willy had made a slipshod investigation of Foster's police plan. (By October, when SLA members were renting an apartment on Oakland's sleazy Seventh Avenue where they could retreat after the shooting, Foster was quietly backing away from his controversial ID plan and was publicly stating his opposition to armed policemen in the schools.) Apparently Willy had forgotten the fact-finding lessons he had learned at Mount Hermon. He was not blamed by the prisoners but he must have felt guilty as Cinque lost face.

At Vacaville and the other prisons where his volunteer work had been to describe to convicts the mood of the community, many former friends of the SLA felt let down. Far from applauding Cinque for declaring with his act of murder that he and his followers were not stoned-out Berkeley yakkers but were willing to go all the way in their fight against repression, the prisoners felt sick, not so much because Foster was dead but because they had been misinformed. One look at the grieving face of any friend of the late Superintendent from the Bay Area was all they needed to know about how seriously they had been misled.

Several sources say that more than one prisoner told Willy, "Cinque's gotta go." Surely nothing could have been more confusing to Willy, who in the preceding months had read everything he could lay his hands on about Uruguay's Movement for National Liberation—Cinque's inspiration and pattern for the Symbionese Liberation Army. Willy had studied the Tupamaros (another name for the members of Uruguay's MNL), whose movement had it roots in the Socialist Party, and he had come to believe that armed struggle was the only way to effect change.

In Pennsylvania, in December 1973, when Willy's father said that he had read of Foster's death and "wasn't that an ugly thing?" Willy answered, "Maybe he deserved it." This was similar to Mizmoon's reaction to her brother's "it's a tragedy Marcus Foster was killed," to which she retorted, "Tragedy? The guy was in it with the pigs." None of the four living onetime members of the SLA (the two Harrises, Russ Little and Joe Remiro) has expressed regret at any time for the shooting itself, although each one has admitted that killing "the jive ass nigger," as Bill Harris has called him, was a tactical error.

Nevertheless, the lives of the SLA members were affected by Foster's death. Cinque, Mizmoon and Nancy Ling Perry, in their "safe house" in Concord, stayed indoors with drawn shades, which led neighbors to believe "the place is a dope den." Inside, Nancy tapped off another message to the press: Because the school authorities had announced there would be no ID program, the SLA nobly agreed to suspend "the death warrant" against all members of the Board of Education. But still on the attack, she went on to accuse the media and those who tried to memorialize Foster as "fascist." She, at least, had no doubt about the righteousness of the hit. And Cinque too, said others who saw him then, "had a strange, new confidence."

In nearby Oakland, meanwhile, the Harrises continued to go back and forth to their jobs from their two-bedroom apartment with its clean linens, sparkling silver and handsome appointments. But they too were making plans. For even as he paid rent for this apartment, Bill was leasing two others in the area, one of which he used for a mail drop and the other, rented under the name William Kinder, for a safe house. Robyn Steiner lived with them until December, when she called it quits and returned to Florida, to be replaced by Angela Atwood, who had gained weight, no longer shaved her legs, wore a bandana around her head and looked, say acquaintances, "like an Italian peasant woman." By then she was having an affair with Joe Remiro, who, according to a friend, "was right for her." Like Camilla Hall, Angela was not yet a member of the SLA but was not turned off either. After all, her lover was involved.

Camilla, without a job at this time, went home to Illinois for the holidays and sent a Christmas greeting from there to Mrs. Soltysik, the mother of Mizmoon, whose attraction for Camilla was as intense as ever. (Mizmoon also sent a card and New Year's letter to her mother but did not go to Santa Barbara to see her family, who would not see her again. Between Thanksgiving and Christmas, Joe Remiro wrote to his mother that he would not be seeing her for some time, and Nancy sent a Christmas card to her mother with no return address.)

When Angela did not write home at Christmas, her sister, Elena, called her at the Harrises'. "Angela said she would be going away for a while but that, whatever happened, I must always remember she was doing something she believed in and that she loved me very much." Neither of the Harrises warned their friends or parents that they were making a change. And it was only afterward that Bill's old SAE pledge brother and war buddy Larry Leach remembered something unusual about Bill and Emily from the time he had visited them and their friends in California. "Only one person I met—and that was Robyn Steiner—talked about any kind of professional career or legitimate business in the future."

Shortly after Christmas, Bill Harris's mother and stepfather visited Bill and Emily in California and suspected nothing. "I saw the Mao poster over the mantel," said Bill's stepfather, who once served with the FBI, "but I put this down as a passing phase, not as a commitment." And Bill's attractive mother enjoyed going to good restaurants with the children and her new husband and thought Bill and Emily were "fine."

Cinque wrote to no one from his Concord safe house but told at least one black friend whom he saw in this period, and to whom he seemed depressed, that he missed his children "and thought a lot about going east to bring them back here." Seldom, even on nights when he consumed more plum wine than usual, did he show his soft side to his troops.

In December, when Joe Remiro moved out of the Bond Street bungalow to live with Angela at the Harrises', Willy moved into Angela's little house at 1834 Delaware Street in Berkeley, only a few blocks from the apartment where Steven Weed lived with Patricia Hearst. Whether he ever had a chance brush with the girl he would help to kidnap as she passed him in the Wash House laundromat nearby or shopped for Steve's supper in neighborhood stores is not known, but that he and Angela before him were aware of her presence in the neighborhood is more than likely. ("No one who lived near Steve and Patty could miss them," says a neighbor. "As Steve and Patty walked along hand in hand in their neatly pressed clothes, they looked like a couple out of the twenties and were as out of character on the Berkeley campus as people in a novel by F. Scott Fitzgerald.") Nor did he ever mention the heiress in his letters home, which he continued to write until close to the middle of December.

On December 7, Willy typed off a letter to his father's wife, Sharon. "This being an electric typewriter," he said, "and the time being 2 A.M., this will prove to be an interesting letter, I'm sure, especially since the typewriter is a bit broken. Things are going well here though hectically. I'll probably only be here shortly, but for the time being you can use this address." He told Sharon to ask Ace to sell two stock certificates "as I need the money." He ended with "I may be coming East for Xmas but don't spread the word, as it may be spreading false hopes."

The weekend after he sent the letter, Willy called his old friend Mike, who was living back in the United States with his sister in Queens after a disillusioning experience as a Franciscan friar in Brazil.

"What happened down in that monastery, anyway?" Willy asked the black man who had been his friend for as long as he could remember. "Why'd you come back?"

"I don't like cow corn three times a day—and roaches on the table—and rats in my bed."

"So you're not a Catholic anymore?"

Mike said that wasn't true. "That's all that pulled me through; I'm just not a monk, that's all."

"Well, that has its advantages," Willy said slyly. 'How are your nights?"

"Busy," Mike said. He told Willy he had been taking care of his mother, "who had a stroke while I was gone." He said his sister who had sent him the money to get home "had spent thirteen thousand dollars for doctors and nurses by the time I got back, so taking over for her here was the least I could do." But now Mike's mother was dead and he had gone back to work.

"For Celanese?"

Mike laughed. "For a company where the boss in our office doesn't make as much after fifteen years as I made my first week at Celanese."

"Where are you?"

"Working for the telephone company."

"You gotta be kidding—why that's the most monopolistic, capitalistic . . ."

"It gives me what I need to help Mary support the house and have a garden out back and . . ."

"You're selling out to the fascists who are wrecking America."

"America didn't look wrecked to me after Brazil; I could have kissed the ground."

"I need to talk to you."

"That's a good idea," Mike said. "Come to see me when you get home."

"I will," said Willy as he hung up. And in another two weeks he was sitting with Mike in his sister's sitting room in Queens. "So it wasn't so good in South America?"

Mike said the natives around the monastery were desperately poor and "everybody had fleas" and there was no money to help anyone "as the church promised when I joined the order and went down there." He said there were Italian, Irish and German monks "and only the Germans had any money" and "outside of the ones from Germany and the bishop, nobody could afford a car, which costs about three times as much down there as here." Mike said he wasn't as critical of American business as he had been when he and Willy lived together. "I've been shaken down."

Willy said Mike should know that everything in America wasn't the way it should be either and that he ought to see the inside of a prison, to which Mike replied that if it wasn't for his religion, which had helped him through a lot of close calls, he might be in one himself— and, no thanks, he'd stay away. Then the two old friends shook hands for the last time. For two weeks later Willy got the call from Bill Harris telling him to get the hell back to the Coast, where his two best friends, Russ Little and Joe Remiro, had just been jailed.

PART FOUR

The Age of Aquarius

Chapter Nineteen

In the month before Willy had left for the East, support had dwindled for the SLA, which in the beginning had taken in as much as a hundred dollars a week from interested radicals. And on his return, with Russ and Joe busted and, with them, their paychecks— and with Bill, Emily and Angela without salaries too—how could they carry on? Knowing that Bill and Cin and the others would be looking to him for a windfall that he had promised to bring back from his father's stockbroker, Willy must have done a lot of thinking as he approached the Oakland railroad station after a transcontinental train trip.

In the station he was met by a young woman in a blond wig and a neat blue pants suit who was pretending to be interested in a plastic glass-studded tower at the souvenir counter. Recognizing the girl as Mizmoon, he stood back as she put down the table decoration and nooded for him to follow her out front, where she slid behind the wheel of a green-and-white Chevrolet van parked at the curb. Without speaking, Willy climbed in beside her. She then told him that the car, bought that day by Bill Harris, was to be used in Daly City, where two days earlier she and Emily had rented a house.

Clearly much had happened to Willy's friends in the weeks he'd been away. And as he rode to the safe house where he would be hiding, he learned what.

To begin with, on the previous Thursday—January 10—Russ and Joe had driven to Concord in their red van with a pack of leaflets they'd had printed for the Symbionese Liberation Army. Something about the van with its red curtains riding through Sutherland Court hours before dawn aroused the suspicion of a policeman who was patrolling the place. So he had stopped and frisked the two in the oddball car and found bullets in the pockets of Russ and a gun on Joe and pulled out a gun of his own.

In the shooting that followed, Joe ducked into the bushes but Russ got nicked and was carted off first to the hospital and then to Concord jail, where he was put behind bars. There he was soon joined by Joe, who had walked down a driveway (with the Walther PP 380 automatic in his pants pocket that police ballistics would connect with the Foster murder) and surrendered to police at 5:30 the next morning after crawling from under a bush and finding the whole neighborhood under siege.

Although Russ and Nancy had been posing as George and Nancy DeVoto on Sutherland Court in Concord and Russ had told the officer who had exchanged shots with him the night before that he was on his way to the DeVoto residence, no one during the day following the shooting visited the house where Russ and Joe had been headed. Still, Cinque, Mizmoon and Nancy could not expect to be left alone for long. So what they had to do was get out, the faster the better, although not before getting rid of everything connected with the SLA.

"What they should have done," said one member afterward, "was to burn up all the papers in the fireplace." But Nancy Ling Perry had another idea. She would destroy the evidence by burning up the whole house, which she attempted (unsuccessfully) a little after six o'clock in the evening.

The weekend after the fire the house on Sutherland Court became a laboratory for crime reporters working on the Foster story and for police officers on the trail of the SLA. And what a lab. There were guns, bullets, drills, cyanide, ambush diagrams, phony ID's, license plates from stolen cars and first drafts of communiqués to the press. And along with all this were fingerprints of Donald DeFreeze, escaped convict; Patricia Soltysik, who was known to have lived with DeFreeze in Berkeley; Nancy Ling Perry, author of the undestroyed communiqués about the murder of Foster; and Willy Wolfe, about whom little was known other than that he was younger than the others, had lived on Chabot Road with Russell Little and on Bond Street with Joe Remiro and was the owner of the Oldsmobile that had been seen racing away from the house on Sutherland Court just before the fire.

His car had not been found when Willy returned to the Bay Area and went with Mizmoon to Daly City for an SLA meeting, which, Bill Harris says, "was not a happy event." Three years after the reunion, when he was interviewed at San Quentin, Bill said, "We were glad to see Willy the way you're glad to see somebody you like at a funeral; you're happy in one way but underneath you're sad." Just a little more time, all believed, and the SLA plan for social revolution would have been under way. But, now, with Russ and Joe locked up, and with the names of possible contributors to the cause in the hands of the police, what was left of the SLA "would have to cut loose its infrastructure of support people," the group knew, and go it alone. Even Willy's hoped-for windfall had failed to materialize.

On the evening Willy returned, he, Cinque, Bill Harris and three of the girls sat on their sleeping bags in the center of the front room in Daly City and talked of the next major revolutionary action to be taken by the SLA. As they thought aloud, Fahizah, introducing herself as Nancy Ling Perry in a letter she was typing, explained to the media that Russ and Joe were not the killers of Marcus Foster, that she had not meant to burn down the house at Concord ("just melt away any fingerprints") and that all units of the SLA had not been dangerous—but now "all will be offensively armed with cyanide bullets in all their weapons." She signed off as she had ended her first communiqué:"DEATH TO THE FASCIST INSECT THAT PREYS UPON THE LIFE OF THE PEOPLE."

"Beginning tonight," Cinque said, "we'll use our revolutionary names *only*. So, I'm Cinque." Then he nodded at Mizmoon, who said, "And I'm Zoya,," and at Nancy, who said, "And I'm Fahizah." Next came Bill Harris, who said, "Teko, that's me," and Emily, who said, "Yolanda," and Angel, who said, "Gelina." Which left only Willy, who said with a bow, 'And I am Kahjoh."

"Cujo?" said Fahizah. "Where did you find that?"

"It's a Central American Indian word."

"What does it mean?"

"Unconquerable."

"Cujo, the unconquerable," said Cinque, adding that he hoped it was a good omen for their first revolutionary kidnapping. Everybody looked up but Nancy, who went on typing. "We know the perfect person to exchange for Russ and Joe."

"Who?" asked Angel.

Cinque nodded at Nancy to open the file folder on the table beside her typewriter and show the others the clipping she had cut out of the San Francisco Examiner just before Christmas. It was a newspaper photo of a moustached young man and a smiling girl who were announcing their engagement. "Here she is," said Cinque, "the daughter of William Randolph Hearst."

Chapter Twenty

Of all who played a role in the SLA story, none was less understood or more abused than Steven Weed, who was living with Patty Hearst when she was kidnapped. Now married to a slim, bright girl of Patty's age whose name is Debby and whose father is a well-to-do doctor in Steve's home town of Palo Alto, he has been living for some time in his own home high in the Berkeley hills, from which he has been driving each day to UC's department of philosophy where he worked until recently as a teaching assistant. Without the droopy moustache and blowzy locks, which in 1974 turned off Americans who associated long hair with hippies and radicals, he looks younger than his years, well groomed and Establishment oriented, and is respected by colleagues and students. And most of the time, he is seemingly comfortable with himself. Until he talks about the Hearsts, that is. Then his frustration comes out. He moves his hands nervously and begins to apologize. "If I could just explain . . .

"I was trying to help," he says, "but everything I would say to reporters or on TV would come out wrong." He tries to smile. "It really got to be funny." He shakes his head. "I wasn't under the same kind of pressure that Patty was under, but . . ." His voice trails off, and one gets the feeling that in the intervening years he has been mulling the mistakes he made in the days that followed the abduction.

231

A shy man, given to pondering before he talks, he obviously wants to talk to someone (mainly Patty) about what it was like to be attacked at every turn for being in with the kidnappers, which was not true, or for being an oaf, which he is not. (He was valedictorian of his high school in Palo Alto, won a scholarship to Princeton and was captain there of the track team.)

The child of divorced parents with no East Coast connections and not uncommonly rich, Steve was not invited to join a club at Princeton and for a time turned to the counterculture for companionship and identity. He wore a beard, played a guitar, raised, sold and smoked a little pot, and helped his roommate, Doug Seaton, who was president of Princeton's SDS, organize a few marches and rallies. But he was never really committed to protesting the American way of life, and in his senior year, as graduation came close, he gave up "bullshitting about not caring about money" and sent out applications for a job.

A Californian at heart and an academician, he wrote to schools on the Coast seeking employment as a teacher and soon got an answer from a private school for girls in Hillsborough, California. "Come for an interview," said the letter from Crystal Springs School for Girls. And he did, and was accepted to teach math to seventh and eighth graders beginning the next fall.

As one of Crystal Springs' few male teachers, Steve received occasional telephone calls from breathy adolescent girls a few years past the age of kids like Vicki Hearst, whom he was teaching. Content in his cottage, which he shared with a young woman of his own age, Steve answered briefly and to scholastic point.

But, then, in 1970, Steve's phone was rung by Vicki's older sister, and this time Steve, who had split from his housemate of the year before, did not brush off his caller, who was new on the campus and a stunner. Yes, he thought he could help her with a junior-year math problem that her own instructor couldn't seem to explain.

So it was that in a matter of days Steve looked out his cottage window and saw a blue MG parked under a tree. And in another few minutes he was in the front seat listening with delight to the laughing, long-haired girl behind the wheel who told him, first thing, she was on the pill. Captivated by his visitor's independence and her social ease, which rivaled that of any college senior he had known in the

232

East, he was soon in bed with Vicki's big sister, who of course was Patty Hearst.

When they became lovers, Steve was twenty-three years old and Patty sixteen, "which would be enough to turn off Patty's parents," say the critics. But friends of Patty's family disagree. "No, Randy fell in love with Catherine when he was in his twenties and Catherine was sixteen, so that wouldn't be a hang-up. It was the Weed guy's style— he's not gutsy like the Hearsts."

Never during their three-year affair, when for most of the time they were with each other daily, did Patty berate Steve for any lack of macho. With money for her every want, she had no need or admiration for a young fellow hellbent to succeed in business. And with an IQ of 130 and the competitive drive to rise to the top of her class in school, she did have a need for Steve's intellectualism and affectionate tutoring, on which she thrived.

In her one year at Crystal, Patty earned the credits needed to graduate from high school a year early. And in the following year, when she went as a freshman to Menlo College (where she signed up to room with a discreet foreign student who told no one that Patty was spending her nights two miles away with Steven Weed), she earned all A's and was the top-ranked student in her class. And then came Berkeley, where Patty, with the knowledge but not the wholehearted approval of her parents, moved in with Steve, who had left Crystal Springs to work as a graduate student at UC. And there again she did exceptional work, which had not always been the case before.

In her years before Crystal Springs Patty had bounced from one convent selected by her mother, who is Roman Catholic, to another. (At one she refused to wear a uniform; in another she told a nun to go to hell; in all, she hated the praying and the discipline.) Bright enough to go from one grade to another even as she hopped around, she had not particularly enjoyed schoolwork until Crystal Springs, where, with Steve's help, she had studied hard and excelled. Then in her first year at college, she had come to enjoy the learning experience itself. Still, she had no special interest (other than to marry Steve and have babies), so at the end of her year at Menlo she took off for Europe, which both her parents and Steve encouraged. In the countries she visited, according to her tour director, she did not notice (or at least did not talk about) the obvious differences in living conditions between the very rich and the very poor, but when she returned to Berkeley she told Steve she was going to stay out of school for a quarter and work, "so I will know what it would be like to earn a living."

At Capwell's department store in Oakland, where Patty was first a salesclerk and then in billing, she got to know workers whose need for a paycheck made it impossible for them to leave a job as she could when working rules seemed unfair. Seeing this, Patty did not attempt to organize workers as Angela Atwood was doing at the same time at her restaurant in San Francisco, but she saw why unions had come about, which she had not thought about before. (And she spoke of this to friends at Berkeley, which she entered in January 1973, planning at first to major in science so that she could be a veterinarian, but switching later to Art History.) But for the most part she took little interest in social problems, concentrating instead on proving to Steve that she was the ideal helpmate. This paid off, and in December her parents announced her engagement.

During the first weeks of 1974, Patty and Steve selected the crystal, china, linen and good antique pieces they would be using after their wedding in June and looked ahead to the good life. But then, on Saturday, February 2, came a warning.

While she was clearing the dinner table about nine o'clock, Patty became aware of figures outside the frosted-glass entrance door of their apartment and called out to Steve. Later she reported that what she had seen were a "weird" woman and a tall, skinny "creepy" man who made her afraid.

Steve, also unnerved, opened the door, and Patty heard the woman outside mumble something about rentals in the building while the man stayed back. There wasn't much talk. After going on for a few seconds about a real-estate agent who had sent her there, the woman departed with her companion into the dark. Later, in a meeting with the FBI, Steve was shown a picture of Emily Harris as she looked at Indiana U and told the agents, "This one right here—grown older and dissipated-looking—could be the woman who was at the door." Whether the man was Willy·Wolfe or not Steve couldn't say, but on the Monday following the incident, when Patty was carried screaming from her apartment and dumped into the trunk of a convertible and driven away by the SLA, Willy was standing guard out front.

Moreover, on the Friday before the kidnapping, Willy met with the kidnappers, who by then had prepared a hiding place for Patty at 37

North Ridge Road in Daly City. "Plenty of closet space," the owner had told the "stewardesses" who came to see his freshly painted three-bedroom house. Opening a door off one of the bedrooms for "Toni" and "Candi" (who were really Mizmoon and Emily Harris), he was pleased to hear one or the other say, "Oh, nice, a walk-in." He sensed the girls were going to take the place, which they did, but for reasons they did not disclose. (Attached to the side of the house was a garage from which a passenger could be brought indoors without being seen from the street. And growing high outside the front picture window, which overlooks small, boxlike houses of working-class people, were tall, leggy bushes that almost covered the glass.) Little did the owner know as he pocketed the $335 the girls paid for one month's rent and a "good faith" deposit that the victim of "America's first political kidnapping" would be brought here on February 4.

As remembered by Patty Hearst, and told under oath, and by Steve Weed and dozens of neighbors, this is what happened that February night. About seven o'clock in the evening a blue Volkswagen, believed to be a scout car, stopped across the street from Patty and Steve's apartment. One of its two occupants, who wore a scarf over her hair and sat on the side near the curb, was probably Mizmoon; the other, described by a passer-by as a "male albino" (a description which she modified after seeing a picture of a suspect who was a large, masculine-looking girl), was probably Camilla Hall. (At the time, Camilla was not a member of the SLA, but on this night she could have been helping Mizmoon.) Neither passenger left the car in the next two hours, during much of which time the VW's motor was running.

Then, a little after nine, two other cars pulled into the street. The first was the green-and-white Chevrolet station wagon from Daly City; the second, a hijacked white Chevy convertible, its stunned owner blindfolded and gagged on the back seat. Each had three visible occupants (Nancy Ling Perry, Emily and Bill Harris, Cinque, Angela Atwood and Willy). And according to reports made later, all the people in the cars (other than Peter Benenson, the owner of the convertible, whose stay with the SLA would be brief) did a lot of switching from one car to another in the next few minutes.

Presently the station wagon backed quietly into the driveway and three figures approached the front door of the apartment. Much later Patty testified that Angela Atwood, "looking really weird in a big black coat," was the one who rang the doorbell. Patty said that she herself had been very tired that night, and after fixing some soup and a sandwich and taking a shower, she was stretched out on the couch in a bathrobe when Steve opened the door. Continuing, Patty said, "The woman was saying that she had a car in the basement and could she just telephone—and then two other people came bursting in behind her." Asked for a description of these two, Patty said that one was black and one was white. "They were Donald DeFreeze and William Harris."

About the ensuing events, there is ample testimony. While the black male intruder tied up Patty, the other man attacked Steve with a rifle butt, sending him to the hospital for a week. Neighbors who came to their doorways felt bullets whiz past their heads. Students who tried to take down the number of the kidnap car were fired on by automatic carbines. And girls who saw Patty carried out of the house watched in horror as the blue bathrobe fell away from her body. One undergraduate co-ed, who watched through a slit in a shade in an upstairs window across the street, left Berkeley the next day, never to return. "Seeing that naked girl thrown into the trunk of that car was too much."

Thereafter, at an unknown rendezvous spot, Patty was moved to the station wagon, and the convertible (with its owner) was abandoned. Then, after another harrowing ride, Patty testified, "The car stopped again and I was taken up a couple of stairs and down the hallway to what Cinque told me was a closet." Patty said that there was something "like carpeting" on the walls and that a foam pad was on the floor.

And there, still bound, she remained for an hour or more, until Cinque came in and told her that she was a prisoner of war and that if anything happened to his two comrades who were held in San Quentin as they awaited trial, the same would happen to her. Until then Patty had taken no account of the story about Little and Remiro (whom Cinque called Osceola and Bo), who, she learned, were being held for murder. Then Cinque told her, as she repeated afterward, that if she made any noise "they'd hang me up from the ceiling" and that if she tried to escape "they had cyanide bullets and would kill me."

Patty does not know how long after that she was left alone, but she

236

was glad a long time later (probably the next morning) to feel the door of the closet open. Cinque came in again, and this time he sat with her on the pad of foam. He was a member of the war council of the Symbionese Liberation Army, he explained, and was the person who had decided she should be kidnapped. He asked her to listen carefully while he read the SLA code of war.

"You are in a people's prison," he said. "And you will be treated in accordance with the rules of the Geneva Convention." He said that she would be provided with adequate food, exercise and medical aid. Then he talked through the door to Angela Atwood, who came in and led Patty blindfolded to the bathroom.

Angela by then seemed far different from the menacing kidnapper of the night before. Her voice was soothing as she sympathized with Patty, who was constipated and getting a cold and whose legs were cut and bruised from having been banged and scraped when she was dragged into the trunk of the getaway car. "I'm going to give you some different clothes," she said when Patty had finished in the bathroom and was floundering down the hall in the blue bathrobe she had worn from home, "but first I think somebody should wash those cuts. I'll get Cujo."

As Cinque had done earlier, Willy, introducing himself as Kahjoh (which sounded to the prisoner like Cujo), sat down beside Patty on the foam pad. Gently he lifted one of her legs and then the other from under the blue robe. Talking quietly about how the SLA was a multiracial group "dedicated to making the earth we share more beautiful," he swabbed Patty's cuts with warm, sudsy water. "There," he said, patting each leg dry. "You're going to be all right."

Patty dared to ask about Steve. "Was he hurt? Will he be all right?"

"He's fine; we heard this morning that he was taken to the hospital last night and released right away." Cujo then went out and came back with slacks and a shirt "which you might want to wear instead of that robe" and a pillow and a blanket "so you will be more comfortable." He said that he would go to the kitchen while she changed "and fix you some mint tea."

Next time Patty was taken to the bathroom she asked Angela, "Who's Cujo? A doctor?"

"His father's a doctor."

"What's his name?"

"Oh, no, you don't," said Angela. "And anyway, it wouldn't do you any good. Cujo's father was out here not long ago and he's completely sympathetic with everything."

What Angela and everyone else in the house did not know was that about the time she spoke these words, Willy Wolfe's father in Pennsylvania was calling the FBI.

Chapter Twenty-one

When Dr. Wolfe called the Bureau in Allentown, which he did on several occasions, beginning before the kidnapping, he was pleading for help.

"My son lived in Oakland with the man who's been arrested out there for killing the superintendent of schools," he told the special agent who talked with him on the telephone the first time he called. "Willy was an idealist who thought the world should be changed, but he would never have anything to do with that Symbionese Liberation Army they've been writing about or with murder." As the FBI man listened quietly, Willy's father told him that Willy had disappeared and he thought he knew why. "He's hiding out from members of the SLA who will be looking for him because he knows too much and because they know he's smart, anyway, and will want him with them."

The agent explained that, as the doctor probably knew, the FBI doesn't look for a mere missing person. "But we can post a stop notice in our FBI Identification Division and let you know if we get anything that way."

"You know," said Dr. Wolfe, "why I'm worried. What would you do if your son had disappeared after he'd been living with Remiro?"

"Remiro?"

"The one in Oakland who's accused of killing the superintendent."

"I'd call anywhere I could think of where he might be."

"Yeah, well, thanks."

Afterward Dr. Wolfe told Roxie that the agent was playing dumb. "Didn't know Remiro; come on."

"He might not know about him," Roxie told her father. "The FBI wouldn't get involved with a local murder."

"If the murder was done by terrorists whose aim is to overthrow the government? Don't be silly."

"So what's our theory now—that Willy's running from the FBI?"

"From everybody," said Dr. Wolfe. "He feels incriminated, and he's running scared."

. That evening Dr. Wolfe called Mike in New York and John in Philadelphia and told both his fears. "Willy left his car out on the Coast with the men who have been picked up for killing Foster." And to this both Mike and John agreed: "Then he's going to be in trouble." Later Mike remembered thinking that he was not as sure as Pete Wolfe that Willy was not the type to become involved with terrorists. And John recalled that Che Guevara was Willy's idol.

That same night Roxie called her mother, who said that she was worried "because I got back a card that I sent long before Christmas to Willy in care of his friends at Chabot Road. Now I get it back in an envelope, postmarked January tenth, which is the day Remiro and Little were arrested, and with nothing on the outside but 'not at this address' in a woman's handwriting. It's a slap—as if Willy's friends are saying they never want to see him again."

"They could be protecting Willy," Roxie said to her father, to whom she repeated the story. But Dr. Wolfe didn't believe it and decided thereupon to call the Coast and talk directly to Willy's friends. But the numbers in his book for both Cindy (who had lived near Willy) and Dave Gunnell were no longer valid.

"Everybody's scared," Pete said to Sharon as they were going to bed after Roxie had gone home. And his wife said, "I don't wonder, from all that's happening, and I think there's more to come." There was— before the beginning of February.

One morning at breakfast the Wolfes heard on the radio that the beige-colored Oldsmobile that Nancy Ling Perry had driven away from the fire in Concord on January 10, after Remiro and Little were picked up, had been found in Berkeley. "The car is registered in the name of William L. Wolfe," said the announcer, "whose name has been linked with the Symbionese Liberation Army. Not much is known about Wolfe other than that he has worked with inmates of California's state prisons through a black studies program that he became interested in when he attended the University of California."

After some mulling, Dr. Wolfe again called the local FBI and talked with special agent in charge, Richard Fritz, who stated that his office had no warrant for Willy's arrest. Whether special agents in the office were cooperating with officers on the West Coast, who by this time wanted Willy for questioning, the FBI man did not say. As far as Dr. Wolfe could tell, Fritz was not particularly interested in talking with Willy, should he show up, which Pete told his wife "he isn't going to do."

"Because they'd look for him here?"

"Because he won't want to get us involved."

Until after the Hearst kidnapping, no news report associated the doctor in Allentown with his son (whose name even in *The New York Times* was spelled Willie Wolf, or Wolff). But twenty-four hours after the abduction, when the case was officially entered by the FBI (which could presume that Patty had been taken over the California line), agents in all states began investigating the tall, thin young man wanted for questioning by the police in Concord, Berkeley and Oakland. (In Concord, Willy's car had been seen leaving the fire that burned "the SLA headquarters." In Oakland, the same car had now been found on a back street, and Willy's belongings in two houses raided by Oakland police tied him to the SLA.)

Interestingly, only in Oakland was a warrant for Willy's arrest ever issued and that was not for arson, espionage or kidnapping but for perjury. On November 5, the day before the ambush slaying of Dr. Foster, William L. Wolfe allegedly made false statements when applying for a driver's license. Apparently thinking back to his childhood when he visited a whaling ship berthed at Mystic, Connecticut, Willy told the clerk, "My name is Charles W. Morgan." Moreover, he gave as his address "1621 Seventeenth Avenue—Oakland—in care of Lynn Ledward." This was a piece of typical Willy carelessness soon noted by reporters, who compared the "Morgan" address with that of a known SLA "drop pad" at 1621 Seventh Avenue, which had been rented by Nancy Ling Perry under the name of Lynn Ledworth and is just seven blocks from the site of the Foster killing. Such clues led reporters and police to look more closely at this guy Wolfe, who, they found, had a father in Pennsylvania, where Willy had last been seen.

Within days both *The New York Times* and the network news announced that Willy Wolfe, who apparently was linked to the Symbionese Liberation Army, was the son of a prominent doctor in eastern Pennsylvania. And this was enough to galvanize a young woman reporter at the Allentown paper into a story she will remember all her life.

Two years earlier, twenty-eight-year-old Joyce Hoffman, a graduate of Boston University, had arrived from a smaller paper to be the first woman general-assignment reporter on the *Morning Call*. Modish and well organized, she likes her job and her town, where by 1974 she had earned a reputation for professionalism. Then she got her first big running story, which came her way, she thinks, because she was more than normally interested in revolutionaries. And this was the result of having seen the beginnings of the Baader-Meinhof movement in Germany, "where I had a fellowship at the University of Munich from '67 to '69."

In November, when the SLA took credit for the Foster killing, Joyce followed the story, "which went quickly from the front to the back pages of *The New York Times*." Remembering the bombings in Hamburg and Munich, she saw the Oakland murder as a possible forerunner of similar violence in America. Then after the capture of Remiro and Little and the Concord fire, Joyce watched the teletype in the *Call-Chronicle* newsroom for more about Nancy Ling Perry and her communiqués. As a result, when Patty Hearst was kidnapped, Joyce knew more than most reporters in the East about the West Coast group.

"One Saturday morning I figured from a story sent special from the Coast to *The New York Times* that Willy Wolfe was the son of an anesthesiologist at the hospital, which is a couple of miles from where I was reading. So I called my editor, who gave me a casual okay to do a story. Well, first I called the hospital, where I got nothing, and then called the Allentown police and got nothing there. So I looked in the tax lists and found the address of a Dr. Wolfe in nearby Emmaus and drove, without calling, to his house.

"I remember that Mrs. Wolfe came to the door and said she would see if Dr. Wolfe would see me and then she came back and said to come in."

What followed for Joyce was an emotional three-hour interview in which Dr. Wolfe, who sat on a piano bench under a life-size painting of Willy and John, said it was "inconceivable" that his son could be a member of the SLA: "He's just not that kind of a guy." He told Joyce, "Willy believes in the philosophy of Mao Tse-tung, but he could never involve himself with the brutal murder of Foster or the Hearst kidnapping. He just couldn't do that, no matter what the end result." He said Willy was the "gentlest" of all his children.

Offering his interviewer a glass of wine "which we make on the place," which Joyce declined, Willy's father sipped steadily as he talked about his recent stay on the Coast, where he met Remiro, "who wasn't my kind of guy," and Little, "who was an absolute delight." He hadn't met DeFreeze or Thero Wheeler (initially thought to be the abductors of Patty Hearst), he said, but he knew his son had visited prisons, "where all the people he was trying to help convinced him that they were innocent no matter what they were sent up for." He said that some time back he had worked briefly with inmates and knew "it takes a mature individual to say 'Knock it off, you're guilty as hell' but still reach out to help."

Repeatedly Dr. Wolfe compared Willy's plight with that of Angela Davis (who was tried for murder after a gun registered in her name killed the judge at the Marin County Courthouse). "And the whole country thought she was guilty until they sat her down in front of twelve people and she was found innocent." Similarly, he talked about Willy's old roommate, "who is in jail for murder because the gun that killed Foster was found in the van he was driving." Then, shifting to Willy, "who must know wherever he's in hiding that he's being judged by implication," his eyes filled with tears. He went to the kitchen, where his winemaker was gurgling, came back with moist eyes and a full carafe, and his guest, as a gesture of sympathy, said yes, she'd have a glass. Thereafter, as Dr. Wolfe drank more wine, he became more and more generous with private memories of Willy, who became in the telling a young Errol Flynn.

"When he was fifteen, he was a cook on a fishing boat," he told Joyce, and "When he was sixteen, he was lecturing to a professional society of anthropologists in Arizona, telling them how to dig up dinosaurs." He said that when Willy went to Europe, "I asked him how much money he needed and he said twenty-eight dollars, and when he came home nine months later from a trip that took him to the Arctic Circle, he gave me nine dollars change." Time after time he came back to Willy's innocence of any SLA connection. "He knew the penal system stinks and felt compassion for prisoners," he said as Joyce at length got up to go. "And he got involved with a group whose ideas were foreign to him and as soon as he was aware of it, he came home."

During the interview Sharon had said almost nothing, but at the door she told Joyce, "There wasn't any indication when Willy was home that he was upset about anything."

"He isn't involved, that's why," the doctor said harshly from the other side of the room."We know that from the FBI."

Joyce turned back. "The FBI?"

"They came out here last night and told us *several* times that Willy's name is *not* on the SLA membership list."

As she made a mental note to call the FBI, Joyce looked back at Dr. Wolfe, who was standing beside the bench near the portrait of Willy. What a picture for her paper! "Would you let us send a photographer to take a picture of you under the painting of Willy?" she asked politely.

"You really would do that," Pete growled at her, "when you know I'm worried to death about Willy."

Puzzled, and embarrassed, Joyce started out the door, only to have her arm grabbed by Dr.Wolfe, who twirled her around. "And you write this up right, see," he threatened, with his big forefinger close to her face, "or I'll say 'That damn broad came in here and drank my wine and messed up the story.' Now, do you get that?"

Joyce nodded and hurried away to her car, where she confronted her distinctly mixed feelings. Here she was on top of a blockbuster story with a contact who was distraught, emotionally bruised and a game-player. From Willy's father she knew she could expect nuggets of truth, fanciful dream plots and a lot of little meannesses, which she would get. (Within weeks she discovered in *People* magazine the very picture of Dr. Wolfe under the portrait of Willy that she had suggested.) Still, she had a good thing going and she knew it as she returned to the paper, where she wrote a five-column Sunday story and then got in touch with the FBI.

244

"Yes, another agent and I made a courtesy call on Dr. Wolfe at his request," Dick Fritz told Joyce. And "No, the FBI has no arrest warrant out for Wolfe as of now." Whether agents in the office were feeding data about Wolfe into the National Crime Information Center the special agent in charge did not say, but Joyce guessed yes. And if Willy turned out to be one of the Hearst kidnappers, this could be as important an investigation as any ever handled by the local office.

About this, Dick Fritz says, ". . . certainly as notorious a deal as we ever got involved in." A graduate of then all-male Lafayette College, Fritz, who was thirty-six years old, had been with the FBI for twelve years. From his first assignment in El Paso, he had been loyal to the FBI and to J. Edgar Hoover, "who made the FBI what it is today." A pleasant, businesslike, prudent man, he is as different in personality from Dr. Wolfe as another man can be. Yet, as the father of three children, he felt deeply sympathetic toward the father of Willy when he went to Emmaus to question him.

"The FBI wants to prevent injuries, not shoot people," he told the Wolfes, who were worried that agents seeking Willy for questioning would go after him with guns. Fritz made a characteristic nervous gesture with his right hand. "And any agent who doesn't believe that shouldn't be in the FBI." To this his young assistant added, "The FBI uses guns in self-defense or to safeguard somebody else, that's all."

Later Dr. Wolfe threatened to sue the FBI for the "massacre" in which Willy was killed, telling the press that the agents who had come to his house had raised their right hands and sworn that "no FBI man will go after your son with a gun." By that time, Joyce Hoffman was cited by Dr. Wolfe as one who could confirm his view, but in her first story about the FBI she simply said that a spokesman had confirmed that Fritz and another agent had gone to the Wolfe home. At a time when no one outside the house in Daly City knew whether Willy was a member of the kidnapping band, she was puzzling whether he was or not. In stories coming in from the Coast, other reporters were asking the same question, which would not be answered until weeks after the kidnapping—not by them or the police of the San Francisco office of the FBI, where the special agent in charge was Charles Bates.

By coincidence, both Mr. Bates and the Randolph Hearsts were in Washington, D.C., on the night Patty was kidnapped. Neither party spoke to the other until both were back in California the next day, but both went into action that night. First, Randolph Hearst called

Clarence Kelley, the new director of the FBI, who got in touch with Bates, who alerted agents in the Bay Area. Subsequently Hearst called the Berkeley police, who said they were asking the media to hold the story temporarily "to give us a little time to pick up the trail of the kidnappers before their descriptions go out." Hearst then called his San Francisco *Examiner* and told reporters to hold up the story.

The embargo lasted twenty-four hours, after which the owner of the Oakland *Tribune*, which had calls about the kidnapping jamming its switchboard, told the Hearsts, "Everybody knows about the kidnapping but us; we're going with the story." After that, reporters and newscasters joined the police and FBI in pursuing the kidnappers, who, many believed from the first, were the SLA. (Even before an FBI man found a cyanide-tipped bullet in Patty's apartment and a neighbor identified one of the kidnappers as DeFreeze, Willie Hearst, Patty's cousin, told his family's lawyer, "This is going to be a political kidnapping," to which, laughing incredulously, the lawyer reportedly replied: "I'd just as soon believe it was done by the police.") Then, on the Thursday after the kidnapping, all guessing stopped. Radio station KPFA broadcast news of a communiqué from the SLA, an ultimatum mailed with half a Mobil Oil credit card from Patty's wallet, which had been stolen by the intruders on Monday. The comminqué was written in the form of a warrant for the arrest and protective custody of Patricia Campbell Hearst, daughter of Randolph Hearst, corporate enemy of the people.

"Should any attempt be made by the authorities to rescue the prisoner or to arrest or harm any SLA elements, the prisoner will be executed," warned Nancy Ling Perry, who signed off as she had ended the execution order for Foster: *Death to the Fascist Insect That Preys Upon the Life of the People*. There was no ransom demand, which puzzled Randolph Hearst, who asked Charles Bates, "What do they want?" He got part of his answer on Lincoln's Birthday in a tape from Cinque, who introduced himself as a black man and General Field Marshal of the SLA.

Until then, the FBI had believed the SLA would ask to trade Patricia for Remiro and Little, but as they listened to the soft, slow voice of Cinque enumerate the sins of the senior Hearsts, they began to anticipate a different bottom line. And they got it. What the SLA wanted was "a gesture of good faith" to the oppressed people of the nation, whose freedom, Cinque said, had been taken away by the corporate state supported in part by the vast Hearst empire and tax monies given out by the UC Board of Regents, of which Catherine Hearst was a member. As a penance for past crimes, the Hearsts were invited to make their "token gesture" in the form of food to the needy—seventy dollars' worth of meats, vegetables and dairy products to all people with welfare cards, social security cards, medical cards, parole or probation papers, or jail or bail release slips. Specifically, Cinque suggested that food be distributed from sixty-five major stores in thirteen California communities, including Watts in Los Angeles and a poor section of Santa Rosa, which was Nancy Ling Perry's home town. The handout, which social service workers said could cost the donors $400 million, was to take place three days a week for a month beginning February nineteenth "or we will assume there is no basis for negotiations."

Both the Hearsts and the FBI had anticipated no such problem, but Randolph Hearst went ahead as best he could, because on the tape from Cinque there was a message from his daughter. All Patty wanted was to be back with Steve and "if you can get the food thing organized before the nineteenth, it would speed up my release." She said she had a few scrapes "that they washed up" and caught a cold "but they're giving me pills" and that she was blindfolded but she wasn't terrified "because these people aren't a bunch of nuts." She was with the SLA, she reminded those at home, "because I am a member of a ruling-class family just as the two men in San Quentin are being held because they are members of the SLA and not because they've done anything."

More than anything, Patty seemed to be afraid of a raid from the police or the FBI. " I am very upset to hear that the police rushed a house, as they looked for me, in Oakland and I was glad I wasn't there." She said that she was with a combat team armed with automatic weapons, "so it won't do any good for anyone to rush in here and try to get me out by force."

In a TV broadcast that night, Patty's father answered. "Tell them not to worry. No one's going to bust in on them and start a shoot-out." He also said, "While I don't see how I can meet a four-hundred-million-dollar program, I just want these people to know that I'm going to do everything in my power to set up the type of program they're talking about." And this he did. Within hours he had made arrangements with Ludlow Kramer, Washington State's secretary of state, Peggy Maze, director of Neighbors in Need, a supplemental food distribution program in that state, and Patrick Potent, an administrative assistant to Kramer, to have them come to California to distribute food (through a tax-exempt charitable organization approved by the state's attorney general) to the poor and needy in the amount of $2 million. (One-fourth of this came from Randolph Hearst's personal bank account; the other $1.5 million from the William Randolph Hearst organization, which donates $3 million annually to charity.) But as he accepted the offer of Sara Jane Moore, who a long time later would shoot at President Ford, to serve as bookkeeper and worked to get the food into warehouses for PIN (People in Need), Patricia' father bumped into one problem after another.

"Anyone on welfare who accepts food in the program should have that amount deducted from his welfare check," said some in state offices. "Can those who take food in this giveaway program be prosecuted for complicity in extortion?" asked an attorney. "Will the food be safe for our people?" wondered a minister after Governor Reagan said, "I hope everybody who eats that food gets botulism."

Several of the churches and community groups suggested by the SLA to oversee the rights of the people in PIN said, "Nothing doing." The United Farm Workers, Black Panthers and the American Indian Movement wanted no food bought with the kidnap money and other activist organizations that agreed to serve in a coalition to protect the rights of the people resented the"condescension" of professionals and society volunteers who rallied around the Hearsts. Members of the United Prisoners Union checked meeting rooms for "bugs." And at least one black organization resented the program's racist overtones.

Through all the confusion the Hearsts moved steadily ahead in their effort to recover their daughter, who seemed to sense this in her second tape, which came just four days before her twentieth birthday. "It was never intended that you feed the whole state. So whatever you come up with is basically okay. Just do it as fast as you can and everything will be fine." To which Cinque added, "We will accept a sincere effort on your part. We are . . . aware of the extent of your capabilities and . . . of the needs of the people."

In this tape, again, Patty expressed fear of the FBI. (If she was blindfolded, she could not have read the newspapers or seen TV, but apparently she listened to the radio because she said, "It's depressing to hear people talk about me like I'm dead—I can't explain what it's like.") She asked her mother to get out of the black dress she wore one day and said that if people got the idea she was dead, "that gives the FBI an excuse to come in here and try to pull me out. I'm sure that Mr. Bates understands that if the FBI has to come in and get me out by force, they won't have time to decide who not to kill. I don't particularly want to die that way."

Because the Hearsts did not want their daughter to die that way either, they turned over all communiqués to the media (as insisted upon by the SLA) but guarded any clues they got to the identity of members of the SLA. As the food program got under way, only Cinque and Nancy Ling Perry had been identified in the news as members. Still, several reporters with an ear to the underground had a "feeling" by this time that Mizmoon Soltysik and Angela Atwood and Emily and Bill Harris were involved, and the FBI was sure of it.

Back in January, when Mizmoon, the Harrises and Angela went underground, the FBI had begun talking to relatives and friends whose names they found in address books left behind in the Concord house and the Harris apartment. And some of these persons, who suspected that their old friends were off on a suicide trip and thought the SLA approach was lunatic, had gone to their local FBI offices (as Pete Wolfe had done in Pennsylvania). One such person was the concerned father of Emily Harris, who went to the Chicago office of the FBI the day after the kidnapping with a letter from his daughter, written to "Mom and Dad"—a letter that shocked middle Americans more than any communiqué written by Nancy Ling Perry. "I've learned a lot from Bill, from other people here in Oakland and from people in prison," wrote this attractive, highly intelligent girl from an upper-middle-class family, "and they in turn have learned a lot from me. One person in particular—a beautiful black man—has conveyed to me the torture of being black in this country and of being poor. He has dedicated his life to eliminating the conditions that oppose people's being able to lead satisfying lives and to replacing these with conditions that make people truly free—so part of the process is to destroy and part is to build."

In the next paragraph Emily said, "Bill and I have changed our relationship so that it no longer confines us, and I am enjoying relationships with other men. I am in love with the black man I referred to earlier and that love is very beautiful and fulfilling." She said that under these circumstances "I feel close communication will only be destructive to us all. . . . I am not the daughter that you know from the past and that I have pretended to be in the more recent couple of years." She said she would keep in touch every once in a while but not regularly and signed off, "Goodbye to the past, forward to the future."

Throughout the country, parents shaken by the changing attitudes of their young toward the Establishment, sex and marriage identified with the Schwartzes and were appalled by the SLA. What was up ahead? More hippies, drugs, Manson cults, bizarre religions, sex with anyone, tacky pads? Enough was enough, and that went for Patty Hearst too. Hadn't she fallen away from the church, lived with a man she wasn't married to, smoked pot any time she wanted? What if she were in it with the others? She and that Steven Weed.

Some in the FBI apparently wondered about this too, because in the hospital and afterward, when he stayed with the Hearsts, Steve was questioned for hours about his old connection with the SDS, what blacks he had known, how much marijuana he had smoked, how often he and Patty had sex. "I got the feeling," he said, "that I could say, 'Hey, you guys, do you know the fucking revolution's coming next month?' and they would say, 'Now, let's see—did you have sex in the morning? In the afternoon? At 2 A.M.?'"

And what about Patty? Hadn't she always been a rebel? So couldn't she have been two-timing old Steve with Cinque, or even with one of the lesbians? From the first, Middle America had doubts about Patty, which would not have entered anyone's head had she been spirited away from a proper girls' school or from her family's estate rather than from a love nest in Berkeley. After all, was she no different from the others in the group? Weren't they all spoiled, rebellious kids? Even Dr. Wolfe, who could not believe that Willy was an SLA member, told Joyce Hoffman, "I've got a feeling that Patty Hearst is in this deal up to her neck!"

Other parents and friends of SLA members were not as outspoken as Willy's father, but they were not as confident as he. Refusing to acknowledge Willy's primary involvement, Dr. Wolfe told Joyce Hoffman, who was making page one in the *Morning Call* day after day with stories about the Wolfes, "Every member of my family is a highly visible target for the SLA. If they could get one of us, they could hold that person up as a hostage and get Willy to turn himself in."

By mid-February, reporters all over the country were discovering that Willy's father was good copy, and several called him to hear the "hostage concept." Few bought it, however, because most thought Willy was more involved with the SLA than his father believed. And, anyway, all thought that before more kidnappings could take place Patty would be home.

On the nineteenth Randolph Hearst told the kidnappers via TV that a prominent San Francisco attorney would serve as an ombudsman to see that Remiro and Little got due process and that in four days he would begin his food program for the poor and needy. "This will be a 'good faith gesture' in the amount of two million dollars." He told a reporter off camera, "I hope that's good enough; it's all that's in the kitty."

On the twentieth, Patty's twentieth birthday, Mrs. Hearst believed that any minute Patty would turn up. So did Charles Bates of the FBI, who said, "I've got a seat-of-the-pants feeling that she'll be coming in." More optimistic than they had been for weeks, the members of the family and Steve waited dinner, hoping it would be a combination homecoming-birthday party. But the celebration did not come off. Instead, the family received word via a taped communiqué left in a telephone booth that Hearst's $2 million food giveaway plan had been rejected as "crumbs to the people." Then the SLA outlined a new way to begin—which required an additional $4 million investment.

So on the night of Patty's birthday all was gloom at the Hillsborough house. Where was Patty anyway? What was she doing? If they could just go to her. And meanwhile, Patty was sitting blindfolded in a closet in Daly City, nibbling daintily on a Rice Krispies "cake" that had been presented to her by Willy.

Chapter Twenty-two

In the first days after her kidnapping, Patricia limped when she was led to the bathroom by Angela Atwood, whose hand she had come to recognize. But by the nineteenth, when she was taken blindfolded down the hall by someone new, her legs were no longer sore. Still, she wobbled, because today's guide, who she sensed was shorter than Angela, was in a hurry.

In the tub, once the new hands had taken the band from her eyes, she sat for several seconds with her eyes closed. From other times she knew that the brightness of this room after her blind world in the closet would be a shock, and she got herself ready. Holding the warm, wet washcloth that was in the tub over her face, she slowly raised her lids. Still screening out the light, she let the cloth spread over the sore place on her cheek where she had been hit with a rifle butt on the night of the kidnapping. Then, finally, she dropped the cloth and looked through a blur toward a masked figure about her size who was standing by the lavatory.

"I'm Fahizah," said Nancy Ling Perry.

As Patricia stretched out in the warm water, Nancy brushed her teeth through the mouth opening of her knit hood. Turning, she said to Patty, "Tomorrow's your birthday."

"The twentieth."

"Cujo's birthday was day before yesterday; he's an Aquarius."

"Oh."

"And you miss being the same by about two hours—you're *barely* a Pisces."

"I know."

"You're both in for big changes this year."

Had either girl been less preoccupied, one or the other might have laughed. As it was, Nancy at the sink flicked water from the brush she had used and handed it and a towel to Patty. "All yours. But hurry up—Cin's waiting."

Patricia could expect one of three kinds of sessions with Cinque when she returned to the closet. He might tell her more about the purpose of the SLA and the kind of society the group wanted to build. Or he might tell her how the FBI wanted to kill her and blame it on the kidnappers, which he had often said. Alternatively, he might interrogate her about the Hearst holdings, which he had done two times before.

"He wanted to know where my parents own property and about the Hearst Corporation," she said later. "And the way he was asking the questions, I thought he already knew the answers." She said that at one point, "Cinque really got mad, and he said that I wasn't answering the questions right, and that he was going to close the door for a while and let me think about what I was saying, that I better get it straight. He said I knew very well what he was talking about. And he went out and closed the door." She said that again, the next day, he came in "to give me another chance to answer the questions." This time he went over the same material again and, according to Patricia, ended the interrogation with: "Your father's got insurance on you, so it does not matter whether you get killed or not."

"Okay, you gotta get out," Nancy said again to Patricia in the tub, "Cin's going to make a tape."

"To my father," Patricia guessed. "What's he going to say?"

Fahizah spit into the sink. "The man's just playing with your life."

"Two million isn't enough," Patty guessed again as she dried herself.

"Your father's not giving up anything; he's going to write the whole thing off."

Blindfolded again and back in the closet, Patricia sat beside Cinque, who spat his contempt for the Hearsts' "good faith" offer into

253

a microphone held near Patricia's ear. "Crumbs to the people," he called the $2 million program. Then he read off a list of the real-estate and corporate holdings (which included TV and radio stations, newspapers and magazines) of the Hearst Foundation, some of which Patricia had known and some of which were new to her. Calling the foundation itself a "tax loophole," Cin asked that $4 million be added to the pledge of $2 million for the purchase of top-quality fresh meat, canned goods, produce and dairy products to be given away to anyone for the asking "or no more communication with the prisoner." As she listened to Cinque's demands, Patricia said later, she believed her parents would try to comply, "but I didn't think they could realistically do what was asked." She knew too, from what had been told her the night after her capture, that Cinque's demand for food was just the beginning. Next would come a demand to exchange Little and Remiro for her, which Cinque hinted at now when he said, "After you get the food that we want, we will begin negotiating for the release of your daughter."

In the week before he made this tape Cinque had been identified by two or three newspapers as Donald DeFreeze, a mentally disturbed escaped black convict. Coming into the news at a time when the deranged black Zebra killers were sending bullets at random into whites on San Francisco streets, this man who talked casually about execution "as a way to save white, black, yellow and red children from a life of suffering and murder" seemed to be encouraging a race war. And this coming after Vietnam and along with Watergate struck terror in battle-weary Americans. Not just wealthy parents of possible kidnap victims but almost everyone who heard him reacted with horror, which Cinque played upon now. "I'm that nigger that you have hunted and feared night and day. I'm the nigger that hunts you now," he continued. "I'm the wetback, the gook, the broad, the servant, the spik. You know us all and we know you—the oppressor, murderer, robber. Now *we* are the hunters that will give you no rest . . . Death to the fascist insect that preys upon the life of the people." Then Cinque snapped off the tape and handed Patty the microphone. Turning to Angela, who stood just inside the closet, he said, "Give the POW her line."

Angela told Patty to listen carefully and then repeat after her. "Today is the nineteenth and yesterday the Shah of Iran had two people executed at dawn." After the rehearsal Cinque said to Patricia,

254

"The Shah gave your parents those Oriental rugs that they own—your father will get the message." When he snapped on the machine, Patty said as instructed: "Today is the nineteenth . . ."

Early the next day the message was taken to Oakland and taped inside a telephone booth on Pine Street (probably by Bill Harris, who had shaved his moustache and dyed his dark hair an ash blond). Afterward, an anonymous caller disclosed the tape's hiding place to the pastor of the Glide Memorial Church, who had volunteered at Cinque's request to serve as a liaison between the Hearst Foundation and the administrators of the PIN program and could be counted on to get the tape to the Hearsts. It was played at the Hillsborough estate on Wednesday night just about the time Patty's birthday celebration was getting under way in Daly City.

As Willy presented to Patty the cake he had made ("We didn't have any flour," one survivor remembered), the others sat down to beans and rice in the kitchen. There, as some drank wine with their supper, they sang a lusty "Happy Birthday, Pretty Patty" for the guest in the closet. They had chalked up a big one and they were jubilant.

By then, all who would be active in the SLA had moved into the kidnap house. The last to arrive was Camilla Hall, who had withdrawn her savings account of $1,500 and driven to the house the night before in her VW, which she sold within days. Gone were all the safe houses. After the murder of Foster, Lynn Ledworth (Nancy) was seen no more at the apartment she had rented on Seventh Avenue near Dr. Foster's office. And soon after the Concord bust, when Bill and Emily Harris gave up their jobs and income, William Kinder (Bill Harris) relinquished his Oakland apartment, and later, as blond Paul Ashford, he and his friends "JoAnn" and "Judith" (Emily and Mizmoon) had moved their things out of the first Daly City house to join the others. Thus all who played parts in the Patty Hearst story were living under the same roof, where in mid-February they talked less about their revolutionary aims than about their negotiations with Hearst and the PIN program, which began distributing food to the poor on February 22.

No one who watched the news coverage of the first handout, in West Oakland, on a wet, gray Friday, will forget the riot scare after more than five thousand (mostly black) people had stood for hours waiting for the food, which came late, failed to meet Cinque's prescription for fresh produce and was not sufficient to go around. In

255

middle-class homes sympathy went out to the Hearsts, whose truckloads of crackers, canned tomato juice, frozen turkeys, Bisquick, and cartons of milk and eggs were ridiculed on camera by some recipients while others turned away to loot stores and throw rocks. Before the day was over more than twenty persons were hospitalized and more than thirty arrested. The giveaway, as far as millions at home could see, was a fiasco, with no end in sight.

That evening Randolph Hearst appeared before the television news cameras to answer Cinque's latest demand. "The size of the latest SLA demand is far beyond my financial capabilities," said the distraught father, his voice hoarse and his face haggard. "The matter is out of my hands." Thereupon Mr. Hearst made way for a representative of the corporation, who said into the microphone, "The Hearst Corporation is prepared to contribute to People in Need a total of four million dollars to the poor and needy provided Patricia is released unharmed." He said that the corporation, "which is not controlled by members of the Hearst family," would contribute $2 million immediately upon Patricia's release and $2 million more in the January following her release. That was all. The pitcher that Cinque supposed would never run dry would pour no more.

A weary Mr. Hearst told Steve Weed he thought the SLA was actually counterrevolutionary. "People pick up the *Examiner*, for instance, and read all that crap the kidnappers force us to print in all those communiqués, and they throw the paper down in disgust." He said, "You can't tell me that doesn't affect their attitudes about the minorities." He told his family, "They can't kill the girl; they'll alienate the entire Left." And even as he spoke, that seemed already true. Denunciations of the SLA had come from Angela Davis, Jane Fonda, Tom Hayden, Jerry Rubin, Dan Siegel, all the Black Panthers and scores of others who had protested American imperialism. Yet, even as they waited for an answer from the SLA to their $4 million "take it or leave it" offer, the Hearsts pushed on, as promised, with their $2 million PIN program, which was better organized for the second go-round, on February 28, when twenty thousand bags of food were given to needy persons in fourteen communities.

Nevertheless, all the way along, news seeping out of PIN headquarters said all was trouble. The staff responsible for the food's distribution fought with suppliers, who ripped them off on one side, and with overseers for the recipients, who ridiculed their efforts on the other. Truckloads of rotten collard greens and bananas had to be dumped; a truck loaded with canned hams was driven off, never to be seen again; fish and eggs were given away or stolen from warehouses maintained by Black Muslims, who presented a bill for $200,000 (and collected); and one packing company that was to supply beef roasts with no more than 30 percent fat sent meat that was 70 percent fat, which had to be thrown away but paid for anyway.

Day after day, as PIN people bought, stored and prepared to distribute food, volunteers in the Hearst faction believed that Patty would be coming home any day. This faith sustained everyone until March 5, when PIN gave away $300,000 worth of food in an orderly way with still no word from the SLA. "That night," says one who worked for PIN, "we began to whisper among ourselves that she might be dead."

Then, on March 6, Remiro and Little smuggled to radio station KPFA a letter stating that Patricia was alive. "Grant us a nationally televised news conference," said the two in San Quentin, "and we will present a list of proposals that can lead to Patty's release." Now, even though the Hearsts had heard nothing directly from the SLA, they felt confident that the men in prison were in touch with the army. And so they were—through letters smuggled to Russ by Nancy and to Joe by Angela, who by this time, according to Bill Harris, had a natural rapport with Patty Hearst.

Later Emily Harris said that she thought Angela was kind of intrigued to discover that she liked this rich kid she had expected to hate. And Patty, in her eulogy of Angela after the Los Angeles fire, was to show that she returned the interest. "Fire and joy," she said in describing her friend. "We laughed and cried and struggled together. She taught me how to fight the enemy within through her constant struggle with bourgeois conditioning."

As she became interested in Patty and vice versa, Angela volunteered more often than anyone except Willy to sit outside the closet, where someone in the group was always posted. And on days when most of the others were out on the streets, she slipped inside the closet and talked.

By then Willy had rigged up a light so that Patty, whose blindfold was no longer a full-time accessory, could read when she was alone. Accordingly, Angela wore her ski mask while inside the closet, but apparently this was something that no longer intimidated Patty. For it

257

was to Angela that Patty poured out her fears about not menstruating (she didn't when she was first kidnapped), not having a bowel movement (she didn't sometimes for a week at a time) and her loss of weight (she had no appetite). And it was from Angela that she got an explanation she could understand of why the SLA was declaring war against the "fascist Capitalist class."

For economic reasons, Angela said, members of the ruling class kept blacks in ghettos, oppressed prisoners, made it impossible for renters to own their own homes, turned their backs on the aged, created laws that forced men and women to stay in relationships that were wrong for them, despised gays, neglected children of the poor and put down women. The SLA (as a multiracial federation of all exploited groups) was dedicated to giving back to people their constitutional rights (liberty and justice) and the right to bear arms to defend their rights.

Who could argue with liberty and justice for all? Not Patty certainly. She may not have thought much about the downtrodden but was bright enough to see with Angela's help that all in America did not get the same breaks. And now that she was thinking about stereotypes, what about the role she had played with Steve? Hadn't she been something of a victim too? There were parallels between Angela's life with the man she married and her own life with Steve, who says now, "I treated Patty, now that I think of it, like a bright teen-ager, which, of course, is what she was." Clearly things were going to be different when she returned to Berkeley, which, as she waited for Cinque to answer her father, is where she says she wanted to be.

In the meantime, however, in early March, Patty left the closet without her blindfold to join Cinque in the adjoining bedroom "where there was just a chair, as I remember, and a little table" to take a "class" in how to break down a shotgun. Told that she would be given cyanide bullets to work with in case of an "attack" by the pigs, she took two or three lessons in how to load and aim a shotgun.

Was Patty being "brainwashed" by her companions at this time? Psychiatrists and lawyers don't agree, but certainly she was living in a controlled and unfamiliar environment in which she was being introduced to new ideas by someone not too different from herself and who admitted to being a convert. And because everything that was being done for her was for her own good, she had ceased to be afraid

258

of her captors. After all, was Gelina, who was raised a Catholic, so different from someone she might have known in the convent before Crystal Springs? And Cujo. Wasn't he someone she could have known (but did not know) on campus?

Next to Angela, Willy, whom Patty knew only as Cujo, spent more time than anyone in the house in the closet. Sometimes he read aloud to her from George Jackson's *Blood in My Eye* or Fanon's *Wretched of the Earth*, but usually he simply talked about what he had learned from his work in prisons. Later Patty was to say, "He taught me the truth as he learned it from the beautiful brothers in California's concentration camps."

Willy told Patty that lobotomies were common at Vacaville and that tranquillizers were fed to prisoners like peanuts to monkeys in a zoo and that beatings by sadistic guards were everyday happenings. He told her about his good friend Death Row Jeff, survivor of a hundred yard fights and years in the hole, where he had lived next to Caryl Chessman, who was executed for murder—and about George Jackson and the love letters he wrote to Angela Davis, and about Thero Wheeler, whom Willy had helped to escape from Vacaville, and about Cinque, who had simply walked away one night from Soledad.

To Patty, who had never been inside a prison, the stories told to her in the closet by Willy, whose vocabulary was like that of the boys she had grown up with in Hillsborough, must have been seductive. To Willy, this little doll who listened without ridicule to what he had learned must have been fascinating. Here, in one girl, was the class of Lydia, the easy California attitude of Nancy Boehm and the don't-push-me-around strength of Mercedes. Whether Patricia also had the sensualness of Eva he did not know, but soon found out.

The opening came from Angela, who told him one night that she had asked Patty if she ever felt horny and had got back, "Well, for Christ's sake, what do you think?"

"So," Angela told Willy, "I asked her if there was anyone here she would like to sleep with and she said, 'Yes, Cujo.'"

According to Emily Harris, who gave her version to *New Times* magazine, everyone kind of laughed when the subject of Patty's sleeping with Willy first came up, but then saw that this could open the way for the others to talk about how the SLA looked at sexual relationships and how they mistrusted monogamous relationships that made for dependencies and weakness. And Bill Harris said that at this time when everybody thought Patty was going to be released any day, he was sure Willy didn't want to get involved and then have Patty go away and never be seen again. But it happened anyway. According to Jack Scott, who "protected" Patty after Willy's death, "She was deeply in love with Willy Wolfe and I believe he was with her." Whatever the case, they slept together, beginning, probably, on the night of March 7.

Long before morning Cinque, who prowled nervously through the house much of every night, began rousting everybody out. "Busy day." Coming up for Willy was a self-defense class, a consciousness-raising session and a trip to San Francisco's Chinatown to see firsthand what kind of food was being handed out by PIN that day. Also a new tape was to be made by General Gelina and Zoya which conveyed the worst to the worried families of Angel and Mizmoon— no doubt about it, their girls were in the SLA. (Shortly before this, both the DeAngelis family in New Jersey and the Soltysiks in Santa Barbara had been questioned by the FBI, and just the day before the tape was broadcast, Angel's brother had received a letter from her saying she was sick of watching poor people eat dog food and that she was willing to die, if necessary, to help liberate the people.) Still, until the strident voices of the two girls came over the air, neither family could believe its daughter was involved.

To make the tape, Angel, Mizmoon and Nancy Ling Perry, wearing their ski masks, removed Patty's blindfold and led her into the bare bedroom, where all sat in a circle on the floor. Cinque (also masked), who had reviewed what all three girls would say, stood in the doorway as the taping began. Pretending to be an angry black woman, Angela laughed at Hearst's offer of $4 million and accused the "fascist corporate state" of trying to get Patty killed to discredit the SLA and of not showing the proper regard for Joseph Remiro and Russell Little. Then she pushed for what she wanted. Remiro and Little "must be allowed to communicate via live national TV," presumably to argue the unfairness of their confinement and the lofty aims of their friends in the SLA. And if the men did not get the air time, she added, there would be no more negotiating for Patty. From that day onward, Angela told the Hearsts, "all communications and negotiations are suspended." Then, after some muttering against the fascist state by Mizmoon and Nancy, who faked black ghetto accents, Angela handed the mike to Patty, who read the party line, embellished with some thoughts of her own.

"I don't believe you're doing everything you can," she told her father, whom she accused of turning the giveaway program "into a real disaster." She questioned his motives in rejecting the original request for seventy dollars' worth of food for every needy person in favor of a continuing program for the poor. (Cinque had told her in one of their rap sessions that this was the "fascist way" of keeping the needy under control.) And she railed about the FBI and other federal agencies "which want me to die . . . because I have become a political pivot point for certain right-wing elements." Referring to hostages at Attica prison and at the Marin County jail who had been killed by law enforcers, she said, "The FBI has never been famous for its concern over hostages."

She said that she did not like being described on the air as an innocent girl who was kidnapped by "two terrible blacks" and that she was "a strong woman and I resent being used this way." Concluding, she said that because she was in danger at all times of being killed, she had been issued a 12-gauge riot shotgun and was receiving instruction in how to use it. "In the event of an attack by the FBI, I will be given an issue of cyanide buckshot to protect myself." She declared that she no longer feared the SLA, "who just want to feed the people and assure justice for the two men in San Quentin" and that "it is only the ones in the FBI who want to murder me." She addressed her mother, her cousin Willie Hearst, and Steven on this tape, but she had changed, and, to all who heard, she seemed far away.

To Dr. Frederick Hacker, a Beverly Hills psychiatrist who later specialized in negotiating with terrorists around the world, Patty's apparent sympathy with the SLA came as no shock. "Don't be surprised if she develops an affinity for her captors," he had told the Hearsts from the first; "it happens all the time." But to others, who had agonized about Patty and prayed for the Hearsts, her shift was seen as an unforgivable betrayal. Some concluded that Patty had been in cahoots all along. Others charged that she was stoned on drugs; still others, that she was hooked on Cinque. But all were wrong. Patty was not a secret member of the SLA before her kidnapping; she was not a drug freak; and although in the nature of things, she slept with Cinque, all reports save some of her own indicate that she clung to Willy.

Gradually Patty had become sympathetic toward the SLA. In part this must have been due to Willy, who talked repeatedly, to others at least, about Tania, the girl who gave up a life of sophistication for his hero Che. And if that is not how Patty came to change her name, the reason remains obscure—because about a month after her first night with Willy, the protected little rich girl who had been kidnapped by the SLA announced to the world that she was joining the SLA and changing her name to Tania.

Chapter Twenty-three

From the night of the kidnapping the SLA did not drive the green-and-white station wagon that was used in the getaway and was parked in the garage. In the driveway, its nose toward the street, was a rented LTD ready at all times to take off. Inside the house, behind its camouflage of scraggly bushes, the shades were nailed down, as they had been at the Concord house, and the doors were barricaded shut.

"A dope den," said some of the neighbors.

"Including my wife," says Lynn Babcock, who lives down the street. "She and I used to talk about the place; we didn't know what to think." He laughs. "But we never thought Patty Hearst was in the closet or Bill Wade and I wouldn't have gone over one Sunday the way we did and cut down the bushes." On that day, Lynn says, "Bill Wade and I were working outside when we looked over and saw those big scraggly bushes at a house that nobody was paying any attention to that was owned by Jim Mazzariello, a fellow we knew. So as a favor to Jim, and because we wanted the street to look good, we went over with our mower and clippers and went to work. Afterward, we figured we were lucky not to get shot."

Patricia remembers the commotion in the house the day the bushes went down. "Lots of times before that, I could hear clicking and noises—like clips going in and out of guns and sometimes the ones in the house would make noises like they were shooting." But this day was different. "There was a lot of running and whispering and moving around." Constantly afraid that the FBI would raid the place, she believed that attack was imminent, and so did others in the house.

Lynn Babcock adds that when he and his friend finished clipping the bushes they just went home, and found out only much later that they had cut down the blind for the SLA. "I guess we kind of shooed the people out; they left in a couple of days."

They did so, according to landlord James Mazzariello, leaving the interior walls filled with BB holes, the refrigerator filled with rotted food, the sink filled with greasy dishes, and the garage filled with an abandoned automobile, which, unknown to him for several months, was the SLA kidnap vehicle.

From Daly City the group moved to 1827 Golden Gate Avenue, in a dreary pocket of San Francisco, where Nancy Ling Perry, posing as Louise Hamilton, put down $250 for two months' rent for an upstairs apartment. Confident after mingling with police at PIN giveaways that they could disguise themselves so as not to be recognized, they did not worry that their new pad was just a mile from the FBI office. In the first place, who would look for them here? And in the second, in this neighborhood of poor blacks and Puerto Ricans and destitute whites, all of whom had benefited from their ransom demand, who would give them away? Once they got their conspicuous captive in the house, they would have little to fear.

To what extent Patty was still captive at this time is a matter of dispute. (Her declared name change came later.) At her trial she said that after the move to the Golden Gate apartment she stayed in a second closet for almost two weeks. On the other hand, Bill Harris says that she spent time in the closet at Daly City only, and that by the time they moved to Golden Gate, she had already decided to stay with the SLA. Whatever the truth, Patricia was beginning to see the SLA members as people by the time of the move.

In mid-March, Catherine Hearst announced on TV that she was accepting Governor Reagan's reappointment to another sixteen-year-term as regent at the University of California, which surprised and enraged her husband. Hoping to appease the SLA, he was revising his food giveaway program in two ways. First, he would organize a giant million-dollar distribution effort for the last Monday of March; then, he would go to New York City to get the board of the Hearst

Corporation to put $4 million in escrow, to be released under the trusteeship of three California liberals on Patty's return.

Also, on his return he paid a visit to San Quentin prison, where he sought the help of Death Row Jeff, who was believed by the FBI to be in touch with the SLA. Encouraged, he returned for a second visit with the FBI's Charles Bates, when all three talked about a possible deal—in particular, safe passage for the SLA to Algeria in return for Patty's immediate release. Thereafter Jeff wrote a letter to his friends, and two days later a bouquet of roses along with Communiqué No. 7 was delivered with half of Patricia's driver's license to the editor of the radical *Phoenix* newspaper in San Francisco. The gamble seemed to have paid off. "Further communications regarding the subject prisoner will follow in—72 hours," said the SLA's Communiqué No. 7, adding that another communication "will state the state, city and time of release of the prisoner." The note was signed by General Field Marshal Cin, SLA.

Steven Weed and the Hearsts were jubilant. But then, on April 3, another message came from the SLA, and all hope disappeared. The first had been an April Fool's Day joke. But this one, delivered to radio station KSAN in San Francisco, was a message from Patty, who said that she had been given her choice of being released in a safe area or of "joining the forces of the Symbionese Liberation Army and fighting for my freedom and the freedom of all oppressed people. I have chosen to stay and fight." In her long, angry diatribe, she told Steven that she had changed and grown "and can never go back to the life we led before." She said that love didn't mean the same to her anymore, that her love had expanded as the result of her experience to embrace all people—"it's an unselfish love for my comrades here, in prison and on the streets." She accused her father of stalling for time with the FBI, of being a liar, of knowing that the corporate state was about to murder black and poor people "down to the last man, woman and child" and that the removal of "expendable excess" had already started. She said that she knew her father, as a member of the corporate state, "would kill me if necessary to maintain power." Then she announced her changed name. Delivered with the communiqué was a shocking photograph of her, grim-faced, shorn of her hair and armed with a gun as she posed in front of a wall hanging of the SLA cobra emblem.

Much later, Patricia testified that she had been told by Cinque about ten days before making this tape that she must fight or die. "He told me that other countries' liberation movements do things like that and that it was a very acceptable way to recruit." She said that when she made the tape she wanted Cinque to think she had joined "so that I could stay alive."

But whether Patty would stay or go was not decided by the group, says Bill Harris, who insists the SLA didn't want a dead weight hanging around. "So once we got to talking about her staying on, we all questioned her relentlessly to see if she really wanted to work with us."

As the group's leader, Cinque had the overriding vote on Patty's destiny, and from the moment he sensed that her attitude toward her old life was changing he wanted her in the SLA. Whether he saw the propaganda coup inherent in such a switch is unclear, but he must have sensed the drama, as did everyone. In any case, he saw to it from the night of April 1 that Patty would be tied into the group by participating in their first bank robbery. (Camilla Hall's $1,500 in savings was by then exhausted.)

Rehearsals for the robbery began the same day the Tania tape was broadcast over the radio. To begin with, Cinque gave everyone a number so that each could see on a chart where and how he or she would function in the operation. Later, Patricia said, "Cinque was number one, and Mizmoon was two; Nancy Ling Perry was three, William Harris four and William Wolfe five; and Emily Harris was six, Angela was seven, Camilla was eight, and I was nine."

The day selected for the robbery was Monday, April 15; the bank, the Hibernia in San Francisco. A week or more beforehand, Cinque said that beginning the next morning the inside and outside groups for the robbery would split up and begin rehearsing separately with the guns they would use. Then he issued each member a gun with a number corresponding to his or her number on the floor plan. In the inside group, Patty was to carry a semiautomatic carbine; Cinque and Nancy Ling Perry, machine guns; Patricia Soltysik, a handgun; and Camilla Hall, a 12-gauge single-barrel sawed-off shotgun. Willy and the others were to carry rifles and machine guns from the "arsenal closet" in the apartment.

Thereafter, Bill Harris sat Tania down and field-stripped her carbine to show her how to operate the trigger and insert the clip and pull the slide back to chamber the round. Then he went off with Emily and Angela to the bank to decide where two cars could be stationed for a quick getaway. Meanwhile, Mizmoon hurried across town to a school where there was space for two switch cars, to be parked so that the getaway cars could be exchanged for them after the holdup.

While the scouts were afield, Patty, Cinque and the others went through their paces like gymnasts. And from then on, day after day, until the Monday scheduled for the holdup, discipline never let up; and as far as the SLA was concerned, the rehearsals paid off. There were few hitches in the Hibernia job, which got under way a little before eight on the fifteenth when several members of the SLA donned wigs.

A few minutes later Willy, Emily, Mizmoon and Camilla took off to pick up four cars that the girls had rented two days earlier with a driver's license found long before by Bill Harris in a discard pile at the Post Office. All the cars were parked in separate spots, but in twenty minutes Willy and Emily, in a red Hornet, and Camilla and Mizmoon, in a green Ford LTD, were finished and waiting out front for Bill and Angela and the other three, who would work inside the bank, and who now moved quietly down the stairs and slipped into their assigned places in the two cars.

At 9:50, Patty and Camilla walked casually into the bank, their guns tucked under their coats, and moved as rehearsed to the far side. Following them came Mizmoon, who abruptly called out, "SLA. Down on the floor and you won't get hurt." At the door, following Nancy Ling Perry, Cinque, meanwhile, lifted a handgun from the guard. "First motherfucker who don't lay down gets shot in the head," said the cool-talking leader, and the guard and all but two of the eighteen customers and employees in the room lay down. Quickly Nancy Ling Perry and Cinque pushed the remaining two to the floor, where she covered the trembling bodies with her machine gun.

Then, while Camilla and Mizmoon went behind the counter and began scooping money out of the tills, Patty introduced herself to the group. "This is Tania, Patricia Hearst," she said in a soft, low voice. She poked a carbine through a hole in her coat, while a hidden camera, activated by an employee upstairs who also called the police, recorded the unlikely sight. Within another five minutes a police siren screamed outside, but by then the deed was done. The robbers had escaped with more than $10,500, leaving two wounded customers behind.

"They were a cold bunch," one of the customers told his wife a half hour later, which was about the time Willy and Camilla, driving the switch cars, were letting one confederate after another off in the ghetto with a couple of sacks full of money to make their way to the Golden Gate place. Then, in another twenty minutes, after the drivers had returned from the parking lot where they discarded the second-string vehicles, they all got together to praise Tania at home.

That night, as Patty and the others dined on the floor on rice and beans, she wore around her neck a small Olmec charm, which Willy had given her beforehand for luck. The little stone face did not leave her person thereafter until it was taken from her on the day she was captured by the FBI.

Chapter Twenty-four

On the day that Cinque and Nancy Ling Perry felled two customers at the Hibernia Bank with their machine guns, one or more blacks shot two white teen-agers waiting for a bus in a black district of San Francisco. Neither boy died, but when the local police station's Z-band barked out word that the bullets in the bodies of the kids came from .32 caliber automatic pistols, city dwellers sucked in their breaths. The Zebras! In the last five months these stealthy assassins—who, according to witnesses, were black—had killed eleven whites and injured six others. And this time again the police had let the gunmen get away. Then at 9 P.M. on the day after the bank robbery, Nelson T. Shields IV, twenty-three, a white visitor from Wilmington, Delaware, was shot and killed by a .32 caliber automatic pistol in front of a flat where he and a friend were picking up a rug. Now the city would have no more.

With Nick Shield's death, Mayor Joseph L. Alioto ordered Operation Zebra, which empowered police to halt black men between twenty and thirty years old and between five feet eight and six feet tall for questioning anywhere, anytime. And then everyone in town was afraid—white men and women for fear they might be cut down at random, black men for fear they might be picked up without warrant or justification, and black women for fear that fear itself was getting out of hand. Thereafter, from eight o'clock at night most neighborhoods looked deserted, and even in the daytime fewer people than usual were on the streets. And an inordinate number of them were in police cars looking for Zebras and the SLA.

Upstairs in their apartment, where they were crammed into a kitchen, bedroom, bathroom and a couple of closets, the nine who had gone to the bank had pockets full of money but were running out of food and were afraid to go out. Cinque, as a black man, could not risk being stopped by a Zebra sleuth. Willy and Bill Harris, whose pictures had appeared in the papers, could not go out "as is" and were afraid to go blackface for fear they, too, would be nabbed by the pigs and found to be in disguise. Until the robbery, the girls had moved about freely in Afro wigs and dark make-up, but now that the police were asking about them door to door they were afraid of close-up contacts. The only way to get food, they decided, was for Cinque to go shopping as a woman, which he did (with the help of Angela's make-up and costume design), but when he saw men along the way eying him, whether from desire or suspicion he knew not which, he gave it up. "Something's got to give as long as this Zebra shit goes on," he told Bill. "In this town now, it's not good to be black."

For several days all nine did not leave the house. And for hours on end they drilled one another for open warfare. At all times three stood guard with carbines at two windows and the door. Nor did tensions ease in the evenings when radio newscasters reported that from eighty to one hundred blacks a day were being stopped and questioned. And when someone on camera one evening said, "Operation Zebra is racist," the soldiers in the apartment shook their fists. "Genocide," they said.

At length, exasperated, Cinque said he was going out and ring doorbells. "With everyone around here up in arms about the Zebra hunt, nobody's going to turn us in. And, anyway, these people are poor and know we're the ones that got the food for them; they'll be glad to know us." Cinque was right.

With a street black's instinct, he slipped down the street to a tenement building at 1743 Golden Gate and there made common cause with at least one tenant, a handsome young black woman named Jamella Muntaz. Speaking softly, he introduced himself as Cinque, and, responding that he was known in the neighborhood as Jesus, Jamella invited him in.

Cinque told Jamella that he and his friends needed someone to go to the store for them and also to find them a new apartment "because the one we're in is too small" and, maybe, to buy a car. And Jamella, either because she was afraid, as she said later, or because she was fascinated or thought there would be money in it for her, agreed to help. Thus a day or so later, after she had received a note from Cinque delivered by Angela Atwood, she and her little daughter and a friend who called herself Retimah X ("like Malcolm X")—who, as Patty Hearst remembers, "was really small"—and the children of Retimah X all went up the block to the SLA.

To the black women and children, Cinque's soldiers, who eyed them with guns by their sides, were awesome, but they were also hungry. And as soon as the black women suggested things they might want for supper, the soldiers relaxed and began hugging their visitors and putting ten-dollar bills in their hands. And soon the two women and the kids were laughing their way to the Lucky Spot market, where they loaded up on everything good they could think of for the soldiers to eat. And after that they and two men they let in on their secret were regular visitors at the apartment, where the outsiders brought news of what people were saying about the bank robbery and the insiders previewed their next communiqué. This, Cinque said, would be a speech from Tania, "your outlaw," which, with the help of General Gelina, was being composed that day.

So it was that a day or two later, at about the time a memorial service was being performed for Nelson Shields in Greenville, Delaware, Tania, in San Francisco, recorded her "bank robbery" message to the people. In it she cut all her ties to the "Pig Hearsts" and to Steven Weed and made an announcement that would shock the world.

In a dead-sounding voice, as played on radio and TV, Tania said that her gun at the bank was loaded, "and at no time did any of my comrades intentionally point their guns at me." She said that the $10,660.02 that she and her comrades had "expropriated" would be used "to insure the survival of the people's forces in their struggle with and for the people." She still believed, she said, that the enemy wanted her dead, "but I am obviously alive and well" and, "as for being brainwashed, the idea is ridiculous."

On the same tape, Cinque explained that the two men at the bank were shot because one refused "to lay on the floor, face down," as ordered, and the other ran down the street to the bank, making combat forces "assume that the subject was an armed enemy-force element." Therefore, that man was shot too. Cinque warned the public that "any citizen attempting to aid, inform, or assist the enemy of the people in any manner will be shot without hesitation. There is no middle ground in war. Either you're with the people or the enemy." Then in the tape's final minute, he expanded on his theory that Operation Zebra was a plot to eliminate black revolutionaries "and by black revolutionaries we mean black people in general."

"The pigs sure are trying," said one of the men who came to the apartment with Jamella and Retimah X with groceries the day after the tape was played. "Around here they're looking mostly for Zebras, but they'd just as soon get you."

Cinque smiled. "I'm sure of it, so I think we'd better move." He gave his new friend a thousand dollars to rent an apartment "that's got more room in it than this one, and buy some kind of car to get us there." He said that the apartment had to be in an all-black neighborhood. "This one's got a lot of whites around that'll turn us in; blacks know we gave them food."

The next morning the black man was back to say that he had bought a green station wagon for six hundred dollars and had given three hundred dollars to a landlord for two months' rent for a flat in the Hunter's Point section, another ghetto, all black.

"And it's a good thing you're going," he told his new friends, "because they're looking for you now from up above." He bent Willy's head down to the window and pointed up. And, sure enough, heads in a small helicopter not far up were looking down.

"We'll leave in the morning," Cinque said.

But the messenger shook his head. "Can't get in the other place until the first."

"Then find us a motel where we can check in sometime tomorrow as blacks."

The next afternoon, as Angela was making up one of her confederates with black grease paint, somebody got the idea of writing on the walls, and soon the whole group was smearing one sign after another on the partitions. No need to hide that they had been there; the pigs would know anyway. So they made a game of it.

"Da da o mi," wrote Willy, as Death Row Jeff had once written to him. "Is it real? To load a gun with a magazine of dreams? No!"

Emily Harris sketched out in big letters. And then Tania, who looked like a scrawny little black boy in her jump suit and Afro hairdo and painted skin, scooped a big gob of paint out of the jar. "Freedom is the will of life," she wrote. *"Patria o muerte, Venceremos."* With a flourish, she signed her revolutionary name, "TANIA."

Mizmoon had been dropping scratched tape and first drafts of communiqués and the plan for the bank robbery into a garbage can. And now she took the whole can into the bathroom and dumped its contents into the tub. Quickly she threw cyanide crystals on top of this pile, as Nancy turned on the tap. One of the others, meanwhile, noticing the toilet was stopped up, went and got a pan and scooped out some excrement. Nancy exulted that Bates would work for his evidence. And, with that, she scrawled on the wall over the tub, "Happy Hunting, Charles."

A witness who saw four or five of the group take off said they looked like a bunch of black kids going off on a bus trip. With all their suitcases and packages (containing guns and ammunition), they had to make more than one trip to the next stop, which was a motel with a mostly black clientele, where they checked into three rooms. (At a later date, when Patty, in hiding, was helping the Harrises get material together for a possible book, she wrote, "There was no room in the cell for bourgeois types of personal relationships," adding, "Once I joined, some of the comrades were afraid that the personal relationship between me and Cujo might become a problem.")

Because the group felt that more than three rooms would be extravagant, and perhaps because he did not trust Cujo and Tania not to skip together, Cinque deputized Mizmoon (or possibly Nancy) to spend the night with the two youngest members of the group. And there they stayed put for three days, until the little band departed for the next place, a rental apartment on Oakdale Street, where they stayed just nine days because by then the heat was on.

By the end of April, Mayor Alioto and every policeman in town were defensive about not finding either the Zebra killers or the SLA. Then, suddenly, on the first of May, everything broke. Through a source they did not reveal, police got wind of a group of Black Muslims called the Death Angels. Between 5:00 and 8:15 in the morning they arrested seven men (four of whom were later tried for the Zebra murders and sentenced to life terms in prison). Then, later the same day, they got a call from the owner of a place on Golden

Gate Avenue, which he said, he thought could have been occupied by the Symbionese Liberation Army.

Like all landlords who rented space to the SLA, this one had thrown up his hands when he saw the aftermath. In the early morning, he said when he brought in the police, the woman below had called to report that her apartment was deluged with cockroaches coming down from upstairs. When he could arouse no one upstairs, he continued, he broke in and found the sink full of greasy dishes and roaches, the walls filled with SLA signs and the bathtub full of God knew what. He had $125 of the group's leftover money to fix the place up, which would cost hundreds.

As they looked at the "up yours" display arranged for the FBI, and after talking to store clerks who thought they had seen Patty Hearst, the cops were determined to "get those bastards." And they and the FBI spread out a dragnet from one end of the city to another.

"They're everywhere," Cinque's black friend, who had put the money down for the Oakdale Street apartment, told the SLA leader, who nodded. "So we've got to move on."

May 3 was the day that the deadline expired for payment of the $4 million food ransom by the Hearst Corporation for Patty's return. When no word was received from the SLA, the money was withdrawn—no more feeding of the multitudes, no more Robin Hood stuff. Patty's father, meanwhile, made plans to go with money itself to the people, and in a few days he offered a reward of fifty thousand dollars for information leading to his daughter's safe return. Would someone come forward now as one had in the Zebra hunt? It seemed the only chance.

On May 4 Cinque gave his friend from Golden Gate more money to buy three vans "that we can live in if we have to." He trusted the friend of Jamella and Retimah X and paid him well. When his purchasing agent showed him two VW buses and a large green van, which he had bought with cash in the names of persons whose drivers' licenses Bill Harris had "confiscated" from stolen purses, Cinque gave him the six-hundred-dollar station wagon they had purchased two weeks before. Then he informed the SLA members that they would be splitting up into three groups.

With the help of a police radio, which they had swiped and were monitoring, the SLA knew on May 8 that Patricia's father had announced a number to call with any tip that could lead to the fifty-thousand-dollar reward. They also learned that some of their neighbors near the Golden Gate apartment were talking to the police and the FBI about having seen them nearby. Cinque figured it was just a question of time before they found the Oakdale pad.

The next night Retimah came by with her family to say goodbye. She pushed forward one of her children, who stood and recited in Swahili the seven principles of the SLA. Then everyone hugged one another and said they would see Retimah again, and afterward, the nine SLA members, alone, took pictures of themselves, the way high-school graduates do at the end of school when they know they are going on to something new.

Whether Cinque, who was in charge of logistics, saw that time for the group was running out, no one knows, but certainly he was concerned by then with getting out of San Francisco, where there was talk on TV that all roads out of the city would be blocked to prevent the evacuation of the SLA. The cops were coming close, Cinque said, adding that they themselves would leave in the morning. And this they did, not in a convoy, but in separate vans, that left the city an hour or so apart.

The first three to go were Cinque, made up to look like a white man, and Mizmoon and Nancy, who set off in the big green van. Next to leave were Willy, Angela and Camilla. And last, in the red and white VW, were the Harrises and Patricia, who said in the "Tania Interview," which she worked out with the Harrises a year later, "Cujo and I were on different teams, not because we were in love and therefore nobody wanted us to be together, but because our military skills complemented different people."

As prearranged, the three cars met in a little park in south-central Los Angeles near a shopping center where Willy, Nancy and Angela had bought supplies and staked out a pay telephone where they would wait for a message from the others about where to go next. Then the other two cars went to look for a house to rent, which they found within an hour at the edge of Watts. And so it was that by midnight the nine comrades were lying in sleeping bags in a little house on 84th Street, where there was no electricity or gas and where the floor under their bags was covered with broken glass left by the last tenant. But for the time being they were safe. Prophet Joe, the owner of the house, who lived in a small cottage out back, had promised Cinque (who had creamed off his white make-up before making the contact) that he would not turn them in.

On their second night in the house, from which no one had stirred since their arrival, Prophet Joe came in to have a talk. "I just don't believe you're the SLA," he told Cinque, who pointed to his most famous soldier. "There's Tania."

Because Patricia had lost fifteen pounds and most of her hair, Cinque told her to put on her long brown wig. "Now do you believe?" he said to Joe, who nodded and left the house. Later he told Nancy Ling Perry, "Well, I love freedom fighters, if that's what you are."

"Prophet Joe's all right," Cinque told the others a few nights later, "but somebody else is going to get suspicious if he sees whites walking in and out. Suppose they think we're undercover pigs? Then we'll be getting offed by my own people." He said they couldn't stay there long. Maybe they should not be in any town for the time being, "until this thing dies down a little." And the next night, when Bill Harris got a ticket for parking his red-and-white VW van illegally in front of the house next door, Cinque said, "That does it. Tomorrow you and Tania and Yolanda [Emily] go out and stock up on supplies for us to take off as three separate groups for the mountains or someplace."

The next morning, May 16, Cinque drove the "Harris van" to the alley out back, and Bill and Emily and Patty walked out past Prophet Joe's house and got in the car as Cinque slipped out. At the last minute, Cujo, who had been talking with Joe, came out and kissed his girl goodbye. "Remember, if something happens that we have to leave here, you're to meet me at the Century drive-in tonight." Tania nodded. *"The New Centurions* is the show.'"

"Just what we need," said Tania.

Cujo smiled, and those who remember the smile from his Berkeley days say that it lit up his face. "I love you," he said.

Chapter Twenty-five

At 4:20 P.M. on Thursday, May 16, the Los Angeles police radio, which Willy monitored with his battery-run set, sent out an excited call about a shooting at Mel's Sporting Goods store on South Crenshaw in Inglewood. The police described the suspects as a Caucasian male, "said to be small but very strong," a Caucasian woman, and a second woman with an Afro hairdo and a pale "nightmare" face who had shot at a clerk from across the street when the clerk attempted to handcuff the male. The trio reportedly had escaped in a red VW van.

Subsequently the regular news stations broadcast the story. The male was said to have tucked a pair of socks up his sleeve after buying and paying for thirty or forty dollars' worth of wool shirts, socks, caps and other clothes. "He is wearing a heavy plaid coat and a rolled-up hat," said one report, "and he has a handcuff on one arm, placed there by the clerk, who struggled with the alleged shoplifter and took from him a .38 caliber Colt Detective Special." The escaped trio, "who may have more than one machine gun," was described as extremely dangerous.

There was no suggestion in the first news reports that the three on the run were in the SLA, but all in the 84th Street house knew that this would come. For the escape vehicle almost certainly was Bill Harris's VW van, which had been ticketed next door.

Then the police radio made a further announcement. The fugitives had stolen a 1970 yellow Pontiac Le Mans with a black vinyl top from a Kenneth Pierre on Ruthelen Street. "The van is parked at 11522; bring it in," said the dispatcher, "and go after the Pontiac, which has been seen heading south on 115th Street." The final announcement, which was headlined on that night's newscasts and brought in the FBI, was, "The alleged robbers, who are armed with machine guns, claim to be members of the SLA."

The time had come. As Emily, Bill and Patty fled into hiding, intending to rendezvous with their comrades at a fallback location in the hills in two weeks, Cinque and his companions packed up their things and moved on. Under cover of night they filled their two vans and made their way through the darkness to a small frame-and-stucco house in south-central Los Angeles, where Cinque's latest contacts, warmhearted, unafraid and drunk, took them in.

"There was always a party at Emma Lee's," says Regina Calloway, a handsome black woman whose small corner house stands a door from the overgrown lot in Watts where the last SLA hideout stood. "People played dominoes on the porch there every day and got drunk and smoked weed at night." She says she was a drunken wife herself in those days, "but I was home in bed on the night the SLA arrived."

"Cinque came to the door, they say, about four in the morning," says Christine Johnson, who lived in the "death house" and now has little gray spots on her emaciated body where her black skin was singed in the fire. "I was livin' in the house with Minnie Lewis—she's the one everybody calls Emma Lee—and she and I and Brenda[Daniels] and Freddie [Freeman] had been drinking wine and playin' the radio in the bedroom when the knock came. I have to take nerve pills, so I'd dozed off, but I know what happened. The one knockin'—that was Cinque—gave Emma Lee a hundred dollars if he and the others he said were stranded in their vans outside could come in and spend the night." Christine says that when Emma Lee said yes, Cinque told her, "I knew you sisters would help."

About this time eighteen-year-old Brenda, who was half asleep herself, came to see who was coming in. "White people," Cinque told her. "Do you mind?" No sooner had she said that color didn't make any difference, Brenda remembers, than "the place filled up with people with more guns than I've ever seen in my life." With the help of Freddie Freeman, the only adult male in the house, Cinque and Willy and the four women out front had brought in suitcases and violin cases filled with handguns, rifles, sawed-off shotguns, knives, automatic rifles, bottles of gasoline, ammo clips, pipe bombs, gas masks and automatic pistols. With quiet efficiency, the white women now arranged their guns and bullets and other war supplies like package goods in the kitchen while Willy moved the two vans from the other side of the street to directly in front of the house. Cinque meanwhile, talked with Freddie.

"The vans are going to be hot; can you think of a place to put them?"

With boozy enthusiasm, Freddie, a suspected car thief, said he knew just the spot a couple of blocks away. "You can put them beside an empty house I know that's behind a board fence." That this was a drop for stolen cars to be broken down and was regularly checked by police Freddie did not think to mention.

"Okay," said Cinque, turning to Nancy, who was standing with her handgun at the front window. "Come on; let's go check out the place. Willy can stand guard."

A half hour after the vans had been stashed away, Freddie and a black man wearing dark glasses and a hunting jacket (Cinque) went from Emma Lee's house to a house for rent on Compton, where Freddie asked a neighbor if "my friend here" could rent the house for a couple of weeks.

"Florence Lishey owns the place," the neighbor told Freddie's companion. "She'll be walking around here later; why don't you talk to her?" Freddie said that Mrs. Lishey also owned Emma Lee's place. "We'll catch her here or there."

Then the two went back to Emma Lee's house, where a co-worker of Freddie's in a downtown parking lot was sitting out front and blowing his horn. "Let's go," he called to Freddie, who shook his head. Then, without letting anyone hear on the street, Freddie walked to the car and whispered, "That dude there is Cinque. The whole SLA bunch is in this house, and I think I see a way to make some dough. You go on; I'm staying here."

Inside the house, Christine had stumbled out to the kitchen and seen the guns. "I'm afraid," she said to Emma Lee and Brenda, who were also anxious. All three drank some wine that was left from the night before and took some of Christine's nerve pills. Then, while Emma Lee went into the back bedroom to wake her two small children and get them ready for school, Brenda talked to Cinque, who asked her to go for beer and cigarettes and lunch meat and other things for sandwiches. He gave her twenty dollars and a grocery list that Camilla had made out and said to duck down the alley to Sam's place on Compton Avenue without talking to anyone. He said that he would be watching. "And he was," Brenda said later, "from in back of the house in the alley." But thereafter, when Brenda came back, Cinque had taken his boots off and was sitting out on the front stoop in his stocking feet. "And he and Freddie stayed out there for a long time talking and smiling at people who walked by."

In the kitchen, the white women were not so affable because by this time the three black women in the house had begun to resent the white ones. When Freddie came in for a drink, Brenda stopped him at the door. "Who asked them here?" she said as she glanced over at Camilla, who was spreading bread for sandwiches on the kitchen table.

Freddie shrugged. "They paid as much for one night as Emma Lee pays for a whole month."

But Brenda would not be pacified. "That big yellow-haired one acts like she owns the place." She said that Emma Lee was getting sick of the SLA people "with all their whispering around." She asked Freddie how he would like it if somebody came in and took over his house "so's Emma Lee's own kids got to stay out of their room." She said that's where most of the others were now. "Back there in the kids' room."

Freddie refused to be drawn in. "So the kids will be going to school pretty soon now anyway." He said he thought Cinque and the big, tall white dude were cool. With that, he flashed a big roll of bills. "See what I mean!"

"Did they give you that?"

Freddie nodded. "To buy them a station wagon." He said the group didn't want to stay anymore than the black women wanted them to. "Besides," he said, "the tall one's got to get out for a ron-day-voo!"

"Who with?"

"With a lady named Tania Hearst."

The FBI, meanwhile, had had a busy night. Starting with one good lead—the parking citation found in the red-and-white VW van—Bill

Sullivan, head of the Los Angeles office, set up a command post at Crenshaw Boulevard and Imperial Highway, near where two stolen cars had been abandoned, and placed agents in strategic locations on the block where the van had been ticketed. Then Sullivan called a meeting for 2:30 A.M. at the Inglewood Police Department to brief his own men and those of the Los Angeles Police Department, the County Sheriff's department and the Inglewood police on the evidence that had led the FBI to believe the SLA was in the 800 block. Sullivan also invited supervisors from the crack Los Angeles Special Weapons and Tactics police unit, known as SWAT.

At a second meeting at dawn, about the time Willy and the others were walking into the house on 54th Street in Watts, the FBI and SWAT and other police units were organizing a task force of heavily armed officers to go into the black ghetto neighborhood (from which Willy and the others had fled) with "sniffer dogs" exposed to wigs and coats left in the abandoned van by Emily Harris and Patty Hearst. In case this tactic failed, the task force had instructions to conduct a house-to-house search.

At 5:30 A.M. an FBI agent intercepted a man leaving the house at 835 84th Street and asked him to look at pictures of four or five young white women. "So the dude asked me if I could identify any of them," the man said later, "and at last I got to say what I'd been wanting to say for a long time. 'Sorry, those white ones all look alike to me.'"

The next neighbor questioned was more cooperative. He picked out the Harrises as having belonged to the house at 833 84th Street. And after several others said they too had seen whites getting out of vans and going into 833, and at least one twelve-year-old had told officers that she had heard Cinque was nearby, the police abandoned the planned house-to-house search in favor of evacuating nearby residents, setting up a defensive perimeter to prevent the SLA's escape, and going directly to the house which they knew by then (from the owner) had been rented for seventy dollars a month by a Ms. Rivera, who distinctly resembled Mizmoon Soltysik.

At nine o'clock, using a public-address system, the police ordered the occupants of the house to come out. "You will not be harmed." When this got no result after an eight-minute interval, the FBI ordered SWAT to fire tear-gas shells into the house, and when the house remained quiet, members of an FBI-SWAT team crashed through the front and back doors to find nobody there.

"Shit," said the first raider to come out the door. But the next ones to emerge had their frustration under control. "There are sacks and sacks of SLA stuff in there, and that stuff's going to help us get those bastards," one flak-vested SWAT man told Bill Hazlett of the Los Angeles *Times*.

"The most useful," Hazlett said later, "were two temporary paper license plates issued for a couple of distinctive vans." So, beginning at ten o'clock, several patrol units were crisscrossing black neighborhoods in south-central Los Angeles looking for the vans.

At a little after noon two SWAT members spotted the vans at the drop near 54th Street, where they regularly checked for stolen cars. They called FBI case agent, Joseph Alston, who was investigating telephone leads to Patty and the Harrises, who had stolen three different cars during the night. Now he sent agents to check the vehicles at the drop—which proved to be the ones they were after. By this time, Alston had received three different reports that both male and female Caucasians with handguns and rifles were staying in a house on 54th Street, and he figured they were with the SLA. He did not know exactly which house was the hideout, but his agents knew that their likely quarry were now in the neighborhood.

Early in the afternoon they met for a briefing with Los Angeles and SWAT officers and neighborhood police at the nearby Newton Area Station, where many in the neighborhood saw the comings and goings and knew that the Man had a plan. For much of the day only the ones in the house on 54th Street and their immediate neighbors seemed unaware that the enemy was closing in.

"I didn't know who was in my house that day," says former actress Florence Lishey, who lives across the street from the property she once owned. "I saw a man sitting on the porch over there, but I didn't know until afterward he was DeFreeze. There were people going in and out, but that wasn't unusual 'cause they partied in that place all the time—folks going in and out all day." And Mattie Morrison reportedly said, "They always partied over there—every day. We didn't think nothing about that or the police either—they're always around." But in midafternoon, when Lee Calloway, Regina's husband, came home from work, he was not so sure. The Man seemed to be everywhere, and by the time he got to his house no one was out in front of Emma Lee's place.

"I'd been playing Ping-Pong over in James Slauson Park," Regina says, "and when I came up on our porch my husband was waiting to ask me why nobody was out on the porch at Emma Lee's place. I didn't know, but just then along came Shirley Davis, and she told us she'd been in the house over there and Cinque and a lot of white women was having an orgy, you know, sleeping with men and women and rollin' weed and drinking."

But Brenda Daniels, who made a second "beer run" for Cinque about noon, said that while members of the SLA passed out beer to anyone who came by, they did not drink much themselves. "We've got to be alert," she had been told by one of the white women, who added that they wouldn't be taking over the house, as some there seemed to think; "we'll be leaving here tonight." After that, the women began loading weapons and ammo into small military-type backpacks. None of those who had arrived in the middle of the night made any secret of belonging to the SLA.

Meanwhile, Freddie Freeman had taken off with the five hundred dollars Cinque had given him. "I didn't know whether he would come back," Christine said, "but the SLA people kept looking out for him, and I heard one of the women tell one of the others, 'The black man is going to steal us a car.'"

This Freddie did not try to do, although he did call a friend and ask to "borrow" his car for Cinque, to which he got a no thanks. Then he called another man and offered to pay forty dollars to "rent his car for the day," to which he got another no. Eventually, hearing reports that police were moving in on a place "where the SLA is supposed to be hiding out," he decided there was no use in trying to go back; he'd never get through the barricade. After four o'clock in the afternoon this would have been true, because it was then that Mary Carr, Emma Lee's mother, got into the act.

Ordinarily three of Emma Lee's five children went after school to Grandma Carr's house, where they lived most of the time. But on this day Mrs. Carr was visiting a friend in the hospital, so the children went to their mother's house, where they bumped into Willy in the front room setting up two automatic guns. Two of the children backed away, but Timmy, who was eleven, went looking for his mother, who had passed out and was lying on the bed across the body of Christine, who also was unconscious. Nodding to a visitor, eighteen-year-old Stephanie Reed, he ran to the kitchen, where he encountered Cinque and the stash of guns.

"Who are you?"

"Your mother's friends," said Cinque. "And we're busy; so you sit down."

But Timmy was suspicious. "You're not my mother's friends," he said, looking hard at the black man. "I think you're Donald DeFreeze. You look exactly like him—I *know* you're Cinque!" And then Timmy was afraid, so he ran out the back door and around to the front, where he bumped into Stephanie's father, who was also anxious.

"I'm scared," Timmy said. "Cinque's in there and he's got a lot of guns."

"Go fetch your grandma," said the gray-haired neighbor, who called into the house for his daughter to come out, which she promptly did. Timmy, meanwhile, reached his grandma's and told her the news. Mary headed in a hurry for Emma Lee's.

"Is everybody around here drunk?" she demanded in the bedroom, where she could not awaken her daughter or Christine. Then she called to Brenda. "What's going on?"

Brenda pointed to the back bedroom, where Angela and Mizmoon were taking a nap on the floor and Camilla was lying on the bed with a gun in her hand. Mary bustled on to the kitchen, where Cinque was talking to Willy and Nancy. "I want you people out of here, do you hear?" And then she talked directly to Cinque. "Right now," she said, "you've got to get out."

Thereupon she grabbed one of Emma Lee's little girls, who lived in the house, and a little boy who had wandered in and stalked back to the girls' bedroom, where the sight of Camilla on the bed infuriated her. "Will you *please* tell me what you think you're doing?"

Camilla did not answer. Instead, she smiled and patted the gun at her side, which was enough for Mary Carr. Overlooking Emma Lee's eight-year-old son, Tony, curled up in an armchair watching TV, she hurried out with the other two children to get the police.

About this time, Clarence Ross, twenty-three, who stopped often at the house, came stumbling through the door, flopped down in the chair next to Tony and went to sleep. Shortly thereafter, Cinque gave Brenda another twenty dollars and dispatched her on another beer run to Sam's. It was to be her last mission, because, returning, she was picked up for questioning by the police. Emma Lee, meanwhile, had come to and run.

In her encounter with the police, Brenda said that she had not seen

Patty Hearst, although "she could have been there." But when Mary Carr saw the police, she said, "Patty Hearst is inside." (Possibly she, like many others, confused Nancy Ling Perry with Patricia.) Mary Carr, however, positively identified Donald DeFreeze and Camilla Hall.

By then the guesswork was over. With Mary Carr in a police car with them, two patrolmen rode down 54th Street where the outraged grandmother pointed out her daughter's house.

"It's the five-room yellow stucco and frame dwelling with a stone front porch at 1466 54th Street on the south side of the street," said an FBI man briefing SWAT patrolmen and others at a command post a few blocks away. "It has a pitched roof with gray composition-type covering. There are two steps on the east and west side of the house leading from the sidewalk to the porch. The house is approximately twenty-one feet wide and thirty-four feet long with seven hundred and fourteen square feet of floor space. It contains two bedrooms, a living room, kitchen and a bath. The house is on a raised concrete foundation approximately eighteen inches from the ground. Air vents in the foundation are evenly spaced along the perimeter of the house."

By this time, Frank Sutter, a contractor whose Lincoln Continental had been commandeered by the Harrises and Patty Hearst, had reported to the police that until 1 P.M. that day the missing heiress and two of her comrades had been riding in his car, in which he had been lying between the front and back seats. "So I *knew* when I heard about the house on 54th Street that had been observed by the FBI for most of the day that Patty Hearst wasn't in there." But, FBI's Alston says, "We couldn't be sure." He says that he, personally, did not think that Patty Hearst was in there, "but there was the possibility that persons who saw her in another place were mistaken or that she had made her way into the house on 54th Street." She had not; even as the police and FBI were trying to determine exactly who was in the bungalow, Patty and the Harrises were on their way to Anaheim, after a series of close calls with the law, in a newly bought, secondhand car.

"We can mix with the tourists [at Disneyland] and nobody will notice us," said Emily as they rode along. She had exchanged her hat for a new wig and was wearing new slacks and shoes. She said later that the three in the car were in pretty good shape by then. "The tension of the last few days was wearing off and we were kind of high."

To which Bill added, "We'd had a lot of close calls, but everything was working out okay for us and for the others. We figured we would lay low in a motel for a couple of days and catch up with them later." (Earlier, the three had heard a radio report that material in the 84th Street house had proved the place was a hideout for the SLA. But at least they could say, "Thank God; they were gone!")

They were in Anaheim and driving into the parking lot of a motel when they heard an updated story about their own escapade. Bill laughed derisively as he switched off the engine to go in to register. But he was somber when he came out. He said some people at the front desk were talking about the SLA. "I think they were talking about this morning's raid," he said, "because they were talking about how the police had their place surrounded."

They heard no more until they had driven around to their room and Bill had switched on the TV set. "And there," Emily said in a later interview, "the whole shoot-out scene came over the screen." She said that she thought the announcer must be describing the raid that had taken place that morning and "it can't be them—it's just a mistake." But Bill said he recognized the sound of carbines from inside the house where the SLA was boxed in. Apparently, the folks at the front desk were not talking about the morning's move on the house on 84th Street. This raid was taking place right then.

By five o'clock in the afternoon Willy knew that the house he and his companions were in was surrounded. Long before Mary Carr had come in and taken away the kids, he had sensed that the Man was near, but now there was no mistake. At least three families across the street had left their homes with undercover men, whom he had seen go up to their doors. And the old woman next door who had sat out front all day with her dogs had been shooed inside. Other than the two drunk zombies and the little boy watching TV in the living room, everyone who had been lying around the place all day had cleared out.

The early-morning rain had not lasted long, and the day had been a scorcher, but now when most everyone would be outside getting a breath of air, there was not a flutter on either side of the street. Occasionally a car filled with stern-faced men would go slowly by the house, but no sirens screamed. Except for the whir of low-flying helicopters everything was quiet.

By a little after five, Cinque, Willy and Nancy had pried up several floorboards with a screwdriver, and Camilla, Mizmoon and Angela had laid out gas masks and were pouring gasoline into bottles for Molotov cocktails. Cinque was suggesting that he, Mizmoon and Willy go down through the bathroom floor in case of a heavy attack and that Nancy, Camilla and Angela go down through the kitchen when Tony came in and told Angela that something was wrong with the TV set. It had just gone off. Cinque reached up and snapped on a light switch, which did not turn on the bulb. "They've turned off the power," he said. "It won't be long now."

"Come on," Angela said to Tony, "we better put you in the bathtub."

"I don't want a bath."

"You don't want to get killed, either, do you?" she said. "Now, you come on."

Angela turned to look out the window and, quick as a rabbit, Tony scrambled out of the tub and ran through the kitchen and living room and out the front door of the house. "Come on out," said a SWAT member, who went to the child, took his hand and led him around the corner to another policeman, who could not believe the boy had come from the house.

"I think he's just lost," he said as Tony yelled for his mother.

But Bob Simmons, the first Los Angeles newscaster on the scene with a microphone and camera, knew better. "Who's in there?" he asked Tony.

"Cinque's in there with white people who've got straps on their chests that're full of bullets." Tony said the people were digging down under the sink, "so water can wet them in a fire."

With that, the police, who had feared all day that the "guerrillas" would dig tunnels to escape, called two more times for the people inside the house to come out. And presently the door opened and out came Clarence Ross, who had no idea what the commotion was all about. Either because he was drunk or just naturally secretive, he could remember no one in the house but one black woman. "I didn't see no white women or guns."

By this time SWAT members had taken up protected positions behind nearby parked cars and houses. And two of the team, who were near the house, said they heard rapid movements inside as the officer triggering the bullhorn continued to call, "You in the house, come out, the place is surrounded." And then, when still no one moved, a SWAT officer crept close to the porch and fired two 40-millimeter tear-gas projectiles through the front bedroom window.

Finally the occupants answered—with automatic weapons fired from posts inside both front and back windows. The SWAT team returned the fire, and in the next forty minutes lobbed fifty tear-gas canisters into the house while continuing to fire at anything that moved inside.

At 6:40 the SWAT leader with the bullhorn saw smoke coming out of the kitchen and said so loudly that he could be heard in the next block, "Come on out. The house is on fire. You will not be harmed."

The message galvanized millions of horrified TV viewers who watched the Bob Simmons broadcast that night on eighty-six different stations. In another two minutes, thick black smoke was belching out from under the roof and thin flames were licking at the sides of the house, but apparently no one was coming out. Or so it seemed outside; inside, Christine had been awakened by a terrible scream and wanted out of her nightmare fast.

Full of "nerve pills" and booze, the black woman had slept through the blazing battle until Mizmoon, at the front window, was shot in the right arm. Bleeding and on fire, Mizmoon ran toward the back of the house to get water, and it was then that her screams awakened Christine, who opened her bleary eyes and found herself in hell. Half blind from tear gas and choking on smoke, she started to stand but was shot in the leg and fell to the floor. With her nose to the carpet, she snaked around a blazing chair, passed Cinque, and somehow made her way to the front door. She heard someone yell, "Don't open the door," but she turned the knob anyway and fell outside, where a SWAT operative hauled her away.

Once the door was open, the entire house burst into flames, and the SWAT officer called once more through his horn. "The house is on fire. It's all over. Throw your guns out the windows." But again the only answer was automatic weapon fire, which came by that time from air vents in the foundation. The ones inside had moved into the crawl space.

"They've got four fire-fighting units out here tonight," the newsman said into his microphone, "but the chief can't send his men to the house over there because of the hostile shooting and the possibility of booby traps."

To this a weeping Bill Harris in Anaheim said, "Bullshit. You're looking at a search-and-destroy operation." He turned to Emily, who

288

stared stony-faced at the TV set, while Patty sobbed into a piece of Kleenex held over her mouth and nose. "We saw it a thousand times in Vietnam—and the folks in the house know it too. That fire isn't a fluke—it's the scorched-earth policy."

"What do you mean?"

"They're going to let them burn."

In Emmaus at almost the same moment, Dr. Wolfe told Sharon, "No matter who's in there, they've got to get them out. They're burning them up like rats." And, even as he said it, a tiny figure came wiggling out of the crawl space under the kitchen, which was completely engulfed in flame. The girl (who was Nancy Ling Perry) was wearing military fatigues and was carrying a gun, which she did not fire, as she crawled five, eight, ten feet from the house. Behind her shortly came a second young woman with cropped blond hair (whom many recognized as Camilla Hall) following the first figure out of the crawl space. This one was firing an automatic pistol in the direction of the SWAT team, one member of which instantly fired a .225 caliber bullet into her brain. Two hands (belonging to Angela) pulled Camilla's body back into the opening, blocking the only way out.

"This is the worst spectacle I've ever seen," Dr. Wolfe wailed, as his wife stared horror-stricken at the screen. Why hadn't the FBI called him? They'd lied to him. He could have flown out to California that day "and hunkered down' with them and got them to come out." He would call the FBI; maybe it wasn't too late. But even as he spoke, the fire filled the screen, and the little figure in the yard twirled and was shot in the back. "Did she shoot at them? What happened there?" But Sharon couldn't say, and, anyway, by then she had the FBI on the phone. "Ask him," Dr. Wolfe shouted, "how in the hell he would like to be watching television and not know if his son was dying in that house. Find out if Willy is in there." A moment later the house collapsed in flame, and Willy's father, sensing the end had come to the boy who carried his dreams, slumped in his chair and sobbed.

At Anaheim, the newscaster explained on TV that later that night or in the morning the bodies would be removed. He said that Dr. Thomas Noguchi, the coroner, had been near the house since the start of the fire and that by the next morning, with the help of dental charts, he would identify the victims. He mentioned that several persons who had been in the house that day had identified Camilla Hall and Donald DeFreeze and that others had thought they had seen William Wolfe and Patty Hearst.

"Well, I'm not there, so maybe Willy's not either," said Patty.

But Bill Harris shook his head. "One tall white male with black fuzzy hair. Who else could it be with the SLA?"

Patty nodded and cried. "I know."

When the firing from the vents stopped and the burning house collapsed on the screen, Patty could take no more and went into the bathroom and turned on the water. Leaning down in front of the mirror, she splashed her face and eyes with cold water and in so doing let the little Olmec charm swing out from her neck on its chain. As she patted her face with a dry washcloth, she saw the little stone face and smiled.

"Cujo was the gentlest, most beautiful man I've ever known," she said on tape a few days later. "We loved each other so much, and his love for the people was so deep that he was willing to give his life for them."

Chapter Twenty-six

Shortly after 5 P.M. on Friday, May 17, Dr. Gerald L. Vale, Chief of Forensic Dentistry in the Los Angeles County Coroner's office, went home and went to bed. "Because I had a feeling that I was going to be busy later on that night," he says, "I thought I had better get some rest." At 1 A.M. the next morning he was notified that bodies taken from the rubble on 54th Street were at the morgue, and for the next thirty-six hours he and his staff compared pictures of teeth and X-rays of bone structure with dental records of known SLA members.

Because the bodies were badly burned and in some cases "shriveled like strips of bacon," the work took longer than expected. (In the beginning, only two bodies could be visually identified as female, one as male. And investigators had to hunt in the ashes for patches of skin that had not been cremated so that coroners could determine each victim's race.) Nevertheless, by Saturday afternoon Dr. Noguchi was able to assure the Hearsts that Patricia was not among the dead.

Throughout the night and morning Patricia's father had been "down, really down," reported a spokesman. "He looked absolutely terrible." But now hope returned to the family at Hillsborough. "It's not her," Randolph called out to reporters when he heard. And over a "splash" before dinner that night he told a friend, "It's a terrible experience to watch a burning inferno and believe your child may be inside." He said he sympathized with the parents of those who had died. "Catherine and I know what they're going through because we've gone through the same thing."

But "Not quite," said the parents of the others, "because your child is alive." By nightfall on Saturday the families of Angela Atwood, Nancy Ling Perry, Patricia Soltysik and Donald DeFreeze knew their children were dead.

With the consent of her husband but over the objections of many in the church she had attended as a child, Angela Atwood was buried with the full rites of the Catholic Church in a plot near her mother's grave. Her body, which contained traces of cyanide from the explosion of cyanide bullets she had carried in her belt, was returned to North Haledon, where her sister finds it hard to believe even today that Angela is gone. "She was an A-1 girl," says Elena, "and I still can't believe that the one they sent home was Angel."

For Nancy Ling Perry there were two memorial services. At one, in a large Episcopal church in Santa Rosa, her father said, "It's over for Nancy now, but it's difficult for me to comment. The Nancy we knew and loved is not the same Nancy that has been described in the last few months." At the other, in a small church for blacks in Berkeley, Nancy's musician husband appeared deeply affected. "It was horrible seeing your wife murdered on television," said Gilbert later. And his mother, who runs a small beauty shop, said that Nancy knew Negroes weren't treated right and wanted to help. "But she shouldn't have gone this far."

The body of Donald DeFreeze, the black leader of the SLA, was claimed by his mother in Cleveland, where his funeral was attended by a thousand mourners. Both Mary, his mother, and Glory, his wife, likewise found it hard to believe that the man they had known was the notorious Cinque.

Pat Soltysik's remains were buried privately in Santa Barbara, where her brother Fred, who made the arrangements, pleaded with the Harrises and Patty and anyone else in the SLA to give themselves up "so their parents and families will be spared the sorrow we have suffered."

Only the parents of Camilla Hall and Willy Wolfe did not comment on Saturday, and there was good reason. Neither family was sure whether its child had been inside.

At midnight on Friday, after the fire, three FBI agents from the

Allentown office had called on Dr. Wolfe. "We do not know that your son was in the house," one was said to have assured him, "but we have been asked to send his dental charts to California." Dr. Wolfe was fearful, "but they said not to worry. . . . They told me for the twelfth time they had no warrant for his arrest." He said that the agents had promised him earlier that he would be notified if and when Willy was located. "And they said it again and promised they wouldn't go charging in with machine guns." According to Dr. Wolfe, he told the men that night that if he found his son had been in the Los Angeles house he would consider it murder.

Not until Sunday night did someone from the Los Angeles County Coroner's office call to inform Dr. Wolfe that his son was dead. ("It almost killed him," Roxie said.) When the representative tried to apologize, Dr. Wolfe refused to accept the explanation. "You took great pains to notify the millionaire newspaper publisher that his daughter did not die. But when it came to calling us, your attitude apparently was 'Let him find out on the radio or television that his son was slaughtered by police.'" He got angrier by the minute. "You behaved atrociously."

"I called my mother," Roxie said, "and I had the strangest feeling that she wouldn't like me if I was the one to tell her that Willy was dead, but she is less emotional than Dad and she said she would call Los Angeles and get ready for the funeral."

Surely, she told this to her former husband, but in his agitated state, Dr. Wolfe got mixed up and flew with Sharon to California, where they were told in Dr. Noguchi's office that his son's ashes had already been claimed by Honey.* "I was almost psychopathic," he says now, and Dr. Noguchi agrees. "In all my years as a coroner, I never had anyone come to my office who was that upset."

Accompanied by a private investigator, hired by himself, and a lawyer from the American Civil Liberties Union, Dr. Wolfe demanded a "war probe." As the little Japanese coroner watched in amazement, the huge doctor from Pennsylvania paced up and down the office shouting oaths against the "storm trooper" tactics of the

---

* Mike Carrerras believes that Dr. Wolfe knew that he should have been informed before the press was that his son was dead. So he flew to Los Angeles, pretending to be coming for the body (which he had to know had been sent to Honey) to put Dr. Noguchi, the coroner, on the spot. The result was more self-inflicted pain.

police and the "stupidity" of the FBI, who, he charged, "burned up that house without knowing who was inside." He demanded to see pictures of the corpse but wept in anguish and pushed them aside when they were brought to him.

Then, returning to the offensive, he stormed, "Why didn't the FBI call me the way they said they would when they went into that first place?" He pounded one big fist on a table and wiped his eyes with the other. He told Noguchi he could have hopped on a plane and been in California before the second raid. "I'd have gotten into that second house and talked Willy into surrendering." Then, in a new outburst of rage against the FBI, he swore that he would sue, a threat that he reiterated in a television interview in Chicago on his way home.

"That broadcast was gruesome," says Joyce Hoffman, but Roxie says, "The people didn't understand. My dad wanted the world to know that my brother had been murdered for no known reason, which is what I feel too." She says her father resented the way the Hearsts were given every consideration by the FBI in comparison with the way he was treated. She believes the house would not have been burned if Patricia Hearst had been inside. "The FBI knew she wasn't there." (The FBI still denies it.)

Nor did Dr. Wolfe's outrage pass with that appalling broadcast. Whereas he had refused to talk about Willy's possible connection with the SLA before the fire, now he could talk of nothing else. A week after Willy's death he granted another interview to Joyce Hoffman, who, he told one of the owners of the *Morning Call*, "always writes a fair story." Inviting the reporter to join him and his family (including Roxie and John and Mike Carrerras from New York), he unleashed an all-day "let's remember Willy" session, at which he acknowledged for the first time that his son undoubtedly was involved with the SLA. "But did he murder? Did he rob? Did he kidnap?" he asked Joyce. "No, no." And therefore he was going to raise "all the hell I can."

"She was sympathetic but professional," Mike said afterward. "When John, who thought she was my date, greeted her with a hug and a kiss, she was embarrassed but kind. She got her story, but she worked harder than you usually have to work for a story."

"The Wolfe story was a very important one in Allentown," Joyce says, "but it had its moments of frustration for me." One such came the morning after the Wolfe family gathering when, without telling her, Dr. Wolfe called CBS in New York and said, "I'm suing the FBI for $100 million." Informed that a CBS film crew from the Harry Reasoner show would interview him, he called several reporters to "get out to the house if you want a story that CBS is coming out to do." But he didn't call Ms. Hoffman, who had been his friend and confidante and had come whenever he called in the past week; now she missed out on the national news event.

The last of the victims to be identified was Camilla Hall, whose dead body had been covered by falling stucco and charred wood and ashes before the others died. Discovered with the body was a letter she had hoped to smuggle to her parents, which said in part, "I know you trust my sincerity even if you haven't come to agree with the course of action I have committed myself to. I am young and strong and willing to dedicate my courage, intelligence and love to the work. I really feel good about what I am doing and want you to, too." A few hours later, the Reverend Mr. Hall told newsmen in Lincolnwood, Illinois, "Camilla was not a martyr in the religious sense. But when people die standing up for what they believe in that makes them a martyr."

In Hillsborough, California, Randolph Hearst did not agree. Notwithstanding the fact the Hearsts and Halls had agonized together waiting for the last (female) victim to be identified, he scorned the Bay Area talk of martyrdom. "Had they been captured, they wouldn't have been martyrs."

Like Dr. Wolfe, Hearst was upset about the fire, but for reasons of his own. He had watched the others burn and did not want his daughter to die that way. "If the authorities had not killed the others, they could have heard the story of the SLA." (He thought the police could have kept the SLA members in the house until their ammunition gave out and taken them alive.) And he feared the martyrdom syndrome: Some who had not approved of the SLA before the fire might now be less critical and help Patty and the Harrises to hide indefinitely. He repeatedly pleaded with Patty to turn herself in, and when he heard nothing, he forgot the sympathy he had felt for parents of the others and blasted out against the ones who had kidnapped Patty, "who would have been looked on as common criminals had they not died." He added, "They weren't martyrs, they were dingbats."

Meanwhile, grief-stricken and depressed, the last of the SLA members worked their way slowly up to the Bay Area, where a rally for

295

the SLA had been announced for June 2 in Ho-Chi-Minh Park. And there, just as Patty's father had feared, the three (who had disguised themselves as old people) made contact with friends and got the help they needed to stay underground. Three weeks to the day after Willy's death, in a small Oakland apartment that Emily had rented for all three, Patty taped their last communiqué, declaring that she could not give up the fight and that the love of her life had been Cujo.

"The name Cujo means unconquerable," she said. "It was the perfect name for him. Neither Cujo or I had ever loved an individual the way we loved each other, probably because our relationship wasn't based on bourgeois fucked-up values. Our relationship's foundation was our commitment to the struggle and our love for the people. It's because of this that I still feel strong and determined to fight."

In all of America, no one was more eager to believe this than was Willy's father. In the days after the fire, more and more evidence had suggested that Willy had been a longtime member of the SLA, and having to come to terms with the evidence was tearing Dr. Wolfe apart.* He could admit that his son might have falsified a driver's license, but he could not allow Willy's name to be linked with murder, kidnap and robbery, as was happening on the Coast. Only days before Patty's communiqué came over the air, he had described Willy as an "angel" to a newswoman who called from San Francisco. "He was the gentlest person that was ever born. He was a good boy." And now a beautiful young woman who admitted to having been deeply in love with his son was declaring to the world what he had said. Only then, and for the first time, could he concede that Willy might have been a serious revolutionary. Swept along in his dead son's glory, Dr. Wolfe called Randolph Hearst in California and suggested that "if we work together we might be able to persuade Patty to come forward." But Patty's father, who had been reviled in the tape as "the pig Hearst," was in no mood to play along. "Dr. Wolfe," said the publisher, "if my daughter was in love with your son, she had very poor taste."

"He was condescending," Dr. Wolfe said afterward, "and I hung up on him."

Tears came to the doctor's eyes the next day as he read a transcript of Patty's statement. "What a difference between the parents of Gabi

---

* His haggard face in *People* magazine shocked all who knew him.

[Camilla] and Cujo [Willy] and my parents," she said. "One day, just before making the last tape, Cujo and I were talking about the way my parents were fucking me over. He said that his parents were still his parents because they had never betrayed him but my parents were really Malcolm X and Joanne Chesimard.* I'll never betray my parents."

Patty was mad at the pigs, she said, for holding up Willy's .45 and his watch "which was still ticking" for reporters and for taking "the little Olmec monkey that Cujo wore around his neck." She said Willy had given her a similar little stone face. And, concluding, she said, the only way the pigs could defeat the guerrillas was to "burn them alive."

Overcome, Dr. Wolfe called Washington to talk to Clarence Kelley, who was out of town. "I want to save some lives," he told an agent at the FBI. "I don't want the FBI to kill Patty and her friends." He wanted them to have "their day in court." This wish would be granted, and, then, as Dr. Wolfe may have foreseen, Willy from his grave would have his say.

* A leader in the outlaw Black Liberation Army.

Epilogue

A year and a half after Willy Wolfe's death, Patty Hearst was captured by the FBI in San Francisco and taken to the San Mateo County Jail, where she signed herself as an urban guerrilla. Since the night when she was carried from her fiance's apartment and tossed into the trunk of Peter Benenson's "confiscated" car, she had burrowed through days in the underground, and, says her cousin Willie Hearst, who saw her the day she emerged, "she had changed." Not only was Patty thin and undernourished; her IQ had dropped twenty points, according to tests made in jail.

As Tania, she had been living with Wendy Yoshimura, a Berkeley artist and activist who had been a fugitive on a bomb charge for three years. Living nearby were the Harrises, who were also brought in. The relationship of Patty and Bill and Emily (who had wept together through the night in Anaheim for their burned comrades) had cooled. And since that time Patty's feeling toward the couple from Indiana has turned to hatred. "They are hideous people who should be locked up forever."

After her capture, Patty did not see Wendy Yoshimura, who was subsequently convicted of possessing explosives and was sentenced to not more than fifteen years in prison. (She is appealing while free on bond and supports herself as a waitress and gives painting lessons to elderly people.) Nor has Patty seen Steve Weed, the man she was going to marry (who talks little anymore about his life with Patty, about whom his new wife, Debby, is tired of hearing) or Steve Soliah, who was Patty's lover for a time in the underground; or Jack Scott, who had not talked to the FBI about any time he may have spent with Patty but has told friends that he and his wife, Micki, and his parents were determined to do anything possible "to prevent a slaughter like the one in Los Angeles."

During her bank robbery trial in 1976, Patty told the jury that she had read her love message about Cujo under threat of death from the Harrises, who say, "she lied to save her own ass." And tall, nimble, careful-talking Jack Scott, who once planned to do a book about Patty and the SLA in cooperation with the Harrises, and now cares no more than Patty for General Teko, agrees with Bill on this one count. "I can say unequivocally that Patty lied about Willy Wolfe on the stand.

"Of all in the SLA," Scott says, "Willy in the only one about whom I've never heard anything but the best. From all reports, he was a thoroughly decent human being." (To this Willie Hearst, now Assistant Managing Editor of the *Los Angeles Examiner*, says, "Maybe so—but remember, Hitler was a patron of the arts and kind to dogs, but was he a good man? Willy Wolfe probably had his good points— but—*I know what he did*.") Scott believes that Patty and Willy were "almost inseparable for the last six weeks of Willy's life," and he says that when Willy died, Patty was almost overcome by grief. "For months, she was the bereaved wife." He says that Patty also did not tell the truth about not being able to go home. "When the Harrises were three thousand miles away, she was offered a ride to her home in Hillsborough, and she would have none of it."

Once emerged from the underground, however, Patty became close again to her parents, sisters and childhood friends. In November 1976, after her trial, after serving fourteen months of a seven-year sentence for bank robbery, Patty was freed on $1.5 million bail pending appeal of her conviction the previous March. She was guarded around the clock by an army of twenty bodyguards, one of whom, Bernard Shaw, Patty says, was in the process of getting a divorce from the mother of his two children. By the following January, Janey Jimenez, then a U.S. Marshal who had become friends with Patty during the trial, sensed that her former charge was in love.

In May of 1978, a year after she pleaded no contest to charges of assault with a deadly weapon and robbery in connection with the sporting goods store shooting (and was sentenced to five years' probation), Patty went back to prison; the U.S. Supreme Court had refused to hear an appeal of her bank robbery conviction. From then until February 1979, when her sentence was commuted by President Carter, she was held at the Federal Correctional Facility in Pleasanton, California, where she cooked lunch and dinner for other inmates at a salary of ten dollars a month. With a gold band on her left hand and an amethyst birthstone on her right, both given to her by Shaw, she looked ahead to her wedding which came off in April.

In the fall of 1978, the Harrises did some plea bargaining which could result in their being "back on the streets," they believe, in 1983. After taking full responsibility "for our participation in the first political kidnapping in this country," Emily went off to the California Institute for Women, in Frontera, near Los Angeles, and Bill went back to San Quentin, where his maximum-security cell is near that of Russ Little.

Russ received his life sentence after a jury heard expert testimony that bullets found near the slain Marcus Foster and in the van in which Russ and Joe were picked up could have come from the .38 caliber pistol that was registered in the name of Chris Thompson, who reported he had sold it to Russ. * Encouraged by his new wife, Dorothy Ballou, a shrewd, young, long-haired legal assistant who met and took to him during one of his trials, Russ believes that neither he nor Joe Remiro will spend all of their lives behind bars.

Joe's fate, like that of Russ, was determined by a gun. On the morning that both men were picked up, Joe was carrying the .380 Walther automatic that had pumped eight bullets into the body of Foster. And, again, many believe this was coincidence and that on the night of the Foster shooting, Mizmoon was wielding Joe's gun. "But you can't tell me," says the Oakland policeman who was at the scene when Foster's body was being carried away, "that those guys weren't involved."

Russ and Joe keep in touch but have not been together (other than

---

* Thompson's story enabled him to collect thousands of dollars in reward money, but is disbelieved by many (including Rudy Henderson, owner of the Fruity Rudy stand, who says Nancy told him that she did the shooting). In court, the defense insisted the Rossi belonged to Nancy.

at trials) since they were booked on the top floor of the Alameda County Court House and tried to escape. (As Russ slugged one guard and Joe jabbed a pencil four inches into the throat of another, the pair came close to success. Remiro had the key to the gun closet in the keyhole when two guards inside the jail came out and helped overpower the pair.) The attempt was costly. "They could beat the murder charge," believes Jack Scott, "but there's a problem with that escape attempt." (The try brought an additional "five years to life," which remained in effect when Little's conviction for murder was overturned by California's Third District Court of Appeal in February 1979.) "Too bad about that."

Russ, still in maximum security, and his blond wife have no conjugal privileges, but their faces light up when they talk through glass by telephone, and they fully expect to have closer contact in or out of prison before long. In the meantime, at San Quentin (where the support of a prisoner costs the American taxpayer between $15,000 and $17,000 a year) Russ keeps fit with exercises, talks occasionally with reporters and keeps in touch with his parents through his sister, JoAnn, who has divorced, remarried and lives nearby.

"She was very close to Willy," Russ says when he thinks of his old friend, and JoAnn says yes. "On the day that he died, my husband and I were walking in the woods behind our apartment house where I picked up a half-buried bleached skull. I felt a premonition, and my husband comforted me, and it was then, I believe, that I conceived my second son. In the evening, when we came down to our apartment, I turned on the TV and saw the SLA people go up in flames. And I remember thinking that I was experiencing death and a new life that night." Nine months later, JoAnn had a son who is as good-looking as her brother and is named Willy.

Joe Remiro, "who is the poet of the Russ-and-Joe pair," according to Public Defender Jim Jenner, is not as outgoing as Russ and is less trusting. At Folsom prison, he sees no reporters and is watched at all times by guards who found a steel bar under his bed and believe he plots to escape. His old acquaintance, Thero Wheeler, the escaped convict who knew many in SLA in its formation period, was believed by police in February 1974 to be the man who bludgeoned Steven Weed on the night of the Patty Hearst snatch. He proved not when he was picked up in Texas and returned to California where he was sent

301

to Vacaville to serve time on an old charge. Eventually he was paroled and he is now free "but comes back to the prison often," says a public information officer, Gary Straughn, "to help convicts in the old Black Cultural Association (active again) to prepare for life on the outside."

Willy's mother says that if Willy had to be in prison or dead, she would prefer that he be dead. "I couldn't stand it if he were in prison." But Jenner says, "If Willy were alive, she would have to ask him which he would prefer—a man can do a lot in prison." But here, Russ Little goes along with Willy's mother. "I don't think Willy could take prison—he was a gentle dude."

Willy's old camping pal Tom Drake, the Andover instructor, agrees. "Willy was a sweet guy." This is the consensus of others in Mount Hermon's class of '69. Few still can quite believe that their old "Wee Willy Wolfe" was in the SLA, although some can see that he might have found an interest in prison work. "He was apolitical," says Nick Monjo, "but he had a feeling for people."

Willy's schoolmates have gone on to professions followed by most well-heeled boys from eastern prep schools. Monjo, the journalist, dines with the likes of Liza Minnelli. Eric Whyte, Mount Hermon's senior class president and man voted "most likely to succeed" applied for medical school eight years after graduation. By then he had gone to Stanford for a year, graduated from Amherst, worked as a journalist, and, finally, returned to school for pre-med at Boston University. He wishes he had gone right into medicine like his old friend Kirk Johnson, son of a Worcester surgeon, who is interning now at Massachusetts General Hospital and going on with his courses in orthopedic surgery through a Harvard Medical School program. According to Eric, Kirk always had success talent. "He won the Williams College Book Prize as a junior, presided over the New England Student Association as a senior, is married to a terribly bright girl from Boston University and is marching right along." Michael Aisenberg is a successful lawyer in Washington, and David West, who tried teaching for a while in his old prep school after going to school in Colorado, went back west for the reason he went out there in the first place—to ski. (He's a full-time ski pro.) The only two in the class who were considered radicals (one was black, the other Chinese) have disappeared into alumni limbo. Most feel they missed the full impact of the sixties, although Kirk Johnson remembers running along with a group of rioters in his first year at Tufts. "I was yelling four-letter words and throwing things with the rest of the mob when I suddenly wondered what I was doing and stopped." He says he is sorry for the arguments about world affairs he had in those days with his father, for whom he has enormous respect. Like Willy's faculty adviser, who is sad that Willy "got caught up in history," Kirk regrets that somewhere along the way Willy did not stop too.

"He was like me when I was a small child and talked about robbing a bank," says Mike. "My friends and I had no money and figured there ought to be a lot of that in a bank. We didn't do it, but if anyone had come along and said, 'Let's go,' we would have trotted along." He says he thinks that's what happened to Willy. "He sat around with a lot of talkers and then someone came along and said, 'Let's go,' and he followed along."

Mike knows that he ended his love affair with his white girl and gave up his glittering job in the office where the boys had big expense accounts and wore suits with vests "because I wasn't ready for that kind of deal." But now he's been doing some thinking. He was as disillusioned with the Church's bureaucracy as with Celanese when he gave up his priesthood. He has, nevertheless, stayed with his faith. "It helps me," he says. But he no longer feels that good living is not for him. Recently he has been elevated from his office job to a position in marketing with the telephone company, and he says, "If I go on as I believe I can go on, I will be ready for the good life this time." (He is taking night courses in business management as he moves up.)

Mike has a girl (white or black, he doesn't say, "and it would not matter") and enjoys himself as he works, studies and goes again to the good restaurants where he ate in the days he was riding high and living with Willy. He is sorry that Willy "never had time to get his life worked out." And he smiles when he remembers how his young friend thought he was in love with Mike's niece, Mercedes. "Really, he liked her mother's cooking and the feeling of that home."

Mercedes is married now to a black accountant. And the other girls in Willy's life have gone on as they were meant. Lydia has been living in Seattle with Michael Bestedo, son of a vice-president of a steel company in Atlanta, who studied for eight years to be a Jungian psychologist but has opted in the last year or so to be a musician. "He has a gig, but in his spare time, which isn't much, he composes," says Lydia. She is now an aspiring actress and modeled as the nurse for the Husky Fever football ads reproduced on T-shirts when the Washington Huskies went to the Rose Bowl. Nancy Boehm, after living in South America, has returned to San Francisco, where she has little to say about anyone she knew in the SLA. And Eva Olsson, Willy's girl from Sweden, has disappeared.

Roxie, who finished college on schedule, worked as a nurse after graduation but now has done a switch. Recently she and Harry Rooney, with whom she has lived for some time, have bought a large home and four acres near Epping, New Hampshire, where they are into breeding goats. She would like to have children, but Harry, who has several children from a finished marriage, has had a vasectomy "so it was either the children or him—and he got the vote." She not only loves him, Roxie says, "but he's my best friend."

The rest of the Wolfe family moves along in character. Because of their Connecticut forebears and their prestige name, the Cheney sons of Honey are thought by those around them to be wealthy and due someday for large inheritances. "That's what Pete Wolfe has always thought," says Ben, "but what money I will have in my life will come from what I make in my own company." Now president of the new Amesbury Industries, which manufactures woven-pile weather stripping, he lives comfortably with his wife, Mary Ann, and three of their school-age children in Hampton, New Hampshire. And Ben's brother, Charlie, and his wife, Susan, and their three children live in Houston, where Charlie, who has his doctorate in anthropology, is a medical anthropologist with the Psychiatric Department at Baylor Medical Center. And Peter supports a wife and baby in Mexico.

John, Willy's younger brother, who is gay, lives quietly with his friend, Frank, in Philadelphia, where he gives private guitar lessons to students of all ages and goes on with his composing and does some performing. More deeply committed than ever to Nichiren Shoshu, John chants with dedication and has pledged to give the world the best that is in him through his music. He says that the organization of NSA, in which he hopes to play an ever-increasing part, suggests no restrictions for anyone's life-style but advocates only that each person (who is on this earth for only a short time) give to those around him his creative best. He believes that his brother was "confused," but after five years he does not criticize or comment on the way of life of his siblings, or of his mother or his father, who lives now in a handsome farmhouse bought for his second family in Hellertown, Pennsylvania.

Like Randolph and Catherine Hearst, who separated in the wake of their ordeal, Pete Wolfe (who Roxie believes was the one in the family "most damaged") was separated for some time from Sharon, who moved to an apartment with Anne and Diane a few blocks from her husband's large Pennsylvania Dutch home. What happened? You will get no answer from Joyce Hoffman, who wrote so many stories about the Wolfes for the Allentown *Morning Call* and once thought of doing a long piece on the family. "Now," she says "the tragedies are too much for me."

Shortly after Willy's death the doctor's contract at the Allentown Hospital came up for renewal and was not renewed. The doctor blamed this on the notoriety of his son's affiliation with the SLA, which a hospital spokesman denies. ("Dr. Wolfe had deep-seated personality problems and at times was extremely rude.") Now, close to sixty, the doctor is a GP in Hellertown, where Sharon says "he is building a good practice."

Protective of her husband, Sharon will say little more than "it's over" about the affair Pete had with a young married mother that titillated their Pennsylvania town during the year of the Wolfes' separation. Now back with her husband after a glamorous reconciliation vacation in Martinique, the present Mrs. Wolfe looks ahead to a settled home life which she knows may or may not come because, as Roxie tells her, "My Dad has a way of complicating things."

Today, Dr. Wolfe still weeps over his loss when talking about Willy, who he knows should have gone to Yale and become a doctor. He realizes that his other sons resented the middle one "because he was brilliant and they know I liked him best." By now he concedes that Willy probably was a terrorist, which middle-class parents in all parts of the world have had to do as their children increasingly wage war against a society they consider corrupt. But he does not go along with those who say that Willy may have taken part in the Foster murder (which Death Row Jeff has suggested) or Patty's actual kidnapping.

Pete Zimmerman still works in Los Angeles, where he feared in '74 that Willy would rap on his door. When the SLA hit town, he headed for Litchfield, arriving along with word that Willy was dead. "Flowers came from Anderson, the painter of Willy's picture, and others, and we had the funeral, which seems like yesterday until you think of how life has gone on."

Honey, who lives handsomely in her Litchfield apartment surrounded by restored antiques left to her by relatives, is now the grandmother of eight. Blessed with affectionate children who keep in touch, she is happy. And only when goaded by a newspaper report, such as one in which prisoners said Willy was the one who killed Foster, does she talk much about her son who is gone.

"It's pretty mean to blame a murder on someone who is dead," she has said, adding, "To me Willy with a gun in his hand is almost inconceivable—but still not as difficult to believe as that Willy would be guilty of sexual assault. That would be impossible." To Honey, the most difficult time other than the night of the shoot-out in Los Angeles was the day when Patty denied in court that she loved Willy. Before that, after the Cujo tape, Honey had consoled herself with a conviction that Willy's last days had been happy. "He was attractive and Patricia Hearst is a beautiful girl—and I could believe that they were in love." She knew that Willy could not have raped Patty ("he was gentle"), but could she be sure that he and Patty were in love?

And then came news of the little Olmec face in Patty's handbag. Relieved, Honey asked one of her sons to ask James Browning, the U.S. Attorney who prosecuted Patty Hearst, if she could have the stone figure that was found under Willy's body, and, if possible, the matching one that was found in Patty's bag. Assured that "once the last legal entanglements are cleared away, she undoubtedly can claim the Olmec charms, which are now locked up in the office of the U.S. Clerk of Court in San Francisco," Honey is grateful. Remembering how the jury reacted when Browning said "there is this little stone face that can't say anything, but can tell us a lot," she smiles. Still pretty, and tranquil now, she looks forward to having tangible proof that Willy's last days were not desolate. Always a romantic, she will be comforted for the loss of her son by the Olmec charms that tell her that he was in love.

Index